Cracking
THE
GOLDEN STATE
EXAMINATION

Biology

The Princeton Review

Cracking

THE GOLDEN STATE EXAMINATION

Biology

by The Staff of The Princeton Review

Random House, Inc.
New York
www.randomhouse.com/princetonreview

Princeton Review, L.L.C.
2315 Broadway
New York, NY 10024

E-mail: comments@review.com

Copyright © 2000 by Princeton Review Publishing, L.L.C.

All rights reserved under International and Pan-American Copyright Conventions.

Published in the United States by Random House, Inc., New York, and simultaneously in Canada by Random House of Canada, Limited, Toronto.

ISBN 0-375-75356-7

Editor: Rachel Warren
Production Editor: Marika Alzadon
Designer: Greta Englert

Manufactured in the United States of America

9 8 7 6 5 4 3 2 1

2000 Edition

Contents

PART I: INTRODUCTION 1
- Chapter 1: About The Golden State Examinations 3
- Chapter 2: Structure and Strategies 11

PART II: THE SUBJECT REVIEW 19
- Chapter 3: The Chemistry of Life 21
- Chapter 4: The Cell 35
- Chapter 5: Cellular Respiration 43
- Chapter 6: Photosynthesis 49
- Chapter 7: Plants 55
- Chapter 8: Life Functions 65
- Chapter 9: Reproduction 109
- Chapter 10: Genetics 133
- Chapter 11: Modern Genetics 143
- Chapter 12: Evolution 155
- Chapter 13: The Diversity of Living Things 163
- Chapter 14: Ecology 171
- Chapter 15: Laboratory Skills 183

PART III: THE PRINCETON REVIEW GSE BIOLOGY PRACTICE TESTS 191
- Chapter 16: The Princeton Review Practice Test I: Session I 193
- Chapter 17: The Princeton Review Practice Test I: Session II 205
- Chapter 18: The Princeton Review Practice Test II: Session I 211
- Chapter 19: The Princeton Review Practice Test II: Session II 223
- Chapter 20: The Princeton Review Practice Test III: Session I 229
- Chapter 21: The Princeton Review Practice Test III: Session II 241
- Chapter 22: The Princeton Review Practice Test IV: Session I 247
- Chapter 23: The Princeton Review Practice Test IV: Session II 259

Part I
Introduction

Chapter 1

ABOUT THE GOLDEN STATE EXAMINATIONS

The Golden State Examinations (GSEs) are a mystery for many California students. The tests are given in thirteen different subjects, and there are many benefits to taking them.

WHAT ARE THE GOLDEN STATE EXAMS?

The GSEs were established by the State of California Board of Education in 1983. (Your parents never took them—that's why they have probably never heard of them and may not understand how important they are.) The tests are designed to offer a rigorous examination in key academic subjects to students in grades 7–12. Students who pass have a variety of advantages over those who don't—including the fact that their school transcript will be more attractive to college and admissions boards.

The GSE program has grown in the last few years, both in the number of different exams offered and the number of students who take at least one GSE. During the 1999–2000 academic year, thirteen different GSEs will be administered, and California students will complete over one million examinations. In 1998, more than 2,100 graduates earned the Golden State Seal Merit Diploma, which recognizes students who have "mastered their high school curriculum"(see below for more information on the Merit Diploma).

You probably purchased this book because a teacher recommended it or because you were told to get ready to take a GSE. Congratulations! This is the most thorough, most complete guide you can own to prepare for the GSE. Our goal is simple—to get you ready for the GSE in Biology.

WE'RE HERE TO HELP

The GSEs are used only to evaluate you as a student—they are not used to measure teacher, school, or school district performance. For that reason, it is easy to see why so many students know very little about the GSEs.

We're here to change all that. Our research and development teams have spent countless hours to ensure that this guide tells you everything you need to know to ace the GSEs. All of the information that is released about the GSEs is in this book. We've also spoken to students and teachers about their experiences with these tests and designed our content review around their feedback. In short, we have the inside scoop on the GSEs, and we're going to share it with you.

What's so Special About This Book?

Golden State Examinations test subject knowledge as well as the application of that knowledge. The goal of this book is twofold. First, we want to help you remember or relearn some of the subject material that's covered in the exam. Second, we want you to become familiar with the structure of the GSE so that you'll know exactly what to do on test day.

We at The Princeton Review aren't big fans of standardized tests, and we understand the stress and challenge that a GSE presents. But with our techniques and some work on your part, you should be able to do well on these tests. There's just one more thing you might be wondering—why *should* I take the GSEs?

WHY SHOULD I TAKE THE GOLDEN STATE EXAMINATIONS?

There are many reasons why you should spend time and energy getting ready for the GSEs. They include:

- **Qualification for a Golden State Seal Merit Diploma**

    The Golden State Seal Merit Diploma is one of—if not *the*—highest academic awards given by the State of California. In the pages that follow, we will detail exactly how you can qualify for a Merit Diploma.

- **Recognition on your transcript**

    If you perform well on a Golden State Examination, you will receive recognition on your high school transcript. We'll tell you later how the scoring system and award processes work.

- **College admissions committees will love you!**

    A strong performance on the GSEs will make you look great to colleges and universities. These are academic awards that will demonstrate to schools that you can excel in an academic environment.

- **They are risk free!**

    First, there is absolutely no fee to take a GSE, so you won't need to worry about spending money on these tests. Second, there is absolutely no penalty if you do not perform well on a GSE. A score that does not give you an award will not appear on your transcript. In fact, only you will know if you did not pass a GSE. Translation—you've got nothing to lose, and a lot to gain!

- **All the things your teacher would say:**

    There are academic benefits to passing the tests as well. If you asked your teacher why you should take these exams, your teacher would probably tell you that, in addition to all the benefits listed above, "These tests provide a great opportunity for you to demonstrate what you have learned throughout high school, with the possibility of receiving numerous awards and titles for strong academic performance. The GSEs are an academic challenge that can enrich your high school experience."

Although we'll be a little less formal in the way we say it, we agree with the teacher's advice. The GSEs are your chance to show off what you know. You should receive recognition for all your hard work, and you should have every tool in your hand to *ensure* that you do well.

HOW ARE STUDENTS RECOGNIZED FOR THEIR PERFORMANCE?

If you score within the highest levels on any one GSE, you will receive one of three awards: high honors, honors, or recognition. Say you take three GSEs, one in history, one in biology, and one in written composition. And (because you used The Princeton Review test-prep books), you are among the lucky one-third of all students who pass the GSEs and earn the awards listed below:

Test	Award
Written Composition	High honors
History	Honors
Biology	Recognition

See how it works? These awards are formally called Academic Excellence Awards. This means that students who receive one of these three awards will receive an Academic Excellence Award from the State of California. This will be recorded on your high school transcript, and you'll receive a gold insignia on your diploma if you get a score of high honors or honors. Now, what exactly do these mean?

- **High honors:** This is the most prestigious award given to students on the GSE. It will be given to approximately the top 10 percent of students. If you receive "high honors" on the GSE, you will receive a special gold seal on your high school diploma, and your award will be placed on your permanent transcript. Further, you can use this result as part of the requirements necessary for pursuing the ultimate award, the Golden State Seal Merit Diploma.

- **Honors:** This is the second most prestigious award given to students on the GSE. It will be given to approximately 12 percent of the students who take the exam (students who score in the seventy-eighth to ninetieth percentile). If you receive "honors" on the GSE, you will receive the same rewards as students who achieved a score of "high honors" (so read above to see what you get).

- **Recognition:** This is the final type of Academic Excellence Award given to students on the GSE. It will be given to approximately 15 percent of the students that take the exam (students who score in the sixty-sixth to seventy-eigth percentiles). If you receive an award of "recognition" on the GSE, you will receive notification of this achievement on your high school transcript. Further, you can use this result as part of the requirements necessary for pursuing the ultimate award, the Golden State Seal Merit Diploma.

Any one of these awards can be very helpful in signaling high achievement to colleges, universities, and employers. Golden State Scholars are also eligible to pursue a Golden State Seal Merit Diploma.

WHAT IS THE GOLDEN STATE SEAL MERIT DIPLOMA?

In July of 1996, the State of California developed a Golden State Seal Merit Diploma program to recognize high school graduates who demonstrate high performance in several different academics areas. The Golden State Seal Merit Diploma is the most prestigious award you can receive through the GSEs. In 1997, the first year that the Golden State Seal Merit Diploma was issued, more than 1,300 high school seniors received the award. This number jumped to more than 2,100 in 1998 and will continue to increase as more students take the GSEs.

In order to receive the Merit Diploma, students must receive high honors, honors, or recognition designations on *six* GSEs. The specific tests and requirements are described below.

Which Six Exams do You Need to Pass to Get the GSE Merit Diploma?

You do not need to apply to receive a Golden State Seal Merit Diploma. You just need to complete four required examinations plus two elective exams, and receive at least recognition for them. School districts track the performance of each student and submit the information to the California Department of Education.

The four exams that students must pass are:

1. English (Written Composition or Reading and Literature)
2. U.S. History
3. Mathematics (Algebra, Geometry, or High School Mathematics)
4. Science (Biology, Chemistry, Physics, or Coordinated Science)

In addition to the four required exams, you will take two other GSEs selected from the following: Economics, Spanish Language, or Government and Civics. You may also complete an *additional* Science, Mathematics, or English exam as one of your electives. For example, let's say you complete both the Algebra and Geometry examinations. In this case, one of them will be counted as the *required* Mathematics exam and the other is counted as an elective.

WHAT MATERIAL IS COVERED ON THE GSE?

The GSEs are developed by a committee of teachers, university professors, and other education specialists. Each examination is designed and tested so that the content reflects the state standards for each subject. In general, you should expect that the information tested on a GSE will be similar to what you've been tested on during the academic year. The style and format of the GSE may be different, but the material should be just like the stuff you studied in class. Unlike many other high school examinations, the GSEs are not designed to trick or trap you. In chapter 2, we'll discuss the specific format, structure, and scoring of the Golden State Examination for Biology.

SO HERE'S THE DEAL

Below are all the frequently asked questions about the administration of the GSEs. If there's anything we don't cover or if you're still confused, ask your guidance counselor or teacher.

How Are Exams Scored?

Every GSE has specific scoring criteria based on its format, structure, and the level of difficulty. See chapter 2 for more specific information about how this GSE is scored.

As we mentioned, there is no penalty whatsoever for poor performance on a GSE. If you fail to receive one of the honors designations, there will be no mention of it on your academic transcript. Further, students who do not receive an honors designation on one GSE should still be encouraged to take additional GSEs. Each test is scored independently—performance on one GSE will have no impact on the scoring of any other GSE.

When Will You Receive Your GSE Results?

Results from the GSEs are first sent to your school district. If you take a winter examination, you should expect to hear about your results in May. If you take a spring examination, you should expect to hear about your results once you return to school in the fall.

If you have any questions regarding your performance on the GSE, you can talk to your high school counselor for more information.

Can I Take the Test More than Once?

No. Students are eligible to take each GSE only once. For this reason, be sure that you are prepared to take the GSE. If you are holding this book, you are well on your way!

How Can I Keep Track of All the GSE Tests and Requirements?

Determining which GSE to take and when to take them can be a confusing process. The California Department of Education has designed some worksheets for use by students that will help you keep track of this information. Ask your high school counselor for a copy of these worksheets.

How Do I Inform Colleges About My Golden State Awards?

If you are applying to a college, university, or military academy, you will want to make sure that any awards you receive on the GSEs are included in your application. If you received high honors, honors, or recognition on a GSE, this will be noted on your high school transcript. In addition to this, you can get a form called the *GSE Status Report for College Applications*. This form is available from your high school counselor, and along with your high school transcript, it will ensure that admissions boards notice your performance on these tests.

> For additional information about the GSE program, contact the Standards, Curriculum, and Assessment Division of the California Department of Education:
> Phone: (916) 657-3011
> Fax: (916) 657-4964
> E-mail: star@cde.ca.gov
> Internet: www.cde.ca.gov/cillbranch/sca/gse/gse.html

HOW THIS BOOK IS ORGANIZED

The next chapter of this book is devoted to giving you the specifics about the test you are about to take. We will discuss test structure, format, and scoring, and we'll also talk about some techniques and strategies that can be helpful to you on the exam. Our goal is to provide you with useful tips you can use throughout this exam.

We will then provide a specific content review of the subject material that's covered on the GSE. Rather than giving you lists of things to know, our goal is to give you information so that you can apply it to the specific way it's asked on the GSE. How do we know what is tested on the GSEs? We have carefully studied California State Curriculum Standards and GSE questions, surveyed high school teachers, and reviewed textbooks to determine exactly what is covered on each test. We'll use sample questions throughout the review to show you how certain topics are tested on the GSE.

Finally, we have prepared and constructed **four** full-length practice tests for the GSE. We will provide you with detailed explanations to each problem, and sample written work when appropriate. Use these tests to recognize the areas in which you need improvement.

WHO IS THE PRINCETON REVIEW?

The Princeton Review is the nation's leader in test preparation. We have offices in more than fifty cities across the country, as well as many outside the United States. The Princeton Review supports more than two million students every year with our courses, books, online services, and software programs. In addition to helping high school students prepare for the GSEs, we help them with the SAT-I, SAT-II, PSAT, and ACT, along with many other statewide standardized tests. The Princeton Review's strategies and techniques are unique and, most of all, successful.

Remember, this book will work best in combination with the material you have learned throughout your high school course. Our goals are to help you remember what you have been taught over the past year and show you how to apply this knowledge to the specific format and structure of the GSE.

AND FINALLY...

We applaud your efforts to spend the time and energy to prepare for the GSE in Biology. You are giving yourself the opportunity to be rewarded for your academic achievement. Don't become frustrated if you don't remember everything at once; it may take some time for the information and skills to come back.

Stay focused, practice, and try to have fun working through this book. And finally, good luck!

Chapter 2

STRUCTURE AND STRATEGIES

It may seem pretty intimidating that only one-third of all students who take the GSEs receives any sort of honors. You might be wondering whether or not you can be one of them...but of course you can! Just remember that most students don't prepare at all before taking the GSEs, so you're already ahead of the game.

In this chapter, we'll tell you exactly which biology concepts are tested, and how. We'll give you an idea of the scoring process, and the structure and format of the test. We'll also show you what you'll need to do to receive an Academic Excellence Award (high honors, honors, or recognition). It's crucial that you use our techniques when you're taking the test. We'll refer to these throughout the book to make sure you incorporate them into your practice.

WHAT IS TESTED ON THE BIOLOGY GSE?

What's tested on the GSE in Biology will be similar to the information you were presented during the academic year. Specifically, the following content areas are covered:

- Molecular and cellular biology

    Including the nature and role of biological molecules; cellular structure and function; cell reproduction (mitosis and meiosis); respiration and photosynthesis

- Functional biology

    Including structure/function relationships; regulatory processes; taxonomic groups including humans, vertebrates, invertebrates, plants, fungi, and protists

- Ecological principles and applications

    Basic ecology, including populations, communities, and ecosystems; energy flow and biochemical cycles; species interactions; human-environment interactions

- Evolution and genetics

    Meiosis; Mendelian genetics; population genetics; patterns and processes of evolution; species concept and systematics; natural selection

In the chapters ahead, we will cover each of the topics mentioned above. We will provide substantial review in each of the topic areas that will be covered on the Biology GSE.

HOW IS THE GSE IN BIOLOGY STRUCTURED?

The GSE in Biology is in two parts, administered in two 45-minute sessions. For example, session I may be on a Tuesday, and session II on a Wednesday.

Session I consists of approximately 30 multiple-choice questions and one written-response question. These questions are designed to test a wide range of biological concepts. You will probably find several of these questions easy, but if you just sat down and took the exam without a thorough subject review beforehand, you would probably find that you'd be unfamiliar with concepts tested in others. But don't worry, we'll review all the material you need to know.

In general, the multiple-choice questions emphasize the concepts and principles of biology. Each of the questions consists of four answer choices. Later, we'll talk about how to use the answer choices to your advantage. You'll get plenty of practice answering written-response style questions as you go through the exams at the end of this book.

Session II consists of one long laboratory task. This lab will expect you to show that you understand common laboratory procedures, are able to document your findings in an accurate way, and are able to support any findings with logical evidence. Because it would be impossible for us to simulate a lab setting, we will instead provide you with a couple of commonly seen laboratories for session II of our simulated exams. You should look through the laboratories and make sure you're comfortable with the procedures, and familiar with the equipment used.

HOW IS THE TEST SCORED?

A machine will score session I, with the exception of the written-response question; biology teachers and other professionals will score the written-response portion of the GSE in Biology exam.

Your performance on session I, combined with your performance on session II of the GSE in Biology exam will determine your overall score. It is important to note that the scoring criterion changes each time the test is administered; it depends on the curve. For this reason, we cannot give you specific information like, "You need to get 80 percent of the questions correct to receive a score of high honors." Every time the test is administered, a new curve is developed based on the performance of the students who have taken the test.

WHERE CAN I FIND A REAL GSE EXAM?

Sample copies of the real GSEs are not available, but you should get enough practice from the four full-length sample GSE in Biology exams in the back of this book, which are followed by explanations and sample written responses. These tests simulate the format and kinds of questions you can expect to see on the GSE.

YOUR BAG OF TRICKS

Have you ever seen the cartoon Felix the Cat? Felix fought crime, solved problems, and got his way out of difficult situations by reaching into his bag of tricks. In this special bag, he'd find the exact tool he needed to resolve any situation. With his bag of tricks, Felix was invincible.

In the first two chapters of this book, we'll help you fill up your own bag of tricks. What will be in the bag? Strategies and tools for handling each type of question on the GSE in Biology exam, as well as general strategies for how to approach the test. It is important to know that being a smart test-taker is just as important as knowing the material tested. Managing your time, knowing when to guess, and knowing what the questions are *really* asking are skills you can learn, and we'll teach them to you. As you'll see, there is a difference between knowing the material and being able to apply it to the test.

Let's take an example of two students, Gretchen and Laurie, each with the same amount of biology knowledge. Now, Gretchen took the same biology class as Laurie, but Gretchen has received additional training. She has learned to think like the people who write the GSE; she understands their traps, fast ways to eliminate incorrect answer choices, and the best techniques to use for certain types of problems. In short, she has learned how to become a solid test taker. Gretchen, with her bag of tricks, is now going to do better on the GSE in Biology exam than Laurie. Why? Not because she knows more, but because she knows how to take this specific test in a smarter way than Laurie does. She understands the rules of the game. Once you know the rules of the game, you know how best to apply your skills to the game.

GENERAL STRATEGIES

Now that you know what's tested on the GSE in Biology and in what format it's tested, we need to talk about the best way to take this test. In the pages that follow, we'll discuss some general tools for you to use as you proceed through the test.

 ### An Empty Scantron Sheet Is a Bad Scantron Sheet

In the past, you've probably taken a standardized test that had a guessing penalty. This penalty meant that points would be subtracted from your raw score if you answered a question incorrectly. Guessing penalties are meant to discourage test takers from answering every question. But guess what? There is NO guessing penalty on the GSE! Your score is only determined by the number of questions that you get correct; it doesn't matter how many questions you answer incorrectly. So when you take the GSE, there is one thing that you must do before you turn in your test: **You must answer every single multiple-choice question.** There are about 30 questions on session I of the GSE in Biology exam. Before you turn in your test, make sure that you have selected an answer for all 30 questions. Earning an Academic Excellence Award may boil down to just one additional point, and leaving a question blank guarantees a wrong answer.

So now you know that you must choose an answer for every question. Now let's talk about how to be an intelligent guesser.

 ### Process of Elimination (POE)

Try the following question:

What is the capital of Malawi?

Unsure? Do you even know where Malawi is located? If not, don't panic. Geography and world capitals are not topics tested on the GSE (especially on the Biology test!). If you had to answer this question without any answer choices, you'd probably be in trouble. You'd just randomly pick a city and most likely guess wrong.

Of course, on the GSE, you will have answer choices to choose from. Rather than closing your eyes and selecting an answer at random, take a look at the choices—you might find some information that can help you:

What is the capital of Malawi?

A. Paris

B. Lilongwe

C. New York

D. London

Now do you know? Can you identify any answer choices that you know are *not* correct? Well, you can probably eliminate choices A, C, and D. Although you probably didn't know that Lilongwe was the capital of Malawi, you could tell that it was the correct answer by eliminating incorrect answer choices. This procedure is called **Process of Elimination**, or POE for short.

Process of Elimination will help you become a better guesser. This is because it's often easier to see incorrect answer choices than it is to pinpoint the correct one. Remember to CROSS OUT any answer choice that you know is incorrect. Then if you still need to make a guess, select an answer from your remaining choices.

It is rare that POE will actually help you eliminate three answer choices like we did in the sample problem above. However, every time you get rid of one answer choice, the odds of getting that question correct go up significantly. Instead of a 25 percent chance of guessing correctly, you might find yourself guessing with a 50 percent (1 in 2) or 33 percent (1 in 3) chance of getting a question right.

So I'll Just Start With #1 and Finish with #30, Right?

Some tests contain an order of difficulty within each section. On these kinds of tests, the first question is generally very easy, and the questions become progressively more difficult, with the last few questions being the hardest. On the GSE in Biology exam, however, there is no order of difficulty on the multiple-choice section of the exam, so doing the test straight through from questions 1 to 30 may not be the best strategy. Your goal on the test is to work as rapidly as you can without sacrificing accuracy. This means that if you find that a question is difficult for you, leave that one for later and move on to another question.

The Two-Pass System
Have you ever been given a question that stumped you, but you were sure you could answer it? Have you ever said, "Just one more minute. I know I can figure this out!" We all have, and we all know that one more minute sometimes means five more minutes, and often, we don't end up with the right answer at all.

Don't let one question ruin your whole day. You've got a certain number of questions to tackle, and allowing one to throw off your timing might set you back. Here's a general rule for the multiple-choice section: *If you haven't figured out the correct answer in 90 seconds, skip the question and come back to it later.* We're not telling you to give up on it—if you can't answer the question, make a small mark on your answer sheet so you can come back to it later. After you complete the section, go back to the questions you weren't able to solve. Remember to use POE on these questions, and make sure you have selected an answer choice for every question before time is up.

We call this strategy the two-pass system. The first time you go through a section, try every question. If a question seems too difficult or you don't know the answer, move right along. Once you've completed the section, go back to those questions. If you still aren't sure how to solve them, use POE and then take a guess.

Oftentimes, when you go back to a problem a second time you'll have a revelation about how to solve it. (We've all left a test and said, "Oh yeah! Now I know what the answer to number 5 was.) Skipping the problem and then going back to it might give you a chance to have this revelation *during* the test, when it will still be useful.

The Written Part
Many students think the written-response section of the GSE in Biology exam is the most difficult part of the exam. As we mentioned, you can practice answering this type of question in session II of the practice exams at the back of this book. But for now, you only need to remember this about answering a written-response question: Start by writing down all of what you know about the topic at hand! Later you can go back and impose a structure on your thoughts and arrange them in a way that answers the question parts clearly and fully.

YOU ARE IN CONTROL
We know that taking the GSE in Biology exam can be a stressful process. With all this built-up pressure, it might feel like this test is totally out of your control.

But the opposite is true—you are in control. Although you can't decide what number pencil (you must bring a #2) to bring to the exam or where to sit during the test, you can decide how you take the GSE. So let's review what we've discussed in this chapter:

- First, you can take advantage of the multiple-choice format of session I. There is no guessing penalty, and you can use POE to add points to your score, even without knowing the correct answer.

- Second, you can answer the multiple-choice questions in any order you want. Spend time with questions that you're comfortable with. If question 12 is really stumping you, move on to question 13 and return to question 12 later.

- Third, you can gain points on the written-response question by providing clear and full explanations.

As you build upon your knowledge of biology by reviewing the chapters ahead, you'll gain more confidence in your ability to handle the exam.

BAG OF TRICKS SUMMARY

Here is a list of what you'll find in your bag of tricks—be sure to make good use of them.

- Process of Elimination (POE)
- Leave no question blank
- A limit of 90 seconds per question
- First write down everything you know about the topic on the written-response question.

Now let's begin the biology review.

Part II

The Subject Review

Chapter 3

THE CHEMISTRY OF LIFE

This section of *Cracking the GSE: Biology* will cover everything you need to know for the exam. The topics in this section should be familiar to you—you've probably seen them in your biology course. But as we go along, we'll quiz you with questions that are just like the ones that'll be on the GSE. This will give you a chance to see how they'll test you on these general topics. After you finish carefully reading through this section, take the four tests at the back of the book and you should be all set for the big test. Now let's get started.

ELEMENTS

Although the countless substances in the universe are chemically diverse, they all have one thing in common: They are made up of **elements**. Elements are substances that cannot be broken down into simpler substances by chemical means. In nature, there are 92 elements, and they are all laid out neatly in the periodic table.

In order to distinguish the elements, scientists have come up with a shorthand notation that employs **chemical symbols**. In this system, the elements are referenced by the first one or two letters of their name. For example, carbon is represented by the letter *C*, and hydrogen, by *H*. While these might seem to make perfect sense, other symbols may strike you as a bit bizarre. Iron, for example, is abbreviated Fe, and lead is Pb! To make matters worse, potassium is K. But as strange as this seems to us, it was a pretty logical nomenclature for the Ancient Romans; in Latin, the word for iron is *ferrum*. In fact, many chemical symbols are drawn from their Latin and Greek names.

Fortunately, you won't have to learn any dead languages in order to recognize the symbols for the elements. All you'll need is the periodic table. If there's ever a doubt in your mind about a chemical symbol, just look it up in the table:

Periodic Table of the Elements

This periodic table is just here for reference. You will probably not need to use it on the exam, but it will be provided, along with a short list of units, definitions, and abbreviations. Much of the information you see on the reference page will not be helpful to you on the exam—the same reference page is included in the test booklet for all of the laboratory science GSEs.

The Essential Elements of Life
Believe it or not, about 99% of living matter is made up of just six elements:

    Sulfur

    Phosphorus

    Oxygen

    Nitrogen

    Carbon

    Hydrogen

The three most common elements are nitrogen, carbon, and hydrogen. These three are particularly abundant in nature and are crucial to many biological processes.

WHAT ARE COMPOUNDS?

When two or more different elements combine in a fixed ratio, they form a chemical **compound**. Since compounds are made up of elements, you would think that they would have the same properties as their constituent elements, but this is not the case. A classic example of this phenomenon is our old pal, water.

Hydrogen and oxygen exist in nature as gases, but when they combine to form water, they turn into a liquid. The combining of hydrogen atoms and oxygen atoms is known as a **chemical reaction**, and can be depicted as a **chemical equation** using the symbols for the elements:

$$2H_2\ (g) + O_2\ (g) \rightarrow 2H_2O\ (l)$$

In a chemical reaction, the starting materials or **reactants** are written on the left side of the equation, while the **products** are written on the right. In the reaction above, hydrogen and oxygen are the reactants and water is the product. The lowercase letters beside the symbols for hydrogen and oxygen indicate the states of the reactants and products. As mentioned above, hydrogen and oxygen are gases (g) that come together to form liquid (l) water.

CARBON: THE VERSATILE ATOM

Now that we've discussed compounds in general, let's talk about a special group of compounds. Most of the chemical compounds present in living organisms contain skeletons made up primarily of carbon and hydrogen atoms. When a molecule contains both carbon and hydrogen, it is said to be **organic**. Most of the molecules that are essential for life are organic compounds.

In contrast, molecules that do not contain carbon atoms are **inorganic compounds**. The most common inorganic compounds found in nature are water and salts. Water plays an important role in chemical reactions and accounts for nearly 70 percent of your body weight. Salts, such as NaCl, supply cells with the ions necessary for many chemical reactions.

To recap:
- Organic compounds contain primarily carbon and hydrogen atoms.
- Inorganic compounds, such as water and salts, do not.

Now let's focus on four of the most biologically important classes of organic compounds:

- **Carbohydrates**
- **Amino acids**
- **Lipids**
- **Nucleic acids**

Carbohydrates

Carbohydrates serve many functions in living things, several of which we'll discuss in this chapter. They are made up of carbon, hydrogen, and oxygen atoms, usually in a ratio of 1:2:1, and can be represented by the formula $C_nH_{2n}O_n$.

Carbohydrates are categorized as **monosaccharides**, **disaccharides**, and **polysaccharides**. But don't let the long words fool you: "saccharide" is just a fancy term for a sugar (just think of *saccharin*, the artificial sweetener found in diet soda). The prefixes "mono-," "di-," and "poly-" refer to the number of sugar units in each molecule. Mono- means "one," di- means "two," and poly- means "many." So a monosaccharide is basically a free-standing, single unit of sugar.

Monosaccharides: The Simple Sugars

Monosaccharides, the simplest of the sugars, serve as an energy source for cells. The two most common monosaccharides are **glucose** and **fructose**.

24 ♦ CRACKING THE GOLDEN STATE EXAMINATION: BIOLOGY

Both of these monosaccharides are six-carbon sugars that have the chemical formula $C_6H_{12}O_6$. Glucose, the most abundant monosaccharide, is the sugar most often found in living things. In photosynthesis, for example, plants produce glucose using the energy from sunlight (we'll discuss this process later on), while animal cells break glucose apart in order to release the energy stored in its chemical bonds. Fructose, though very similar to glucose, is not quite as common. It is found, among other places, in fruits.

Disaccharides

What happens when two monosaccharides are brought together? A hydrogen (–H) from one sugar molecule combines with an hydroxyl group (–OH) from another sugar molecule. What do –H and –OH add up to? Water (H_2O)! So, when two sugar molecules combine, a molecule of water is removed. This process is called **dehydration synthesis**: *Dehydration* refers to the removal of water, and *synthesis* refers to the manufacturing of the new molecule. Through dehydration synthesis, the two monosaccharides are now chemically linked, forming a **disaccharide**. Maltose is the disaccharide formed by the combination of two molecules of glucose:

What if you want to break up the disaccharide and form two monosaccharides again? Well, just add the water molecule that was removed when we combined them. This process is called **hydrolysis**:

Polysaccharides

Many biologically important carbohydrates are made up of repeated units of simple sugars. These chains of sugars are called **polysaccharides**. The most common polysaccharides (which you'll need to know for the test) are **starch**, **cellulose**, and **glycogen**. Polysaccharides serve as storage forms of sugar and lend structure to cells. Starch and glycogen, for example, are polysaccharides used for storage; starch is found in plants, while glycogen is found in animals. Cellulose is found only in plants and enables them to have rigid cell walls. These solid walls provide structural support, giving some plants their sturdy trunks, branches, and stems.

Amino Acids

Amino acids are organic molecules that serve as the building blocks of proteins. They contain carbon, hydrogen, oxygen, and nitrogen atoms. Every amino acid has four important parts: an **amino group** ($-NH_2$), a **carboxyl group** ($-COOH$), a hydrogen, and an **R group**. Here's a typical amino acid:

Amino acids differ only in their R groups, which are also called their **side chains**. The best way to recognize an amino acid is to start by looking for nitrogen (the letter N). Once you've found the N, make sure it's part of an amino group (–NH$_2$), then look for the carboxyl substituent (–COOH). If you see all of these together, odds are you're looking at an amino acid.

Polypeptides

When two amino acids join, they form a **dipeptide**. In bonding, the carboxyl group of one amino acid combines with the amino group of another amino acid. Here's an example:

here's the peptide bond

This is the same process we saw earlier: dehydration synthesis. You may have figured that out when you saw a water molecule being removed in the process. The bond between two amino acids has a special name—a **peptide bond**. When several amino acids are joined together, the resulting chain is called a **polypeptide**. Once a polypeptide twists and folds on itself, it takes on a specific, functional shape, and is called a **protein**.

There are 20 different amino acids commonly found in proteins. Amazingly, all the proteins that exist in nature are made up of different arrangements of those same 20 amino acids.

Lipids

Like carbohydrates, **lipids** consist of carbon, hydrogen, and oxygen atoms, but not in the 1:2:1 ratio typical of carbohydrates. A lipid consists of three fatty acids and one molecule of glycerol. A fancy name for lipids is **triglycerides**. The most common examples of lipids are **fats, oils,** and **waxes**.

To make a lipid, each of the carboxyl groups (–COOH) of the fatty acids must react with one of the three hydroxyl groups (–OH) of the glycerol molecule. Again, this happens through the removal of water, but a lipid requires the removal of *three* molecules of water. This is yet another example of dehydration synthesis.

Lipids function as structural components of cell membranes, a source of insulation, and a means of energy storage.

Nucleic Acids

The fourth major class of organic compounds is **nucleic acids**. Like proteins, nucleic acids contain carbon, hydrogen, oxygen, and nitrogen. In fact, nucleic acids are molecules made up of simple units called nucleotides. Two kinds of nucleic acids we'll be seeing quite a bit of later on are **deoxyribonucleic acid (DNA)** and **ribonucleic acid (RNA)**. DNA is important because it contains gene segments, and genes are the hereditary blueprints of life. RNA is essential for protein synthesis. We'll discuss DNA and RNA in greater detail when we discuss genetics.

CHEMICAL REACTIONS

Now that we've introduced organic compounds, let's figure out how organisms use them. Organic compounds like carbohydrates store energy in their chemical bonds. Through a series of complicated steps and intermediaries, cells use this energy to perform the functions necessary for life.

Let's talk about chemical reactions. As you probably know, during the course of a reaction, the chemical bonds holding compounds together are broken and new bonds are formed. This process—taking molecules apart and reassembling them—either requires or gives off energy. Here's something you need to remember: *Every type of chemical reaction involves a change in energy.*

What Are Enzymes?

Chemical reactions don't occur haphazardly in the cell. Can you imagine what would happen if they did? The inside of the cell would be an explosive mess! In order to control the chemical reactions that take place within their walls, cells rely on complex control mechanisms that employ specialized protein molecules called **enzymes**. Enzymes are organic **catalysts**, which means they speed up the rate of reactions without being changed themselves. In other words, they don't get used up in the process and can be recycled.

The Enzyme-Substrate Complex

Different types of enzymes have different ways of helping reactions along. But generally speaking, the reactants in an enzyme-assisted reaction are known as **substrates** and, during a reaction, the enzyme's job is to bring the substrates together. It accomplishes this by virtue of a special binding region it contains called its active site. When substrates are brought together at the active site, they form a short-lived **enzyme-substrate complex**.

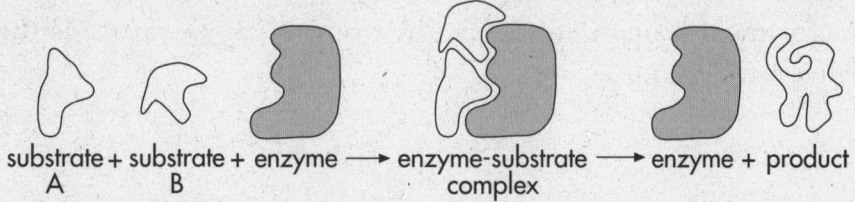

Once the reaction has occurred and the product is formed, the enzyme is released from the complex and restored to its original state. The enzyme is now free to repeat this process over and over again.

How Do Enzymes and Substrates Fit Together?

Originally, scientists thought that enzymes and substrates came together the way keys fit into locks. That is, they thought a given substrate just plugged right into the active site of an enzyme. This theory was known as the **lock-and-key theory**. Recently, however, we learned that enzymes and substrates don't fit together quite so perfectly. It appears that the enzyme's shape changes slightly to accommodate the substrates, in what's known as an **induced-fit** mechanism.

When discussing enzymes, we often mention the concept of **enzyme specificity**. This term refers to the fact that enzymes are very particular: Each enzyme catalyzes only one reaction. For example, there is a specific enzyme that breaks down maltose into two glucose molecules. Since this is the only reaction this enzyme carries out, the enzyme is called *maltase*. Many enzymes are named this way, by replacing the suffix of the substrate in the reaction they catalyze, with *-ase*.

Enzymes Don't Always Work Alone

Enzymes sometimes need a little help in catalyzing a reaction. Well, this help is provided by a class of molecules known as **coenzymes**. Vitamins are examples of organic coenzymes, but coenzymes can also be inorganic. For example, some cells use metal ions (Fe^{+2}) as coenzymes, and these inorganic helpers are known as **cofactors**.

FACTORS THAT AFFECT REACTION RATES

Enzymatic reactions can be influenced by such factors as temperature, pH, and the relative amounts of enzyme and substrate.

Temperature

Generally speaking, rates of reactions increase with an increase in temperature. This occurs because an increase in the temperature increases the chance of collisions among the molecules. As more and more molecules collide, a greater number of enzyme-substrate complexes are formed, which leads to an increase in the overall reaction rate. But all enzymes operate most effectively at optimal temperatures; for most human enzymes, the optimal temperature is the normal body temperature (37 °C):

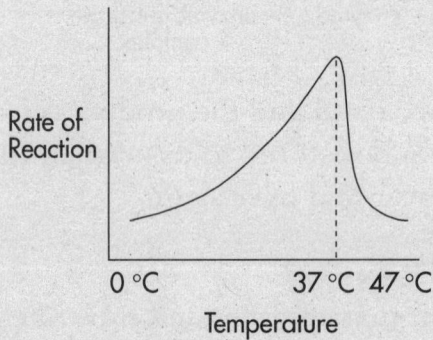

As you can see from the chart above, while the reaction rate peaks at 37 °C, it rapidly drops off above this optimal temperature. Excessively high temperatures cause the structures of enzymes to change, rendering the enzyme unable to function. When this occurs, an enzyme is said to be **denatured**. Denatured enzymes are no longer able to form active complexes with their substrates.

pH

Enzymes also function best at their specific optimal pH. Chemical reactions are influenced by whether the solution in which they occur is **acidic**, **basic**, or **neutral**. The acidity or basicity of a solution can be measured using a **pH scale**.

The pH of a solution refers to its concentration of hydrogen ions (H⁺). A solution with a relatively high concentration of hydrogen ions is acidic, while one with a low concentration of hydrogen ions is basic.

When an acid is put into solution, it fills the solution with free hydrogen ions. Lemon juice, cola, and coffee are all examples of acids. Bases, on the other hand, do not release hydrogen ions in solution. They release hydroxide ions (OH⁻). Solutions with high concentrations of hydroxide ions are said to be **alkaline** (another term for basic). Soap is an example of a base.

The pH scale runs from 1 to 14, and the midpoint (7) is considered neutral. A solution with a pH below 7 is considered acidic, while one with a pH above 7 is basic. Since pH is a measure of the concentration of hydrogen ions, we can sum up the pH scale in this way:

- An increase in hydrogen ions causes a decrease in the pH.
- A decrease in hydrogen ions causes an increase in the pH.

The scale below illustrates the relative pH's of some common substances. Notice that stronger acids have lower pH's:

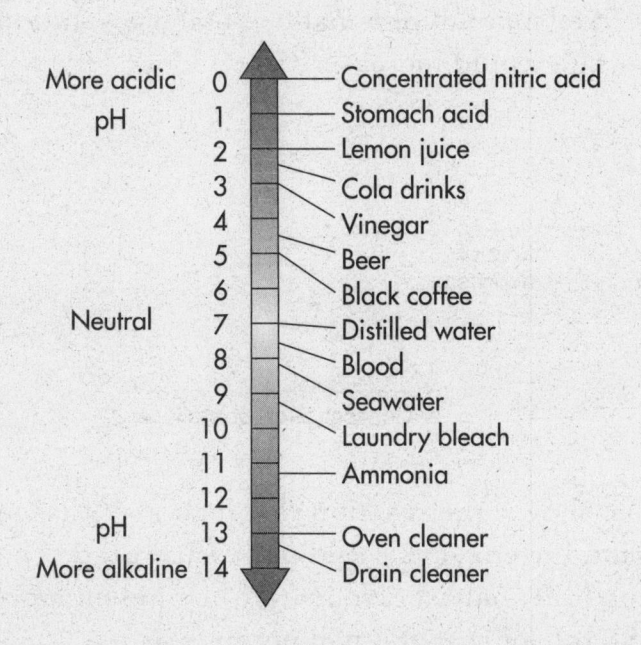

	pH	Substance
More acidic	0	Concentrated nitric acid
pH	1	Stomach acid
	2	Lemon juice
	3	Cola drinks
	4	Vinegar
	5	Beer
	6	Black coffee
Neutral	7	Distilled water
	8	Blood
	9	Seawater
	10	Laundry bleach
	11	Ammonia
	12	
pH	13	Oven cleaner
More alkaline	14	Drain cleaner

Returning to our discussion of enzymes, we said earlier that enzymes function best at their particular pH. Most enzymes function best in a neutral solution, that is, at a pH of around 7, but there are other enzymes that function best in other types of environments. For example, pepsin, a digestive enzyme found in the stomach, functions best at a pH of about 2, which is a pretty acidic solution! This is convenient for the stomach (and for us!) because hydrochloric acid (HCl) is secreted by the stomach lining—we'll talk about this in the chapter on digestion.

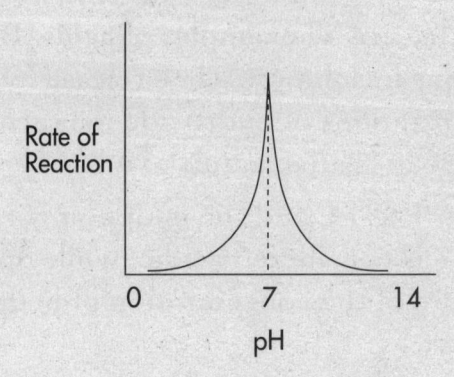

[Graph: Rate of Reaction vs pH, peaking at 7]

Note that enzymes are usually active over a pretty narrow range of pH. This is because beyond this range in either direction, enzymes are denatured.

Concentration of Substrates

The rate of a reaction can also be affected by the amount of substrate available. If we were to take a fixed amount of a maltose-maltase solution and add more maltose, the reaction rate would increase. Take a look:

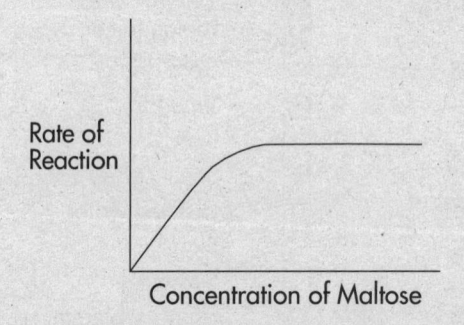

[Graph: Rate of Reaction vs Concentration of Maltose, increasing then leveling off]

As the chart above shows, the reaction rate increases to a certain point, then levels off. At this point, the enzyme is said to be **saturated**. That is, there's too much maltose and too little maltase. No matter how much more maltose we add beyond this point, the rate of reaction will not increase.

Here are a few questions to make sure you have a handle on the material in this chapter.

LET'S TEST WHAT YOU'VE LEARNED

1. Which substances are inorganic compounds?
    1. Water and salts
    2. Proteins and carbohydrates
    3. Fats and oils
    4. Enzymes and nucleic acids

2. Which chemical formula represents a carbohydrate?
    1. CH_4
    2. $C_6H_{12}O_6$
    3. CO_2
    4. $C_3H_7O_2N$

3. Which compounds represent the building blocks of a lipid?
    1. A water molecule and a fatty acid
    2. A glycerol molecule and a fatty acid
    3. An amino acid and a water molecule
    4. A carboxyl group and an amino group

4. Which is a true statement about the relationship between pH and enzyme action?
    1. All enzymes work best at a neutral pH.
    2. Adding more acid does not affect the rate of activity of an enzyme.
    3. Enzymes function only in a pH range of 4.0 to 5.5.
    4. The activity of an enzyme is affected by pH.

5. Maltose molecules are formed from glucose by the process of
    1. dipeptide synthesis
    2. intracellular digestion
    3. dehydration synthesis
    4. biological oxidation

THE CHEMISTRY OF LIFE

Chapter 4

THE CELL

LIFE'S BASIC BUILDING BLOCKS

All living things are composed of **cells**, and biologists have spelled out the importance of the cell in an idea known as the **cell theory**. According to this theory, the cell is the most basic unit of structure and function in all life forms, from those invisible to the naked eye, to the largest of living creatures. It is the smallest unit of living material that can carry out all the activities necessary for life. The cell is the basic building block of all complex organisms.

WHAT MAKES UP A CELL?

Our knowledge of the existence of cells dates as far back as the seventeenth century, when Anton van Leeuwenhoek first peered through a microscope. But it wasn't until this century and the development of the electron microscope that biologists were able to figure out what actually goes on *inside* cells. Now, based on our studies of the inner workings of different types of cells, we know that they come in two distinct types: **eukaryotic** and **prokaryotic**. In this chapter, we'll pretty much limit our discussion to eukaryotic cells.

Eukaryotic cells are filled with a jelly-like fluid known as **cytoplasm**. Embedded in this cytoplasm are tiny structures called **organelles** (literally "little organs"), as well as a membrane-bound structure known as a **nucleus**. While the organelles enable the cell to carry out all the functions necessary for life, the nucleus serves as the cell's command center, directing all the activities within the cell. As we'll see later on, the nucleus also plays an important role in cell reproduction. Fungi, protists, plants, and animals are all made up of eukaryotic cells.

Prokaryotic cells, which are smaller and more ancient than eukaryotic cells, lack a nucleus and many of the membrane-bound organelles we'll be examining in this chapter. Bacteria are examples of prokaryotic cells.

ORGANELLES: THE CELL'S MACHINERY

You can think of a eukaryotic cell as a microscopic factory filled with specialized machines (organelles), each of which handles some part of the business of life. Let's take a tour of a eukaryotic cell, looking at the structure and function of the cell's principal organelles. Here's a picture of the inside of a typical cell:

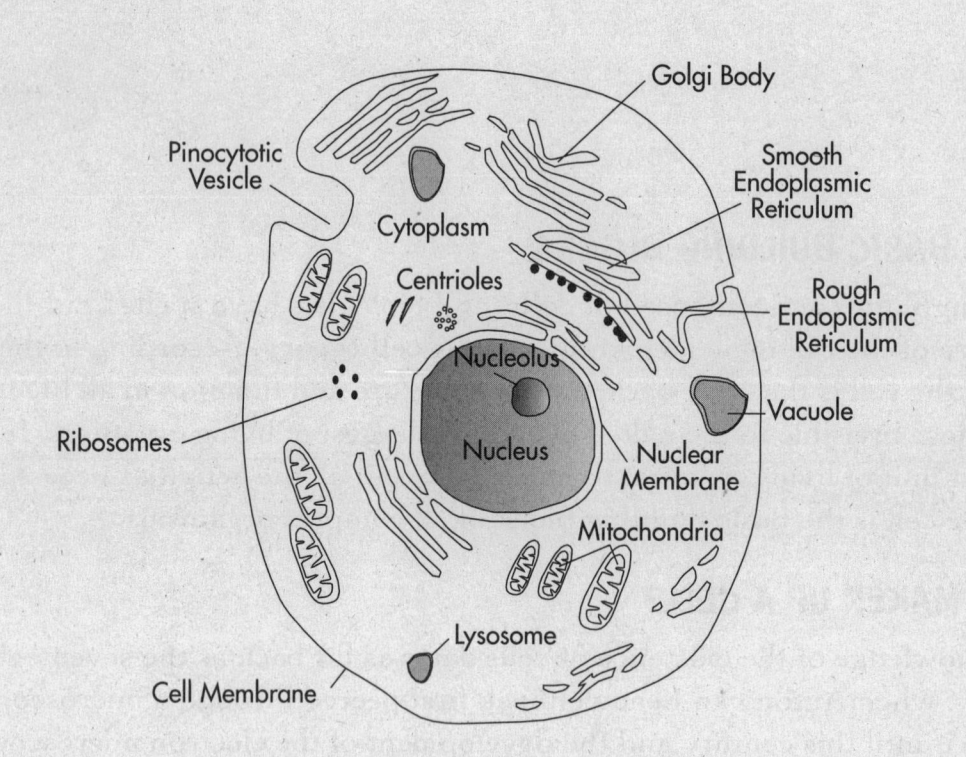

Plasma Membrane

You'll notice from the diagram above that the cell has an outer envelope surrounding it. This envelope is known as the **plasma membrane**. Although the plasma membrane appears to be a simple, thin layer that surrounds the cell, it's actually a complex structure made up of proteins and two layers of phospholipids:

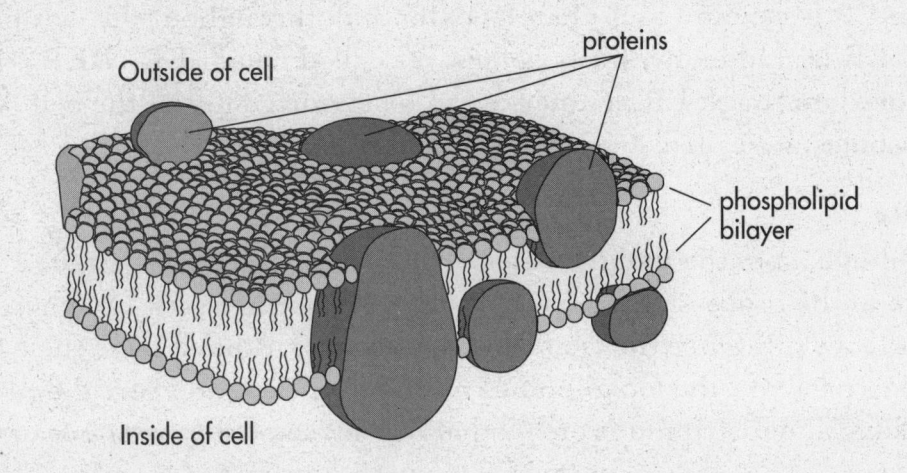

Notice that the proteins float in the double-lipid layer like icebergs in the ocean. You'll also notice that the round "heads" of the lipids face out; one layer toward the outside of the cell, and the other toward the inside of the cell, while the "tails" of the lipids point in toward the middle of the membrane. This arrangement of lipids and proteins is known as the **fluid-mosaic model**.

The plasma membrane is very important because it allows the cell to regulate the movement of substances into and out of the cytoplasm. The membrane is semi-permeable, meaning that only certain substances move across it.

The Nucleus

Our next stop will be the **nucleus**. The nucleus, which is usually the largest cellular organelle, is the command center of the cell. As we mentioned earlier, the nucleus not only directs the inner workings of the cell, it also enables the cell to reproduce. It is here that the cell's DNA is located, bunched into large structures called **chromosomes**. As you probably already know, DNA contains the software that runs the cell and allows it to make copies of itself.

The most visible structure within the nucleus is the **nucleolus**, which is a specialized structure that is formed from various chromosomes and is active in the synthesis of ribosomes.

Ribosomes

Ribosomes are located in the cytoplasm and are the sites of protein synthesis. Their job is to help manufacture the proteins required by the cell. Ribosomes are round structures composed of RNA and proteins. They float freely throughout the cell or are associated with another structure called the endoplasmic reticulum.

Endoplasmic Reticulum

Not all proteins are constructed on free-floating ribosomes; some are synthesized by ribosomes that are attached to the surface of the **endoplasmic reticulum (ER)**. The ER is a continuous channel extending throughout the cytoplasm. When the ER is studded with ribosomes, it's called **rough ER (RER)**. Proteins manufactured on rough ER are marked to be exported out of the cell. When ER lacks ribosomes, it's called **smooth ER (SER)**.

Golgi Bodies

Now let's move on to the **Golgi bodies**. The Golgi bodies are flattened sacs that participate in the processing of proteins; these structures pick up where the ribosomes leave off. Once the ribosomes on rough ER have done their part in synthesizing proteins, the Golgi bodies modify, process, and sort the products. They package and distribute proteins that are subsequently sent out of the cell.

Mitochondria

Another important type of organelle is the **mitochondria.** Mitochondria are often referred to as the powerhouses of the cell. They are responsible for converting the potential energy packed in organic molecules into a form of energy the cell can use. The most common energy source used by the cell is **adenosine triphosphate (ATP)**. From each molecule of glucose a cell takes in, it can produce 36 molecules of ATP. We'll see exactly how this is done a little later on.

Mitochondria are usually pretty easy to identify. They have a unique oblong shape (like tiny, overweight footballs) and distinct inner and outer membranes.

Lysosomes

Throughout the cell are small membrane-bound structures called **lysosomes**. These tiny sacs release digestive (hydrolytic) enzymes when they fuse with worn-out organelles or debris. Lysosomes are the cell's clean-up crew. These exist only in eukaryotic cells and not in prokaryotes.

Centrioles

The centrioles are small, paired cylindrical structures that are found near the nucleus. The role of centrioles is to assist in cellular division. When the cell is ready to divide, the centrioles produce **spindle fibers**, which help in separating chromosomes and moving them to opposite ends of the cell. Although centrioles are common in animal cells, they are not found in plant cells.

Vacuoles

In Latin, the term vacuole means *empty cavity*. But vacuoles are far from empty. They enable the cell to store water, food, wastes, salts, and pigments.

Cilia and Flagella

Some cells have whip-like structures called **flagella** or hair-like structures called **cilia** on their surfaces. These structures are often associated with two particularly well-known microscopic organisms: *Euglena*, which has a flagellum, and *Paramecium*, which is covered in cilia:

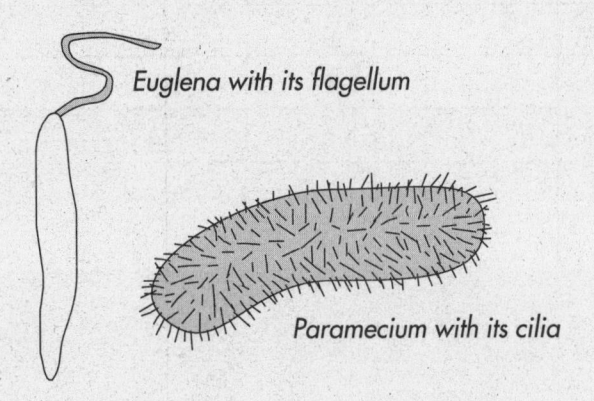

Euglena with its flagellum

Paramecium with its cilia

Cilia and flagella enable these unicellular organisms to move about in their watery environments.

PLANT CELLS VERSUS ANIMAL CELLS

Plant cells contain most of the same organelles and structures found in animal cells. However, plant cells also contain a tough **cell wall** (made of cellulose) and **chloroplasts** (structures involved in photosynthesis). Chloroplasts contain **chlorophyll**, the light-capturing pigment that gives plants their characteristic green color. Another difference between plant cells and animal cells is that most of the space within a plant cell is taken up by a single huge vacuole. In mature plants, this vacuole contains the cell sap.

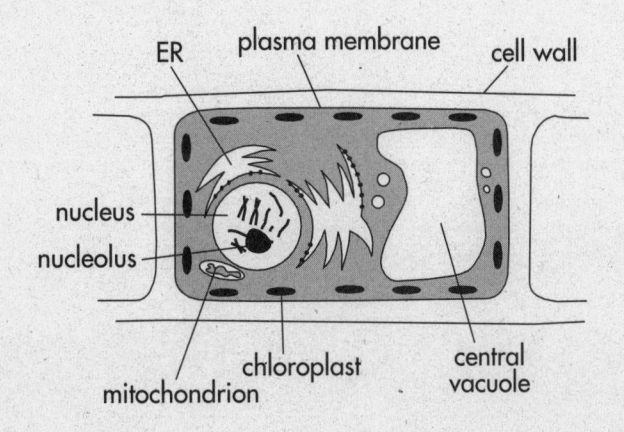

To help you remember some of the most basic differences among prokaryotes, plant cells, and animal cells, we've put together this simple table:

STRUCTURAL DIFFERENCES AMONG CELL TYPES			
Structure	Prokaryote	Plant Cell	Animal Cell
Cell Wall	Yes	Yes	No
Plasma Membrane	Yes	Yes	Yes
Organelles	No	Yes	Yes
Nucleus	No	Yes	Yes
Centrioles	No	No	Yes

LET'S TEST WHAT YOU'VE LEARNED

1. Which of the following organelles is a continuous channel associated with protein synthesis?

    1. Ribosomes

    2. Golgi bodies

    3. Rough endoplasmic reticulum

    4. Mitochondria

2. A major difference between plant cells and animal cells is that plant cells have

    1. A plasma membrane

    2. Mitochondria

    3. A cell wall

    4. Vacuoles

Directions: (3–5): For each statement in questions 3 through 5, select the organelle from the list below that best describes that statement.

   Organelles

    1. Nucleus

    2. Lysosomes

    3. Centrioles

    4. Vacuoles

3. A large membrane-bound, fluid-containing sac

4. Paired organelles that migrate to opposite poles of a dividing eukaryotic cell

5. An organelle that contains hydrolytic enzymes

Chapter 5

CELLULAR RESPIRATION

Nearly everything the cell does requires energy. But where does the cell get the energy it needs? In nature, there are some organisms that make their own food, and others that must obtain it from their environments. Members of the first group are called **producers** or **autotrophs**, and those in the second group are known as **consumers** or **heterotrophs**. As you'll soon see, these two groups have evolved very different strategies for acquiring their nutrition. However, they do have one thing in common: all living things, whether autotrophic or heterotrophic, use ATP as their primary energy source.

ADENOSINE TRIPHOSPHATE

Adenosine triphosphate can be thought of as the cell's energy currency. The structure of ATP is shown on the next page:

Adenosine triphosphate (ATP)

In the diagram, you can see squiggly lines that connect the phosphate groups to the adenine-sugar molecule, adenosine. Each of these represents a high-energy bond. When a cell needs energy, it takes a molecule of ATP and splits the third phosphate through the addition of a molecule of water, or **hydrolysis** (remember that one?). This release of an inorganic phosphate group, P_i, leaves the cell with a molecule of adenosine diphosphate (ADP) and energy.

$$ATP \rightarrow ADP + P_i + energy$$

How the energy from this reaction is used is entirely up to the cell. When the cell wants to store energy, the reaction above merely goes in the opposite direction. The cell attaches P_i to the ADP molecule via dehydration synthesis, and this results in the formation of another energy-rich molecule of ATP.

CELLULAR RESPIRATION

Adenosine triphosphate is produced in a process known as **cellular respiration**. In cellular respiration, certain compounds are broken down in order to release the energy contained in their bonds, and this energy is used to produce ATP. You'll recall that many organic molecules are important to cells because they are energy-rich, and this is where that energy comes into play. In the shorthand reaction, cellular respiration looks something like this:

$$C_6H_{12}O_6 + 6O_2 + 6H_2O \rightarrow 6CO_2 + 12H_2O + ATP$$

(glucose)

Notice that we've taken sugar and combined it with oxygen and water to produce carbon dioxide, water, and energy in the form of our old friend ATP. However, as you probably already know, the actual picture of cellular respiration is far more complicated than this. Luckily, you will not have to know each step in the process of respiration for the GSE. You'll pretty much just need to know what goes into it originally, and what is produced. This is true of many of the biological cycles you'll be tested on.

Generally speaking, we can break cellular respiration down into its two different forms: **aerobic respiration** and **anaerobic respiration**. If oxygen is present, ATP is produced via aerobic respiration. If oxygen isn't present, cells rely on anaerobic respiration for energy production. Since anaerobic respiration is much less efficient than aerobic respiration, most organisms rely on aerobic respiration to meet their energy needs. So let's start by taking a look at aerobic respiration, the more important (common) of the two processes.

Aerobic Respiration

Aerobic respiration consists of two major stages: (1) **glycolysis** and (2) the **oxidation of glucose**. While we could go into much more detail about each step in these stages, we'll stick to the essentials. Let's begin where the cell does—with glycolysis.

Stage 1: Glycolysis

Glycolysis, which takes place in the cytoplasm of the cell, involves the splitting up (-*lysis*) of a molecule of glucose (*glyco-*). Glucose, as we already saw, is a six-carbon molecule. In the numerous reactions in glycolysis, glucose is split into two three-carbon molecules. Each of these three-carbon structures is known as a molecule of **pyruvic acid** (We're only providing the carbon backbones here—they're the most important parts to remember.):

$$\text{C-C-C-C-C-C} + 2\,\text{ATP} + \rightarrow \text{C-C-C} + \text{C-C-C} + 4\,\text{ATP}$$

glucose 　　　　　　　　Two molecules of pyruvic acid

Notice that we must invest two ATP in order to split glucose and make four ATP. It's like the expression, "You have to spend a little to make a little." In order to make four ATP, we had to invest two. Our net profit? Two ATP. While this may not seem like a lot, keep in mind that this is only the first stage of cellular respiration.

Also keep in mind that glycolysis is an *anaerobic* process. It occurs in all living cells and requires no oxygen. The products of glycolysis—the two molecules of pyruvic acid—can now be used in aerobic respiration (if oxygen is present) or anaerobic respiration (if oxygen is absent). Let's first see what happens in cases where oxygen is present.

Stage 2: Oxidation of Glucose

When oxygen is present, the pyruvic acid formed in glycolysis travels to the mitochondria. Through a complicated series of steps involving many enzymes and intermediate molecules, pyruvic acid is converted to 34 ATPs, water and carbon dioxide. We can sum up this process as follows:

$$2 \text{ \{C-C-C\}} + 6 O_2 \rightarrow 34 \text{ ATP} + 6CO_2 + 6H_2O$$
$$\text{Pyruvic acid}$$

You may have already seen a much more complicated version of this stage in your biology textbook. The oxidation of glucose, as mentioned so briefly above, does involve many intermediary steps, including the **formation of acetyl CoA**, **the Krebs cycle**, and **oxidative phosphorylation**. You should know that those three steps are part of the oxidation of glucose, but you will not be tested on them specifically. Just make sure that you memorize the names of all the key processes, and you should be all set. The most important thing to keep in mind about the oxidation of glucose is the outcome: From two molecules of pyruvic acid, the cell produces 34 ATP. You'll recall that in glycolysis the cell had already produced two ATP, so the net result of aerobic respiration can be summed up this way:

AEROBIC RESPIRATION		
Glycolysis	Occurs in the cytoplasm	Produces: 2 ATP
Oxidation	Occurs in the mitochondria	Produces: 34 ATP
		Net: 36 ATP

What about Anaerobic Respiration?

Some organisms can't undergo aerobic respiration because they're anaerobic; they can't use oxygen to make ATP. How do anaerobic organisms get energy? Well, since glycolysis is an anaerobic process, they can make two ATP from this series of reactions. However, instead of continuing on to stage two of aerobic respiration, these organisms carry out a process called fermentation. You should remember that, under anaerobic conditions, pyruvic acid is converted to either lactic acid or ethyl alcohol (ethanol) and carbon dioxide.

Unfortunately, anaerobic respiration is not very efficient. It only produces 2 ATP for each molecule of glucose that's broken down. As you can see from the chart below, there are two major end products of anaerobic respiration:

$$1 \text{ glucose} \xrightarrow{\text{glycolysis}} 2 \text{ pyruvic acid} \xrightarrow{\text{fermentation}} \begin{cases} \text{lactic acid} \\ \text{ethanol and } CO_2 \end{cases}$$

What types of organisms can undergo fermentation? Yeast cells and some bacteria. While yeast cells always produce ethanol and carbon dioxide, some bacteria produce lactic acid as a result of fermentation.

By the Way—Your Muscle Cells Can Ferment!

Did you know that your muscle cells ferment? It's true. Although we're aerobic organisms by nature, we can actually carry out fermentation in our muscle cells. Have you ever had a cramp? If so, that cramp was the consequence of anaerobic respiration.

When you exercise, your muscles require a lot of energy. To get this energy, they convert enormous amounts of glucose to ATP. But as you continue to exercise, your body may not get enough oxygen to keep up with the demand in your muscles. What do your muscle cells do? They switch over to anaerobic respiration. Pyruvic acid produced from glycolysis is converted to lactic acid. This lactic acid causes the pain in your muscles.

LET'S TEST WHAT YOU'VE LEARNED

1. According to the summary equations below, what is the net gain of ATP molecules from the complete oxidation of one glucose molecule?

    (1) 1 glucose + 2 ATP → 2 pyruvic acid + 4 ATP

    (2) 2 pyruvic acid + oxygen → carbon dioxide + water + 34 ATP

    1. 34
    2. 36
    3. 38
    4. 40

2. Two species of bacteria produce different respiratory end products. Species A always produces ATP, CO_2, and H_2O. Species B always produces ATP, ethyl alcohol, and CO_2. Which conclusion can be drawn from this information?

    1. Only species A is aerobic.
    2. Only species B is aerobic.
    3. Species A and B are both anaerobic.
    4. Species A and B are both aerobic.

    Directions: (3–5): For each statement in questions 3 through 5, select the term from the list below that best describes that statement.

    Cellular respiration
    1. Pyruvic acid
    2. Lactic acid
    3. Alcoholic fermentation
    4. Water

3. A method of anaerobic respiration

4. A molecule that is produced during the oxidation of glucose

5. A substance that accumulates during strenuous muscle exertion

Chapter 6

PHOTOSYNTHESIS

In general, plants and algae seem to have it pretty easy. No running around chasing prey, no long lunch lines. As producers, all they have to do is bask in the sun, churning out the glucose necessary for life. But this is no easy feat—in fact, it's pretty complicated. In order to make glucose, plants perform a series of reactions collectively called **photosynthesis**. Here's a very simplified overview of photosynthesis:

$$\text{sunlight} + 6CO_2 + 12H_2O \rightarrow C_6H_{12}O_6 + 6O_2 + 6H_2O$$

You'll notice from this equation that carbon dioxide and water are the raw materials plants use to manufacture glucose. But remember, there's much more to photosynthesis than the simple reaction shown above. You'll soon see that this beautifully orchestrated process occurs thanks to a host of specialized enzymes and pigments. Before we take a look at the many stages of photosynthesis, let's talk about where photosynthesis occurs.

THE ANATOMY OF A LEAF

Photosynthesis takes place in the leaves of plants. Here's a cross-section of a typical leaf:

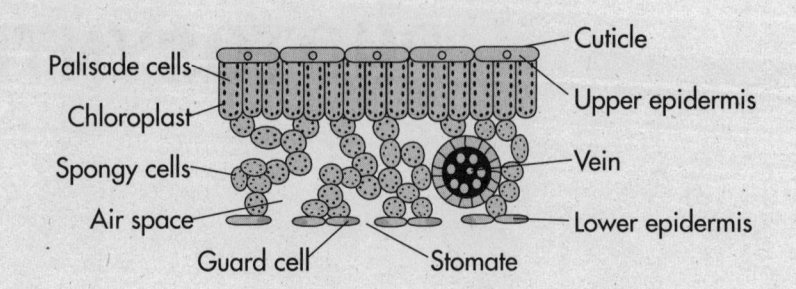

If you look closely at a leaf, the first thing you'll notice is its waxy covering called the **cuticle**. The cuticle is produced by the upper epidermis and protects the leaf from water loss through evaporation. Just below the upper epidermis are the tightly-packed cells of the **palisade layer**. These cells contain lots of chloroplasts, making them the primary sites of photosynthesis.

Now let's take a look at an individual chloroplast. If you were to peel back the membrane of a chloroplast, you'd see a fluid-filled region called the **stroma**. Inside the stroma are structures called **grana** which, as you can see from the diagram below, look like stacks of coins:

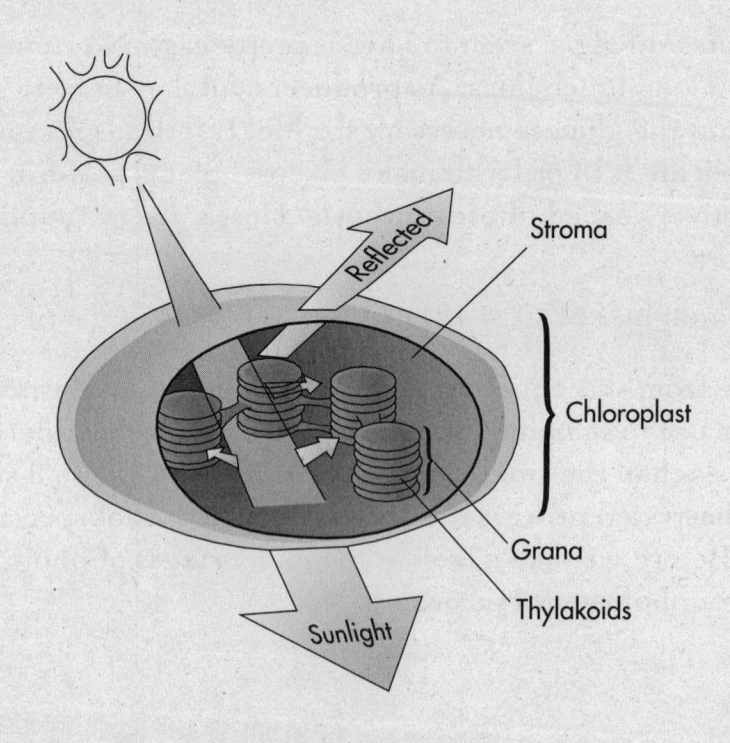

Comprising each "stack" of grana are **thylakoids**, which contain the pigment that drives photosynthesis: chlorophyll. As we mentioned before, chlorophyll also gives plants their characteristic green color. It does this by absorbing the red and blue spectra from sunlight and reflecting back the green.

Now let's talk about the structures in the leaf that are not directly involved in photosynthesis. Look back at the diagram. Just below the palisade layer, you'll see the irregularly shaped cells of the **spongy layer**. The conducting tissues are found in this layer of the leaf, including the xylem and phloem. At the **lower epidermis** are tiny openings called **stomates**, which allow for gas exchange. Surrounding each stomate are **guard cells**, which control the opening and closing of each stomate.

A CLOSER LOOK AT PHOTOSYNTHESIS

There are two stages in photosynthesis: the **light reaction** and the **dark reaction**:

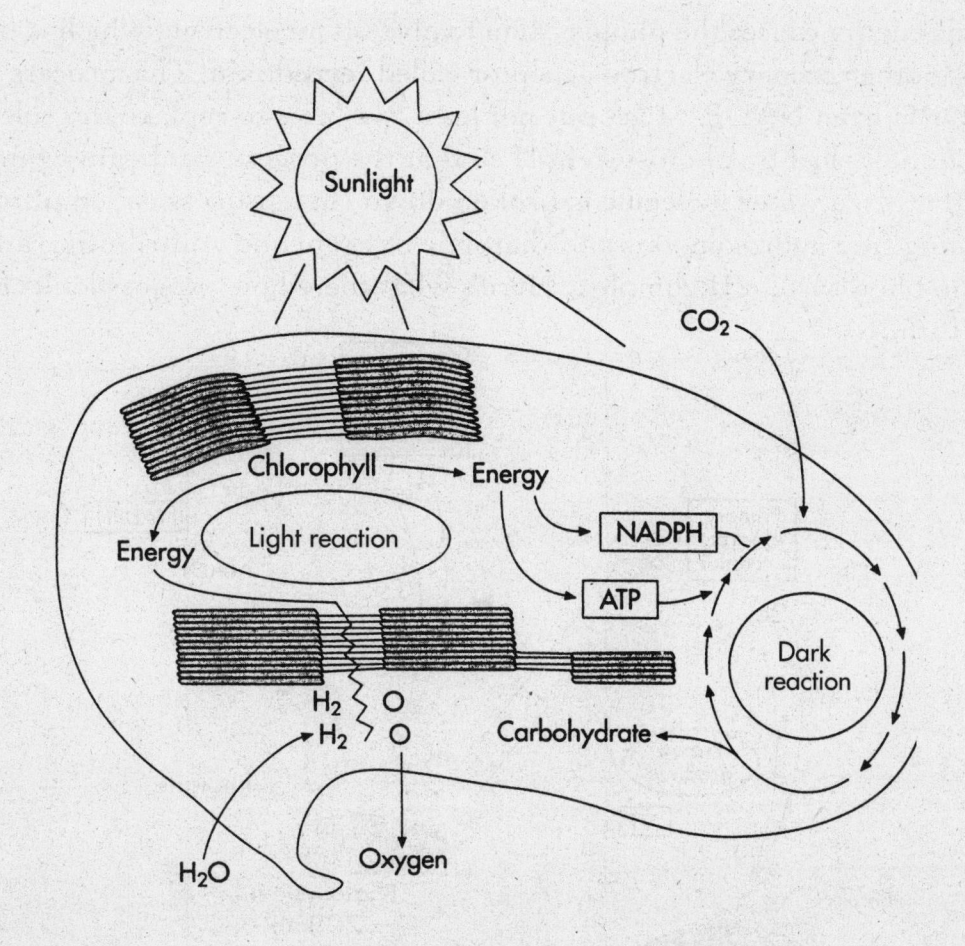

PHOTOSYNTHESIS ◆ 51

The Light Reaction

Photosynthesis begins when **photons** (energy packets) of sunlight strike a leaf, activating chlorophyll and other light-absorbing pigments by exciting their electrons. The energy enters the leaf cells and is absorbed and transferred to a series of chlorophyll molecules within a complex cluster called a **photosystem**. The first photosystem involved in this transfer is called **photosystem II**; this photosystem contains chlorophyll molecules that absorb light with the wavelength of 680 nm (This photosystem is abbreviated P680.). When the complex in photosystem II is activated by light energy, it gives up electrons that are then absorbed by a primary electron acceptor. From there the electrons move to **photosystem I**. During these transfers, hydrogen ions are pumped from the stroma into the interior of the thylakoid, and as these hydrogen ions leak back across the membrane through special carrier proteins called **ATPases**, ADP is phosphorylated (meaning that it receives another phosphate group), forming ATP.

Photosystem I absorbs light with a wavelength of 700 nm and is abbreviated P700. This energy causes the photosystem to give off an electron, which is transferred to another primary electron acceptor called **ferredoxin**. This process creates NADPH from NADP$^-$. Last but not least, we have to replace the electron that was initially lost by photosystem II so that the process can begin again. In order to do this, a water molecule is broken down (in a process called **photolysis**), forming free hydrogen ions and diatomic oxygen, and contributing an electron to the photosystem II complex. Here's what the whole process looks like in diagram form:

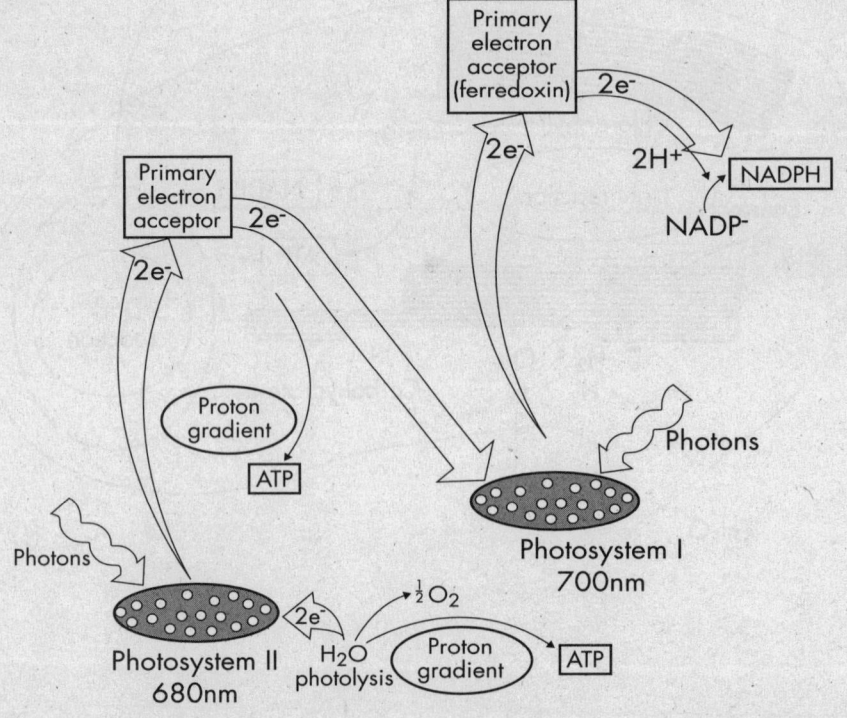

The Dark Reactions (Also known as the Calvin Cycle)

Now let's take a quick look at the dark reactions. The dark reactions use the products of the light reaction—ATP and hydrogen atoms—to make glucose. We now have the energy to make glucose, but what do plants use as their carbon source? Carbon dioxide, of course. The process begins when three molecules of CO_2 combine with a five-carbon molecule called ribulose biphosphate (RuBP) to form a six-carbon compound that's immediately split into two molecules of 3-phosphoglyceric acid, or PGA. Overall, six molecules of PGA are formed.

In the second step of the reaction, the six PGA molecules are converted into six molecules of 1, 3-diphosphoglyceric acid, or DPGA, in a reaction that consumes ATP. (This is the ATP made in the light reactions.)

Next, the DPGA molecules are converted to phosphoglyceraldehyde, or PGAL, and then some of these PGAL molecules are used to produce glucose. The dark reactions are also called the **carbon fixation reactions**; and they occur in the stroma of the chloroplasts.

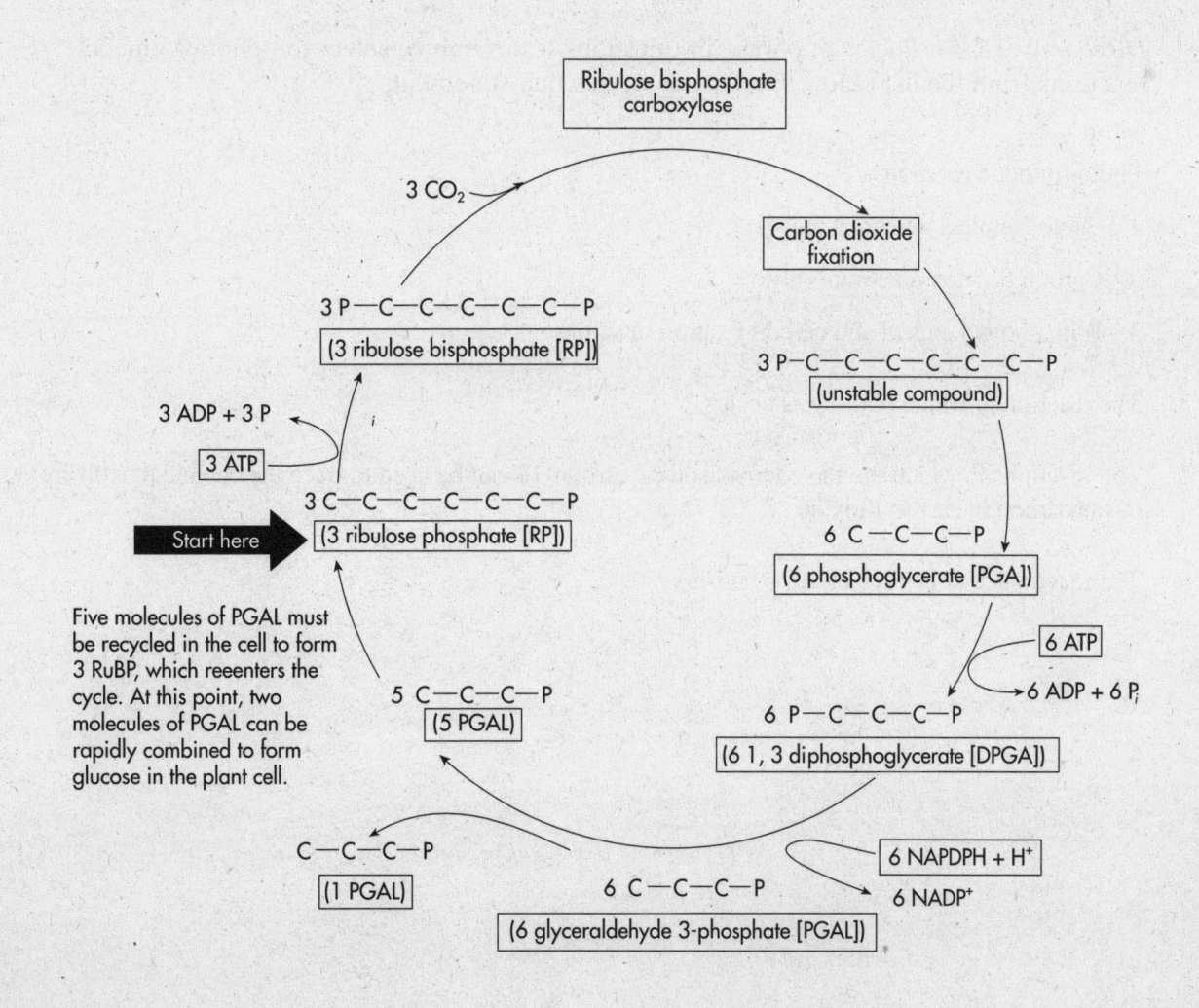

PHOTOSYNTHESIS ◆ 53

LET'S TEST WHAT YOU'VE LEARNED

1. A wet-mount slide of photosynthetic protists was prepared and then exposed to light that had been broken up into a spectrum. When viewing this preparation through the microscope, a student would most likely observe that most of the protists had clustered in the regions of

    1. yellow and blue light
    2. orange and green light
    3. green and yellow light
    4. red and blue light

2. Which of the following plant structures regulates the opening of the stomates?

    1. Guard cells
    2. Thylakoids
    3. Grana
    4. Stroma

Directions: (3–5): For each phrase in questions 4 through 6, select the photosynthetic reactions from the list below that best describes that statement.

Photosynthetic reactions

1. Photochemical reactions only
2. Carbon fixation reactions only
3. Both photochemical and carbon fixation reactions

3. The reaction in which photolysis occurs

4. The reactions in which the radioactive isotope carbon-14 can be used to trace the chemical pathway of the carbon in carbon dioxide.

5. The reactions that involve electron carriers

Chapter 7

PLANTS

The plant kingdom is incredibly vast. As you probably already know, plants are everywhere, from the tropical seas to the Arctic tundra. There are over 260,000 species of flowering plants alone! Here's what we have learned about plants so far in our review:

- They are multicellular, eukaryotic organisms.
- They have a cell wall made of cellulose.
- They are photosynthetic—they convert light energy to chemical energy.

Plant Classification

Now let's discuss the classification system for plants, starting with a simple flow chart of the different subdivisions of plants:

```
                    Plant Kingdom
                    ↙         ↘
            Bryophytes      Tracheophytes
                             ↙         ↘
                      Gymnosperms    Angiosperms
```

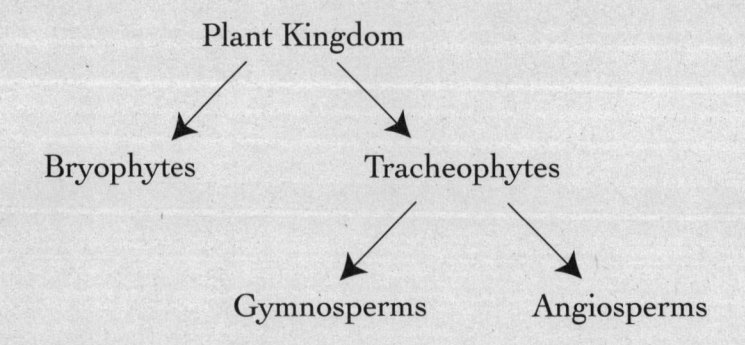

All plants fall into two major categories, or phyla: **bryophytes** and **tracheophytes**. Bryophytes are primitive plants that lack true stems, roots, and leaves; mosses are an example of bryophytes. Tracheophytes are more advanced plants that have specialized conducting and vascular tissues (the xylem and phloem we saw briefly in the last chapter.) Gymnosperms are "naked" plants like pine trees, while angiosperms are the flowering plants.

Bryophytes

Bryophytes are the simplest plants; they are characterized by a lack of true stems, roots, and leaves. Common bryophytes include mosses and liverworts. The fact that bryophytes do not possess specialized transport systems means these plants are unable to store water to be used in times of drought. Consequently, bryophytes have a hard time surviving very far from a water source. To make matters worse, these plants need water for reproduction! Without an abundant supply of water, reproduction is nearly impossible for them. Without water, there is no way for the sperm to reach the egg. For this reason, they generally live in damp, shady places and are covered by a waxy cuticle that helps them retain water. In addition to this, the embryos they produce (during reproduction) are produced inside a protective shell that helps keep them from desiccating.

Tracheophytes

Plants of the other phylum, tracheophytes, are far more numerous. These plants contain vascular tissues and are found all over the world, in all environments. Vascular tissues make it possible for tracheophytes to thrive on land by helping them transport and store water and nutrients. As we saw earlier, these plants contain two types of vascular tissues: **phloem** and **xylem**. Phloem carries nutrients such as glucose throughout the plant. Xylem is tissue that conducts water and minerals *up* the plant from its roots.

Roots have special features in their outer layer called **root hairs**, that increase the surface area of the roots for the absorption of water and nutrients. So roots not only anchor plants, they also absorb water and nutrients from the ground. But how does water move up through a plant? Well, there are two forces at work: **cohesion** and **adhesion**.

- Water molecules have a strong tendency to stick together. That is, water exhibits **cohesive forces**. As water molecules evaporate from a leaf, they tug on nearby water molecules further down the vessel, pulling them up the stem in a microscopic, continuous stream.

- Water molecules also tend to stick to other substances. This is known as **adhesion**. If you've ever tried to separate two glass slides that are stuck together by a film of water, you know how strong this force can be. Basically, adhesion makes the water stick to the sides of the vessel, and cohesion allows those molecules that are climbing up the vessel to drag others along with them.

Both of these forces—cohesion and adhesion—account for the ability of water to rise in the thin vessels of plants.

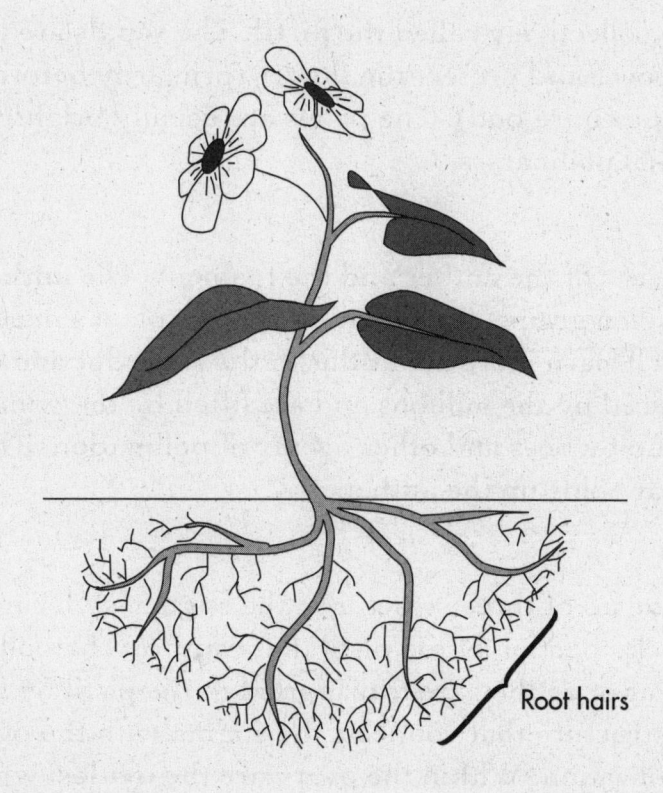

Root hairs

Flowering Plants

From an evolutionary standpoint, the flower is a remarkable example of successful adaptation. Let's take a look at its structure and see why this is so:

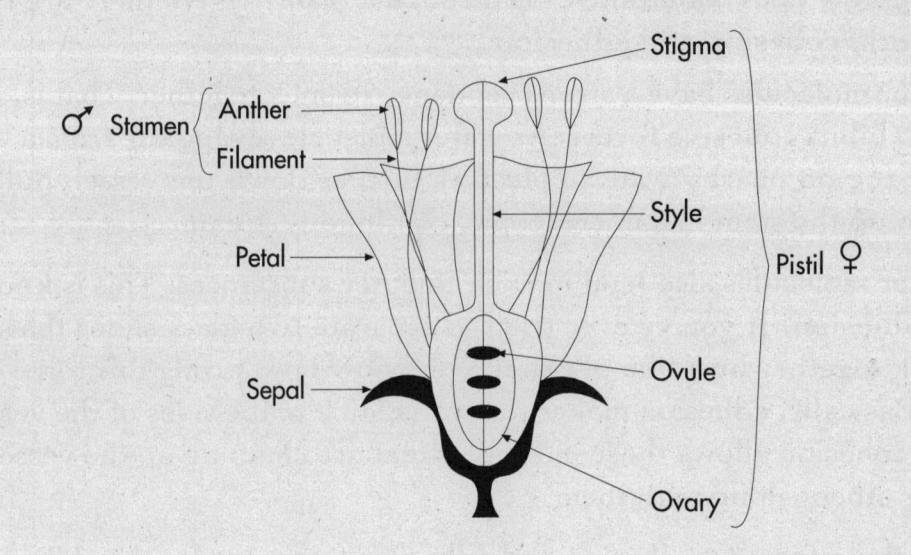

The male parts of the flower are collectively called the **stamen**, while the female parts are collectively called the **pistil**. The **sepals** are the green leaf-like structures that cover and protect the flower (primarily before it has blossomed, when it covers the entire bud). The petals are usually brightly colored in order to attract potential pollinators.

The Stamen

The stamen consists of the anther and the filament. The **anther** is the structure that produces pollen grains. Pollen grains are the plant's male gametophytes, or sperm cells (you'll learn more about this in the reproduction chapter). Pollen grains are produced by the millions and are lifted by the wind into the air; they are also picked up by bees and other agents of pollination. The **filament** is just the thin stalk that holds up the anther.

The Pistil

The **pistil** is made up of three structures: the stigma, style, and ovary. The **stigma** is the sticky portion of the pistil that captures the pollen grains as they fly through the air or as they are transported to the pistil by an insect. The **style** is the tube-like structure that connects the stigma with the ovary, and the **ovary** is the site of fertilization. Within the ovary are the **ovules**, which contain the plant's equivalent of female gametophytes. The ovary of fertilized plants is what eventually develops into the fruit. Apples, pears, and oranges are all fertilized ovaries of flowering plants, if you can believe that. The female gametes of plants undergo meiosis to produce eight female nuclei, including one monoploid egg and two polar nuclei (Again, we'll explain this in greater detail in the reproduction chapter).

As you might suspect, some flowers can pollinate themselves in a process called **self-pollination**. Other flowers are fertilized solely by pollen grains from other plants. This is called **cross-pollination**. The primary agents of pollination are insects, birds, water, and wind.

PLANT REPRODUCTION

Now that we've seen both the male and female organs in plants, let's take a look at how plants reproduce.

Double Fertilization

Flowering plants carry out a process called **double fertilization**. When a pollen grain lands on the stigma, it germinates and grows a thin pollen tube down through the style. The pollen grain divides into two sperm nuclei that descend the pollen tube into the ovary. One sperm nucleus (**1n**) fuses with an egg nucleus (**1n**) to form a zygote (**2n**). This zygote will eventually form a plant. The other sperm nucleus (**1n**) fuses with two polar nuclei (**2n**) in the ovary to form the **endosperm** (**3n**), which ends up as food for the plant embryo. Double fertilization produces two things: a new plant and food for the plant embryo.

Let's review the steps involved in double fertilization:

- Grains of pollen fall onto the stigma. The pollen grains grow down the style in a pollen tube, into the ovary.

- The monoploid nucleus divides into two sperm nuclei, which meet up with the female gametes in the ovule.

- One sperm nucleus unites with an egg nucleus and eventually develops into an embryo.

- The other sperm nucleus unites with two polar nuclei that turn into food for the developing plant.

Embryonic Development

As the embryo germinates, different parts of the plant begin to develop. The **cotyledons** are the first seed leaves of the embryo. They are responsible for temporarily storing all the nutrients for the plant. The **hypocotyl** is the stem below the cotyledons. This portion will eventually develop into the roots of the plant. The **epicotyl** is the section at the tip of the plant that later becomes the stems and leaves:

Epicotyl Hypocotyl
Cotyledons

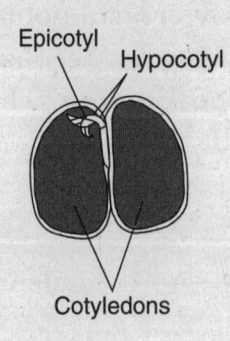

PLANT GROWTH

How do plants grow? Plants have undifferentiated, actively-dividing groups of cells called **meristems**. There are two types of meristems: **apical meristems** and **lateral meristems**. Apical meristems are the regions of active cell division located at the tips of a plant's roots and stems. These dividing cells increase the overall length of a plant.

Lateral meristems are dividing cells that give girth, or width, to a plant. They're responsible for annual growth in stems and roots in woody plants such as trees. These dividing cells are located on the sides of stems and roots. Another name for the lateral meristem is the **cambium**.

Tropisms

Plants need light, and this is pretty easy to prove: Just stick a houseplant (preferably not one of your parents' favorites) in a closet for a week and see what happens. Because it is rooted in its pot, the plant cannot open the closet door and move to an area with more light. As a result, the plant will die.

Although you wouldn't think so from your houseplant's reaction, plants do in fact, move. Not enough to escape from the closet, but enough to ensure that they get maximum amounts of sunlight wherever they are. Notice that all the plants in your house lean or bend toward the windows. This movement toward the light is known as **phototropism**. As you also know, plants also generally grow up and down: The branches grow upwards, while the roots grow down into the soil in search of water. Growth of a plant that occurs relative to the gravitational pull of the earth is called **gravitropism**.

A **tropism** is a turning response to a stimulus, and as you should remember for the exam, plants exhibit three basic types of tropisms. They're easy to remember because their prefixes indicate the stimuli that induce them:

- **Phototropism** refers to how plants respond to sunlight. Plants always bend toward light.

- **Gravitropism** refers to how plants respond to gravity. Stems exhibit negative gravitropism (i.e., they grow up, away from the pull of gravity) and roots exhibit positive gravitropism (i.e., they grow down into the earth).

- **Thigmotropism** refers to how plants respond to touch. For example, ivy grows along a post or trellis.

Plant Hormones

The plant responses mentioned above are initiated by hormones. The major plant hormones are known as **auxins**. Auxins promote growth on one side of the plant. For example, in phototropism, the side of the plant that faces away from the sunlight grows faster, thanks to the plant's auxins. This makes the plant bend toward the light. Imagine yourself on crutches. If your left crutch were longer than your right, you would wind up tipping to the right. This is precisely how a plant bends or leans toward the sun: It makes one of its sides (the side that faces away from the sun longer).

Generally speaking, auxins are found in the tips of the plant—the roots and stems—since this is where most growth occurs. Auxins are also involved in cell elongation and fruit development. Another hormone involved in the ripening of fruit is **ethylene**. Ethylene causes fruit to ripen by hastening its deterioration. Ethylene is a gas, so it can spread from fruit to fruit, and this gives truth to the phrase "One bad apple spoils the lot!"

Some other plant hormones that influence the growth and development of plants are **gibberellins**, **cytokinins**, and **abscisic acid**. You will probably not be tested on the effects of these, although you might be expected to recognize them as plant hormones.

LET'S TEST WHAT YOU'VE LEARNED

Two plants were observed to have the characteristics indicated in the chart below. An X indicates that the characteristic was present:

Specimen	Multicellular	Photosynthetic	Vascular Tissue	Roots	Stems	Leaves
Plant A	X	X				
Plant B	X	X	X	X	X	X

1. According to the chart, which statement about these plants is correct?
    1. Plant A is a tracheophyte and plant B is a bryophyte.
    2. Plant A has xylem and phloem, but plant B does not.
    3. Plant A could be a pine tree and plant B could be a moss.
    4. Plant A is a bryophyte, and plant B is a tracheophyte.

2. The function of the cotyledon in a seed is to
    1. form the upper portion of the plant
    2. form the lower portion of the plant
    3. protect the ovary from drying out
    4. provide nutrients for the germinating plant

Base your answers to questions 3 and 4 on the diagram below of a flower, and on your knowledge of biology.

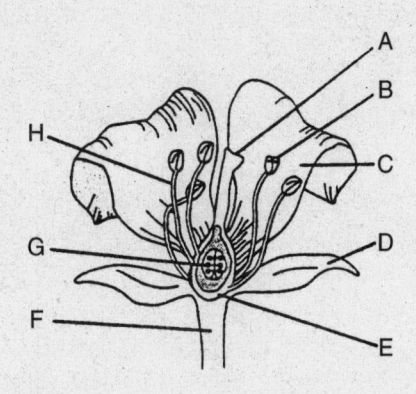

3. Which structures form the stamen?

    1. A and F
    2. B and H
    3. C and D
    4. E and G

4. During pollination, pollen is transferred from

    1. B to A
    2. C to D
    3. B to G
    4. F to H

5. Growth in higher plants most often takes place in regions of undifferentiated tissue known as

    1. meristems
    2. lenticels
    3. palisade layers
    4. vascular tissues

Chapter 8

LIFE FUNCTIONS

All organisms must perform certain activities in order to survive. These activities are known as life functions. The principal life functions are listed below:

- **Nutrition**
- **Respiration**
- **Transport**
- **Excretion**
- **Regulation**
- **Locomotion**
- **Growth**
- **Reproduction**

This chapter will deal with each of these functions. Naturally, different organisms have evolved different ways of meeting the challenges of staying alive. For each life function, we'll look at the principal ways in which organisms as simple as *Amoeba* and as complex as *Homo sapiens* carry out these activities. This is a long chapter, but you should familiarize yourself with all of the information pertaining to life functions for the GSE Biology exam. There will be places where a working knowledge of a topic will be sufficient for the exam, and we'll point these topics out as we go along.

NUTRITION

All organisms need nutrients to survive, but where do these nutrients come from? The answer to this question varies widely, depending on whether the organism is an autotroph or a heterotroph. As you may recall, autotrophs make their own food through photosynthesis, drawing almost all of the building blocks from their immediate environments. Heterotrophs, on the other hand, can't make their own food. They must find sources of energy in the outside world.

When we say **ingestion**, we're talking about the taking in of food from the environment. After food particles are taken in, they're broken down into simpler compounds in a process called **digestion**. Digested molecules are then absorbed by the cells, and used to carry out many different activities. Undigested food particles must also be eliminated from the body, and this process is known as **egestion**. In fact, everything we'll discuss concerning nutrition boils down to two simple questions: How do organisms acquire what they need in order to survive, and what do they do with it once they get it?

Unicellular Animals

Single-celled organisms like protists are able to absorb materials directly across their cell membranes. In some cases, these single-celled creatures rely on specialized structures in order to guide food into an appropriate location to be absorbed. *Paramecium*, for example, uses its cilia to move food into an opening called an **oral groove**. Once the food has been digested, wastes are excreted through an **anal pore**. *Amoeba*, on the other hand, surrounds its food with flexible extensions of its body known as **pseudopodia**. These tiny arms-like structures reach out, close around a chunk of food, and gather it in forming a **food vacuole**. This food vacuole acts like a tiny stomach: It contains digestive enzymes that break down the food particles. The vacuole then recombines with the cell membrane, squirting the waste products out into the environment in a process called **phagocytosis**:

Pseudopodia

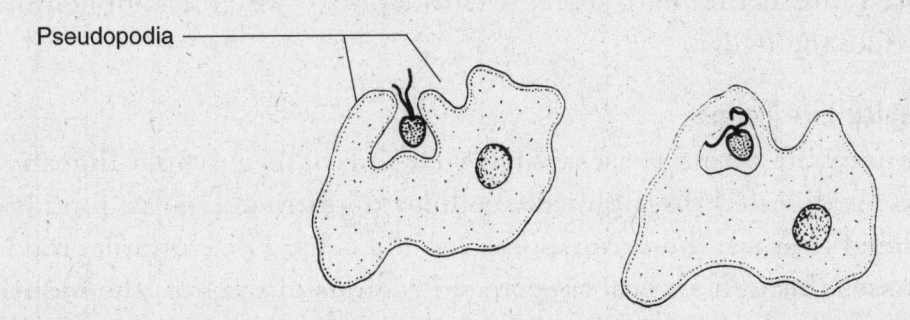

Simple Life Forms

More complex organisms don't have it as easy, however, as the unicellular ones. Since multicellular organisms cannot just absorb food across their cell membranes, they have evolved a variety of ways to obtain their nutrients. In the simplest cases, a single cavity serves as both the digestive and the respiratory system. This type of system is known as a **gastrovascular cavity**. The **hydra** is an example of an organism that possesses such a system:

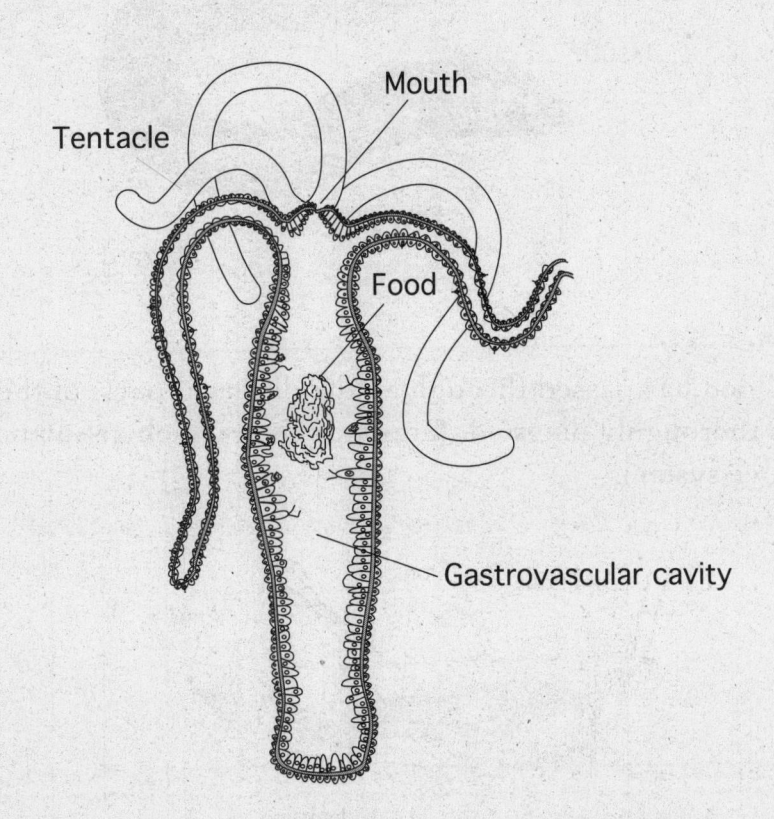

Mouth
Tentacle
Food
Gastrovascular cavity

The hydra sweeps food into its mouth with its tentacles. Specialized cells then release digestive enzymes into the gastrovascular cavity. Food is dissolved, and the nutrients pass directly into the cells lining the cavity. Interestingly, the same opening is used for both nutrition and excretion: Wastes pass out through this mouth as well!

As horrifying as that may seem, it works pretty well for simple multicellular creatures like the hydra.

More Complex Life Forms

More complex life forms possess what we think of as a proper digestive tract, in which food is digested through extracellular digestion. That is, food is digested in specialized cavities, then transported to the cells. For example, food in earthworms passes through several specialized regions of the gut: the **mouth**, **esophagus**, **crop** (a storage organ), **gizzard** (a grinding organ), **intestine** and **anus**:

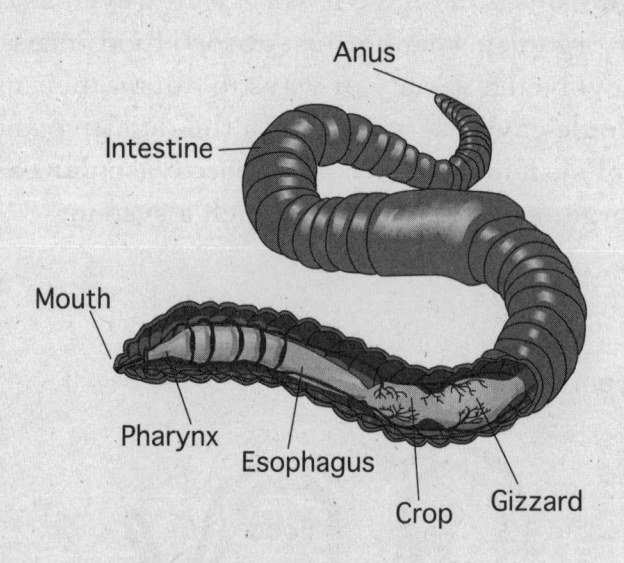

By the time food has passed through all the different parts of the earthworm's gut, it has been thoroughly digested. Grasshoppers, which are arthropods, have a similar digestive system:

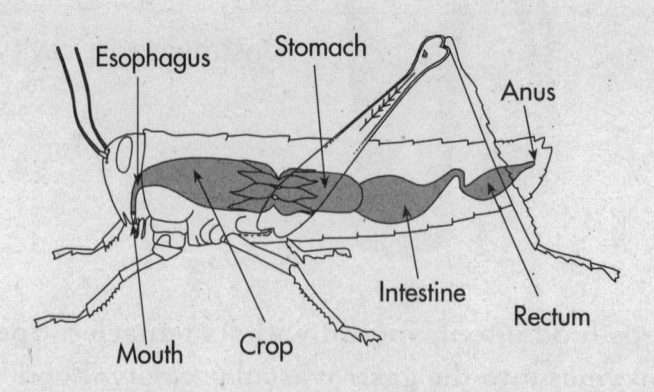

In addition to the organs pictured above, grasshoppers also have **salivary glands** (which secrete saliva) and **gastric caeca** (which contain digestive enzymes). These specialized organs enable the grasshopper to digest its food more effectively.

Different organisms have very different digestive systems (Cows, for example, have four stomachs!). However, few are as well understood as the human digestive system. In this book, we will concentrate primarily on the human digestive system—not only because it is the type of digestive system most often encountered on the GSE, but also because the study of animals (such as the cow or tapir) belongs to a higher branch of science known as zoology.

The Human Digestive System

The human digestive tract consists of the **mouth, esophagus, stomach, small intestine, large intestine** and **accessory organs**.

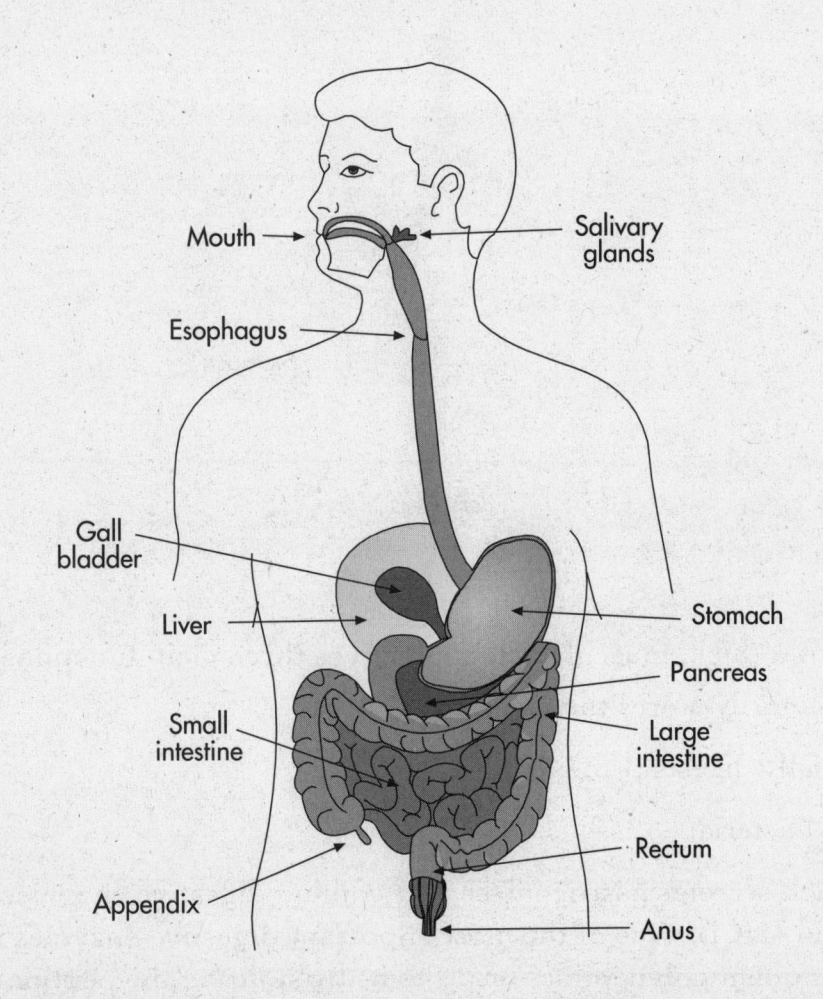

Three groups of molecules are broken down by our digestive tract: **starch, proteins,** and **fats**.

The Mouth

The first stop in the digestive process is the mouth, or **oral cavity**. When food enters the mouth, the teeth begin to chew, softening and mechanically breaking it down. Chewing is a form of *mechanical* digestion. In addition to tools for mechanical digestion, the mouth also contains **saliva**. Saliva, which is secreted by the **salivary glands**, contains an important enzyme known as **salivary amylase**. Salivary amylase begins the chemical digestion of starches into maltose. This explains why a cracker will melt in your mouth while a piece of steak will not: Crackers are made mostly of starches.

Once chewed, the food moves into a muscular tube called the **esophagus**. Food moves through the esophagus in a wavelike motion known as **peristalsis**. These waves of contraction push the food toward the stomach:

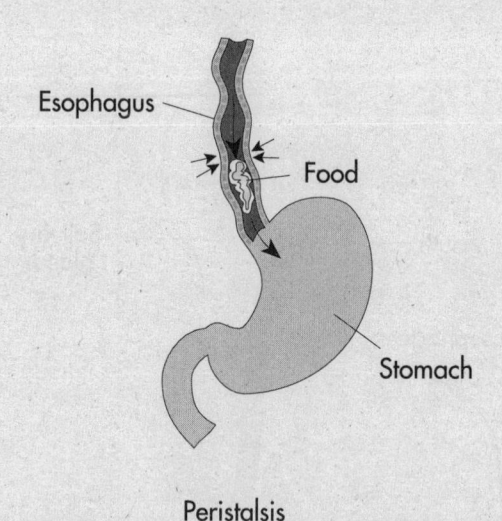

Peristalsis

The Stomach

The stomach is a thick, muscular sac that serves three main functions:

1. It temporarily stores the ingested food.
2. It partially digests protein.
3. It kills bacteria.

The stomach secretes gastric juices that contain digestive enzymes and hydrochloric acid (HCl). One of the most important digestive enzymes is **pepsin**. Pepsin breaks down polypeptides or proteins by splitting the peptide bonds between amino acids. (Remember our discussion of peptide bonds? How about our discussion of the naming of enzymes? *Pep*sin gets its name from the *pep*tide bonds it breaks apart.)

Pepsin works best in an acidic environment. When HCl is secreted by the lining of the stomach, the pH of the stomach is lowered, and this activates pepsin. The lining of the stomach is also covered by a thick coat of mucus that protects the structural tissue from its own acidic secretions. Lastly, HCl kills bacteria found in foods ingested into the stomach.

Once food is broken down into a partly-digested mush (biologists call this mush **chyme**), it travels into the small intestine, where the process of digestion continues.

The Small Intestine
The small intestine might seem like a silly name for this part of the body. After all, an average man's small intestine is about 23 feet long! However, this organ earns its name not from its length, but from its width: The small intestine is only about an inch in diameter. As you've probably already figured out, the large intestine, which we'll look at in just a bit, is much thicker.

Starches, proteins, and fats are completely digested in the small intestine. Although the walls of the small intestine produce enzymes known as **proteases** that help breakdown proteins and dipeptides, the main digestive enzymes are produced by the **pancreas**.

The Pancreas
The pancreas releases digestive enzymes into the small intestine. Among these enzymes are **protease, lipase,** and **amylase**. Protease breaks proteins and dipeptides into amino acids, lipase breaks down lipids down into fatty acids and glycerol, and amylase breaks down starch into simple sugars. These enzymes are all dumped into the small intestine via the **pancreatic duct**:

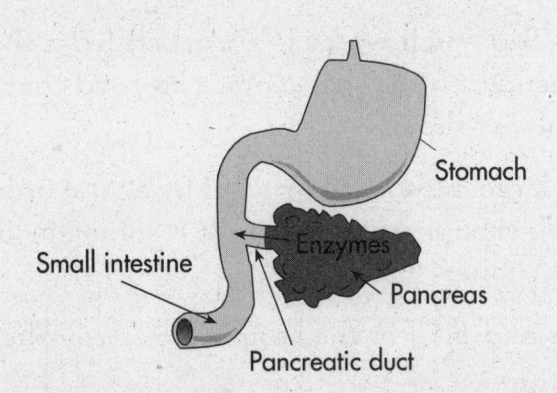

Finally, there is one more substance in the small intestine worth noting: **bile**. Bile is not a digestive enzyme; it's actually an **emulsifier**, which means that it coats tiny, individual drops of fat and prevents them from coalescing. This, in turn, allows the pancreatic lipase to break down the drops of fat more efficiently. Here's something else you should know for the exam: *Bile is made in the liver and stored in the gallbladder.* The **gallbladder** secretes bile into the **duodenum**, which is the first section of the small intestine after the stomach.

Once food is broken down, it's absorbed by tiny finger-like projections called **villi**. Villi are folds that increase the surface area of the small intestine for maximal food absorption. Upon these villi are even smaller projections called **microvilli**. With all of these villi and microvilli, the surface area available for absorption in your small intestine is comparable to the size of several tennis courts! Within each villus is a capillary that absorbs the digested nutrients and sends them into the bloodstream, where individual cells pick them up.

The Large Intestine

The last opportunity for absorption in the digestive system is the large intestine. This intestine is much shorter and thicker than the small intestine (it's about 3 feet long), and performs a relatively simple function: It reabsorbs water and salts from waste materials. The waste material in the large intestine becomes compacted as it moves along, losing water to the body. The large intestine also harbors many bacteria, one of which is *E. coli*. These bacteria reside in the waste material that passes through, and in the process of metabolizing the material, produce odiferous gases such as methane. Some of the bacteria also produce vitamin K, which the body needs and absorbs. The undigested material, called **feces,** then moves out of the large intestine and into the rectum.

Digestive Disorders

What happens when the digestive system malfunctions? Any of several disorders may develop. Here's a list of the most common ones:

- **Constipation**—Too much water is absorbed from the waste material in the large intestine, so that it becomes so hard that it is difficult for the body to eliminate them.

- **Diarrhea**—The large intestine is irritated by a viral or bacterial infection and fails to absorb enough water properly, resulting in loose, watery stool (feces).

- **Ulcers**—Pepsin and HCl in the stomach destroy the stomach lining, causing lesions.

- **Appendicitis**—Infection leads to the inflammation of the **appendix**, a small pouch located at the junction of the small and large instestines. Though the appendix is a "vestigial" organ (i.e., it once served a purpose but is no longer used for anything, like wisdom teeth), appendicitis is extremely dangerous if not properly treated.

- **Gallstones**—Hardened masses of cholesterol lodge in the gallbladder, producing excruciating pain when they attempt to pass through the duct that leaves the organ.

Now that we've looked at digestion, let's move on to respiration.

RESPIRATION

All cells need oxygen in order to survive. Once they've gotten their oxygen, they need to get rid of the waste products that result from their use of it. As we saw in chapter 3, oxygen is necessary for cellular respiration in aerobic organisms, and CO_2 is one of the byproducts of cellular respiration. High levels of CO_2 in the cells can be just as detrimental to the body as a total lack of oxygen, so you can imagine how crucial it is for the body to rid itself of gaseous wastes!

Respiration, then, refers to the process by which organisms complete both of these tasks: the acquisition of oxygen, and the excretion of gaseous wastes.

Microorganisms

Microorganisms have no specialized structures for respiration. As is the case in nutrition, respiration in unicellular organisms is very simple: Gases diffuse directly across the cell membrane. When CO_2 builds up in the cytoplasm as a result of cellular respiration, it passes by the process of diffusion to the outside of the cell (down a concentration gradient). Similarly, low levels of oxygen inside the cell result in the diffusion of oxygen directly into the cell. It's that easy. (We'll look at diffusion in greater depth in the section on transport.)

As we move into the multicellular organisms, respiration becomes a bit more complicated. Let's start by taking a look at plants.

Plants

Plants have special structures called **stomates** and **lenticels**, both of which facilitate gas exchange. Stomates are pores found on the surface of leaves, and lenticels are pores found in woody stems. The majority of gas exchange occurs in the stomates; oxygen and CO_2 pass into these openings. (Remember that plants need CO_2 to carry out photosynthesis!) Gas exchange among plants also occurs via simple diffusion.

MORE COMPLEX ORGANISMS

As is the case with unicellular organisms, many smaller multicellular organisms obtain vital gases through simple diffusion. The hydra, for example, is only two cell layers thick. This enables all of its cells to exchange gases directly with the environment, whether through the exterior cell layer, or into their gastrovascular cavity.

In more complex multicellular organisms, however, not all cells are in direct contact with the environment. These organisms must find other ways of getting oxygen into their systems. Some organisms, such as earthworms, can breathe directly through their moist skin. Oxygen, once taken in, enters the earthworm's circulatory system and is distributed to those cells not near the outside environment.

Other organisms, like grasshoppers, have hard, chitinous shells that make it impossible for them to exchange gases directly with their environments. Grasshoppers and other insects solve this problem by breathing through special tubes called **tracheal tubes**. Air enters the tubes through tiny openings called **spiracles**. Once oxygen passes through the spiracles and into the tracheal tubes, it is transported throughout the grasshopper's body.

Vertebrates rely on two different types of respiratory structures: **gills** (found in fish and amphibians) and **lungs**. Gills are found only in creatures that live in watery environments. They work in much the same way as an earthworm's skin: They allow gases to diffuse directly into and out of the environment. However, unlike an earthworm's skin, gills are highly specialized organs that have evolved solely for the purpose of respiration.

Since gills work by simple diffusion, they have to be in contact with their environments. On land, gills would dry out very quickly, and as they dried out, gas exchange would become more and more difficult. Have you ever seen a fish on dry land? Well, fish can survive for some time on land—certainly longer than we would be able to under water! They don't die immediately because they're still able to breathe: Oxygen and CO_2 continue to diffuse into their blood via the gills. Eventually, however, the fish's gills dry out and the fish dies.

Interestingly, lungs can be thought of as little more than internal gills. It was because of this adaptation (the internalization of the organs used for gas exchange) that organisms were able to make the transition from a watery or *aqueous environment* to land, a *terrestrial environment*. In order to understand how lungs work, let's take a look at the human respiratory system.

The Human Respiratory System

When we breathe, air enters through the **nose** or **mouth**:

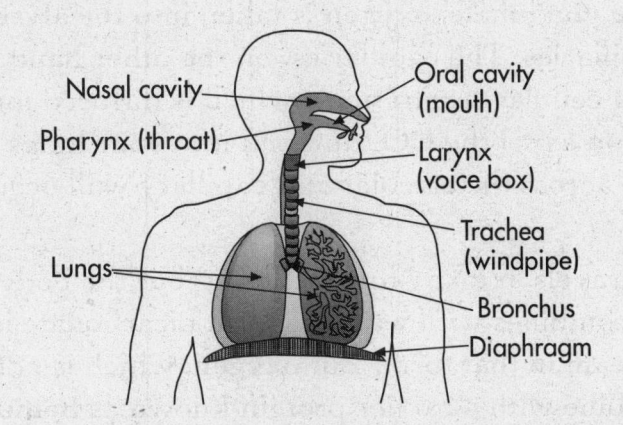

The nose cleans, warms, and moistens incoming air and passes it on through the **pharynx** and **larynx**. Next, air enters the **trachea**, a tube lined with rings of cartilage. The cartilage enables the trachea to remain open as air rushes in.

A special flap called the **epiglottis** covers the trachea and prevents food from entering it. If food does enter the trachea or "windpipe," breathing becomes impossible. This is precisely what happens when someone is choking. The Heimlich maneuver, in which a second person forcibly squeezes the choking person's abdomen and ribs, is a first-aid technique used to help someone in this predicament. By squeezing a choking person's abdomen and ribs, you force air upwards, which expels the stuck piece of food.

As you can see in the diagram below, the trachea branches into two tubes: the **left** and **right bronchi**, which service the lungs. In the lungs, these two passageways break down into thousands upon thousands of smaller tubes known as **bronchioles**. Each bronchiole ends in a tiny air sac known as an **alveolus**. Alveoli provide the lungs with an enormous surface area. If you were to lay out all your alveoli, they would cover an area equivalent to that of a high-school basketball court! Let's take a look at one of these tiny air sacs:

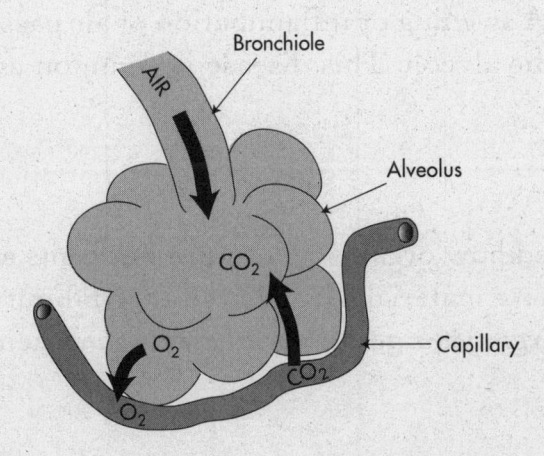

You'll notice that alongside the alveolus is a **capillary**. Oxygen and CO_2 diffuse in opposite directions across the membranes of both the alveolus and the capillary. Every time you inhale, oxygen is taken into the alveoli, which then diffuses into the capillaries. The capillaries, on the other hand, contain excess CO_2 (a byproduct of cellular respiration), which is diffused into the alveoli. When you exhale, you expel the CO_2 dumped into your lungs by the rest of your body. Gas exchange across the alveolar and capillary wall occurs via passive diffusion.

Carbon dioxide travels in many forms throughout the body. Most CO_2 enters red blood cells and combines with water to form bicarbonate ions and travels around the bloodstream in that form. But oxygen, which is not very soluble in water, needs to combine with a carrier protein known as **hemoglobin**. Each hemoglobin molecule can carry up to four oxygen molecules, transporting them to and from the lungs.

The Mechanics of Breathing

What happens to your body when you take a deep breath? Well, your rib cage expands and your diaphragm contracts. The **diaphragm** is a thin muscle that forms the bottom wall of something called the **thoracic cavity**. You can see it in the preceding breathing diagram. This action increases the volume of the lungs, allowing air to rush in. This process of taking in oxygen is called **inspiration**. When you breathe out, pretty much the opposite occurs, and you're letting CO_2 out of your lungs in a process called **expiration**.

Respiratory Disorders

Here are some respiratory disorders you should be familiar with:

- **Asthma**—An allergic reaction in which the bronchi are constricted. Asthma usually results in wheezing and difficulty breathing.

- **Bronchitis**—An inflammation of the bronchi resulting in a severe cough.

- **Emphysema**—A swelling or inflammation of air passages due to a loss of elasticity in the alveoli. This disease is common among individuals who smoke.

TRANSPORT

We've already discussed how organisms acquire nutrients and essential gases. But how exactly are these materials distributed throughout their bodies? In other words, how do organisms get these nutrients *into* their cells?

As we've already seen, this is no problem for simple organisms such as protists. Single-celled organisms in a watery environment have no trouble moving materials directly across their membranes. Even relatively simple multicellular organisms, such as the hydra, manage to do the same. But what about complex organisms like humans?

Traffic Across Membranes

Before we discuss transport, let's review the cell membrane. You'll recall from our discussion in chapter 4 that animal cells possess a plasma membrane. This plasma membrane is **selectively permeable**, which means that certain substances, such as water and lipids, can move freely across the membrane according to their concentration gradients, while others are kept in or out. The substances that move freely across the membrane do so by **passive transport**.

We already encountered passive transport in our discussion of respiration. Basically, whenever there's a higher concentration of a substance outside the cell than inside, the substance will move into the cell. The opposite is also true—whenever there is a higher concentration of a substance inside a cell than outside, that substance will move out of the cell. Passive transport is just diffusion across a cell membrane. The cell spends no energy moving substances across the membrane in the process of passive diffusion—and this is important to remember for the GSE.

One important type of passive transport is called **facilitated diffusion**. Facilitated diffusion occurs with the help of carrier proteins that are embedded in the cell membrane. (Remember our discussion of the fluid-mosaic model in chapter 3?) In a mechanism that is still unknown to us, these carrier proteins shuttle certain molecules and ions across the membrane with their concentration gradients. This is a unique type of passive diffusion that uses membrane proteins but does not require energy.

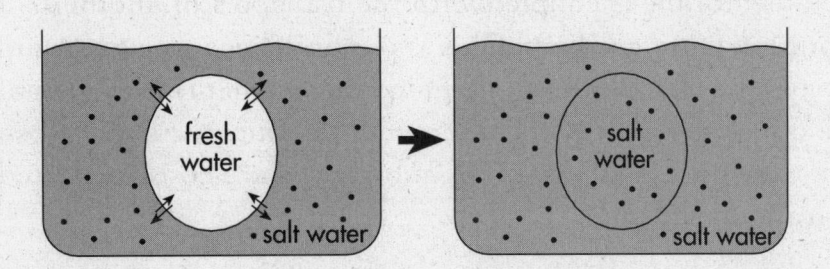

So what do we know now about passive transport?

- It is also known as **diffusion**.
- Substances move from a region of higher concentration to one of lower concentration along a concentration gradient.
- This type of transport does not require energy.
- Facilitated diffusion is a unique type of passive transport in which a membrane (carrier) protein is employed to shuttle ions and molecules across the membrane. No energy is expended.

One last thing. When we speak of the movement of water across a membrane (as a result of diffusion) we call it **osmosis**.

Active Transport

Suppose the cell needs to move a substance in the *opposite* direction, from a region of lower concentration to one of higher concentration. This requires energy in the form of ATP. Movement across a cell membrane and *against* a concentration gradient is called **active transport**.

The ATP molecules are used to activate specialized proteins embedded in the plasma membrane (hearken back to our discussion of the fluid-mosaic model, in chapter 3). These specialized proteins allow the cell to bring substances into and out of the cell against their gradient. A classic example of this type of transport is the sodium-potassium pump. This cell-membrane pump is one of the basic active transport mechanisms you should be familiar with for the GSE. This pump shuttles three sodium ions out of the cell for every two potassium ions it takes in, hydrolyzing ATP in the process.

One last term you should be familiar with (as far as transport mechanisms go) is co-transport. **Co-transport** occurs when normal diffusion of a substance across the cell membrane is coupled with the transport of another substance against its concentration gradient. This is possible because as a pump shuttles a substance across the cell membrane (against its gradient), the substance tends to diffuse in the opposite direction back down its gradient. As the substance leaks back through transport proteins, other substances are co-transported against their concentration gradients.

Endocytosis

What happens when the particles that want to enter a cell are just too large to pass through the membrane by either passive or active transport? Well, the cell takes these particles in by forming a pocket from a section of its cell membrane, in a process called *endocytosis*. The pocket pinches in to form either a vacuole or a vesicle.

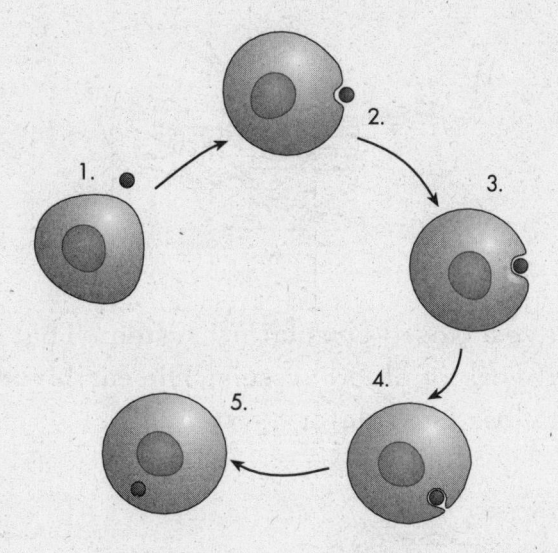

There are three main types of endocytosis: pinocytosis, phagocytosis, and receptor-mediated endocytosis. In **pinocytosis**, the cell ingests fluids ("cell drinking"), by an infolding of a section of its membrane into a tiny vesicle filled with extracellular fluid. In **phagocytosis**, the cell ingests large particles ("cell eating"); a section of the cell membrane folds in and pinches off a large vacuole that fuses with a lysosome. You'll recall from our discussion of nutrition that *Amoeba* accomplishes this thanks to its pseudopodia, which act like arms, wrapping around the large particles. In **receptor-mediated endocytosis**, specific molecules bind to receptors on the cell surface, which signals the cell membrane to pinch off and carry the molecules into the cell in vesicles.

Now that we've looked at some of the ways organisms move substances across the plasma membrane, let's jump to more complex means of transport.

Circulatory Systems

Larger organisms can't use the same strategies as their smaller counterparts to supply all their cells with the necessary materials. Too many cells are not in contact with the environment. These organisms, therefore, need special systems to accomplish internal transport. There are two types of circulatory systems: **open circulatory systems** and **closed circulatory systems**. In an open circulatory system, blood is carried along by open-ended blood vessels that spill blood into the body cavity. In grasshoppers, for example, blood is pumped by the heart through vessels that open into large spaces known as **sinuses**:

Heart

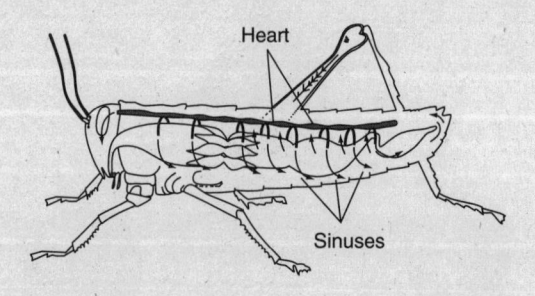

Sinuses

Other organisms have a closed circulatory system. That is, blood flows continuously through a network of blood vessels. The earthworm is an example of an organism that has a closed circulatory system."

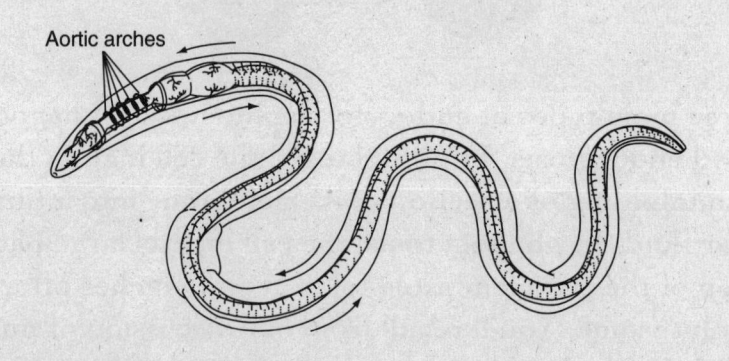

Aortic arches

Closed circulatory system of an earthworm

As you can see from the diagram above, earthworms have five **aortic arches** that pump blood throughout the body. Now that we've looked at a couple of invertebrate solutions, let's move on to the human circulatory system.

The Human Circulatory System

As you already know, the heart pumps blood throughout the body. If you stop to think about it, the heart's job is pretty amazing. In your lifetime, your heart will beat more than two billion times, pumping about 180 million liters of blood!

The heart is divided into four chambers, two on the left and two on the right. The four chambers of the heart are the **right atrium**, the **right ventricle**, the **left atrium,** and the **left ventricle**. Take a look at the heart pictured below:

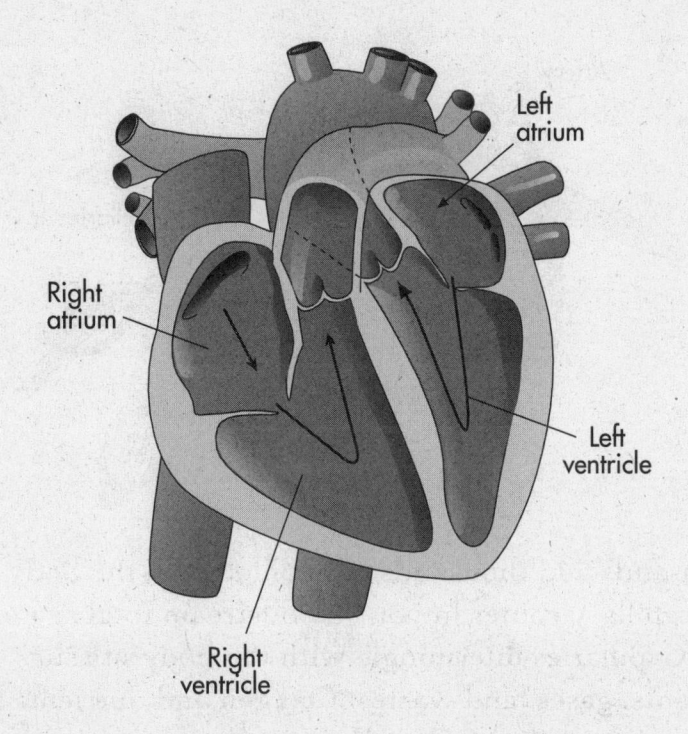

As you can tell from the arrows, the heart pumps blood in a continuous circuit. Blood flows from the left atrium to the left ventricle, then out of the aorta toward the body. It then returns via the right atrium, flows into the right ventricle and leaves again via the pulmonary arteries.

Let's go back for a moment to the point in the circulatory system at which the blood exits the left ventricle. When blood leaves the left ventricle it starts its long tour of the body. This tour is called the **systemic circulation**.

Systemic Circulation

Blood leaves the heart through a large blood vessel called the **aorta**; the largest artery in the body. It carries blood away from the heart and quickly branches out into smaller vessels called **arteries**. Arteries always carry blood away from the heart. Just remember: "A" stands for "away" from the heart. Arteries are thick-walled but elastic vessels. Their strength and elasticity make it possible for them to manage the high-pressure flow as blood is pumped away from the heart.

The arteries branch into even smaller vessels called **arterioles** and finally into the smallest vessels, **capillaries**—tiny tubes no more than one cell thick. In fact, blood cells pass single-file through capillaries:

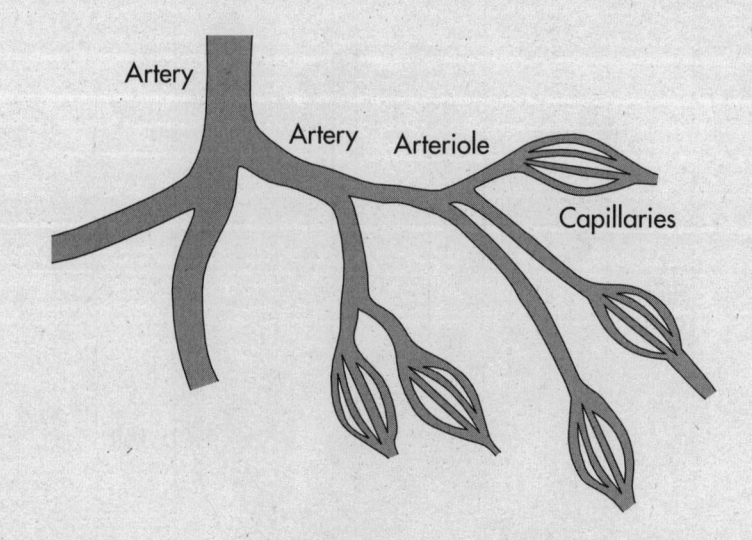

There are thousands and thousands of capillaries in the body. In fact, some estimate that the capillary routes in your bloodstream total as much as 100 kilometers in length! Capillaries intermingle with the body's tissues, facilitating the exchange of nutrients, gases, and wastes. Oxygen and nutrients leave the capillaries and enter the tissues, and CO_2 and wastes leave the tissues and enter the capillaries:

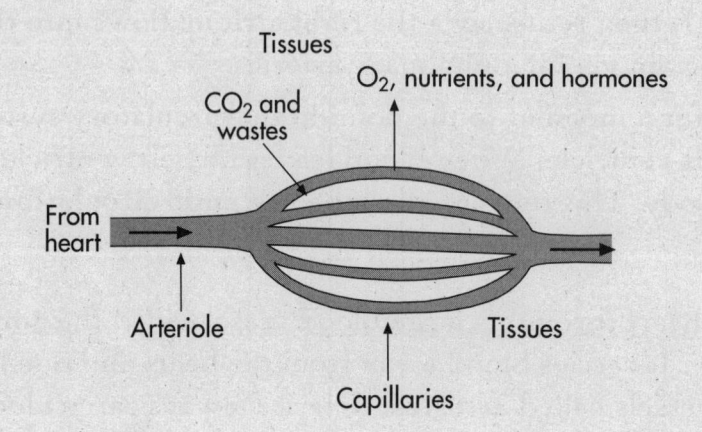

Back to the Heart
After touring the body, the blood has very little oxygen left—most of its oxygen has passed through the capillary walls to the body's cells; the blood is **deoxygenated**. In order to get a fresh supply of oxygen, the blood now needs to travel to the lungs.

However, the blood doesn't go directly to the lungs. It must first return to the heart to be pumped out again:

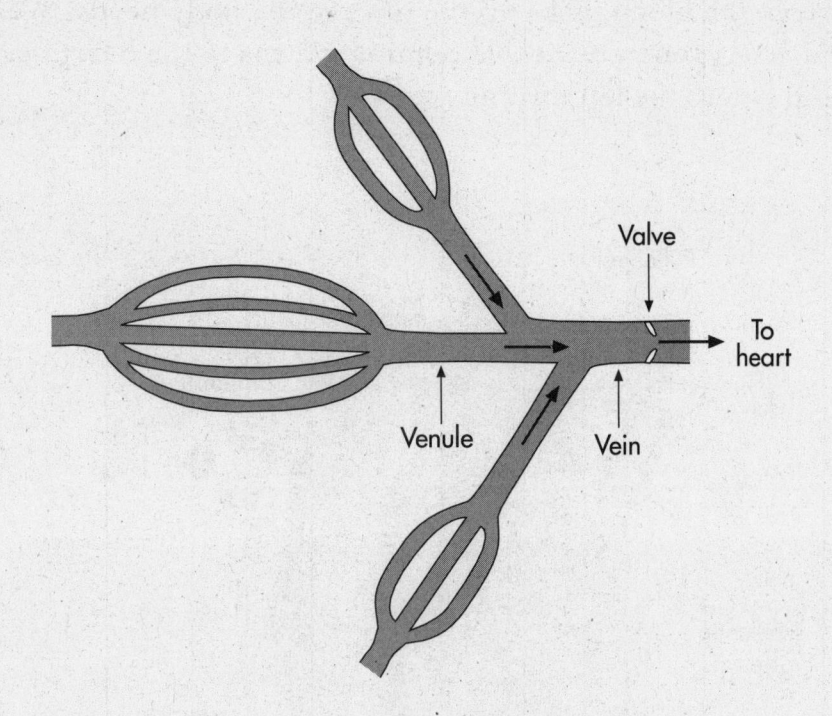

From the capillary beds, blood travels through vessels called **venules**, then into larger vessels called **veins**. Veins carry blood *toward* the heart. They are thin-walled vessels with one-way valves that prevent the backward flow of blood. The deoxygenated blood finally reaches the heart, entering through the inferior vena cava, into the **right atrium.**

The blood is then pumped from the right atrium to the right ventricle. From the right ventricle, blood will travel out again into the body, but this time toward the lungs, in what's called the **pulmonary circulation**.

The Pulmonary Circulation
Blood leaves the right ventricle through a large artery known as the **pulmonary artery.** Remember what we said about arteries? Blood vessels that leave the heart are called arteries. The pulmonary artery branches into right and left pulmonary arteries, which lead to the lungs. These arteries then become smaller vessels called **arterioles** and finally **capillaries.**

We mentioned above that the blood that arrives in the right atrium is deoxygenated, having delivered its oxygen to the body. When it leaves the right ventricle, it heads to the lungs in order to pick up fresh oxygen and dump its load of CO_2. Does this sound vaguely familiar? It should. This is the gas exchange we discussed before when we looked at the respiratory system. Keep in mind that the capillaries in the lungs are wrapped around alveoli, which are tiny air sacs.

At the alveoli, the blood picks up the oxygen the body needs. We now say that the blood is **oxygenated**. At this point it returns to the heart via the **pulmonary veins** and enters the left atrium:

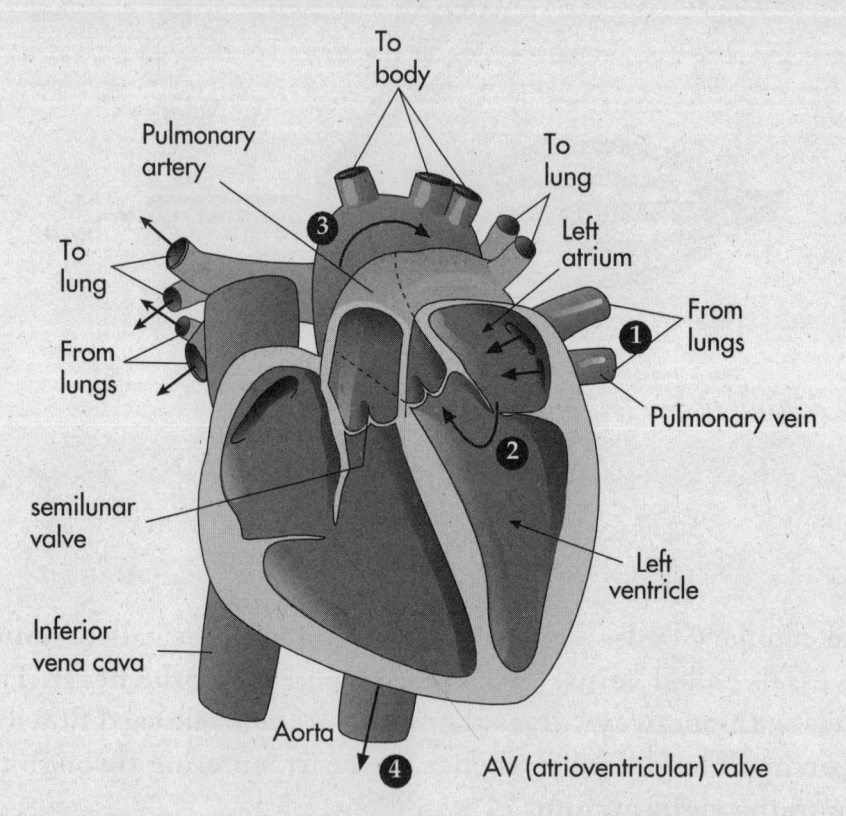

Once the blood moves to the left ventricle, it's ready to start its circuit all over again.

The Contents of the Blood
Now let's take a look at blood itself. Blood consists of two things:
1. Fluid (called **plasma**)
2. Cells suspended in the fluid

Blood doesn't just carry oxygen and CO_2 throughout the body. It also carries three types of cells: **red blood cells (erythrocytes), white blood cells**, and **platelets**. Red blood cells (erythrocytes) are the actual oxygen carriers in the blood—they contain **hemoglobin**, a specialized iron-complexed protein that transports oxygen.

Blood also contains **white blood cells (leukoocytes)**. These cells fight infections, and there are five types of leukocytes: lymphocytes, basopils, eosinophils, monocytes, and neutrophils. You will not need to know the different names of the white blood cells for the exam, but you should be aware of the function of white blood cells. Some white blood cells eat bacteria and debris that's produced from our own dead cells, and some white blood cells produce other cells that give rise to **antibodies**, which defend the body against infection by foreign agents. Leukocytes come from bone marrow (which is located in the center of bones); bone marrow also produces erthyrocytes. This is important, so don't forget it.

Platelets, the last active component of blood, are not actually cells; they can be thought of pieces of cells (they have no nuclei). They are involved in blood clotting, along with a plasma protein called **fibrinogen**.

Blood Types

Blood comes in four different types: **A**, **B**, **AB**, and **O**, and if a patient in the hospital is given the wrong type of blood during a transfusion, it could be fatal! Why? Because blood cells clump when they're exposed to the wrong blood type. For example, if you have blood type A and you receive a blood transfusion of blood type B, your blood will start to clump as the body produces antibodies that bind to the surface of the foreign blood cells. There are two fairly unique properties of blood types:

- Type O blood is the universal donor.
- Type AB is the universal recipient.

This means that anyone can receive a blood transfusion of type O blood, which produces no immune response, and that those with type AB blood can receive any kind of blood.

Cardiovascular and Blood Disorders

Here are some common cardiovascular and blood disorders you might be interested in. You probably won't be tested on these in too much detail, but try to be vaguely familiar with them:

- **High blood pressure**—The arteries become narrowed, which reduces the flow of blood to the heart. If left untreated, this condition can cause damage to the heart muscles and blood vessels. The primary cause of narrowed blood vessels is a buildup of fatty deposits or "plaque" on the walls of the arteries.

- **Anemia**—A condition in which the blood doesn't carry enough oxygen because the number of healthy red blood cells is below normal. This can occur as a result of insufficient levels of iron in the diet and often manifests itself in the form of extreme fatigue.

- **Leukemia**—A blood disease in which there is an uncontrolled production of immature white blood cells. Leukemia is a type of cancer.

The Immune System

The **immune system** is the body's defense system. We've already talked about leukocytes, which are white blood cells involved in the body's immune response. As we saw, specific types of leukocytes trigger an immune response when they detect an **antigen**, or foreign invader. In addition to these cells, the immune system includes a network of **lymph vessels** that run along the same routes as the blood vessels:

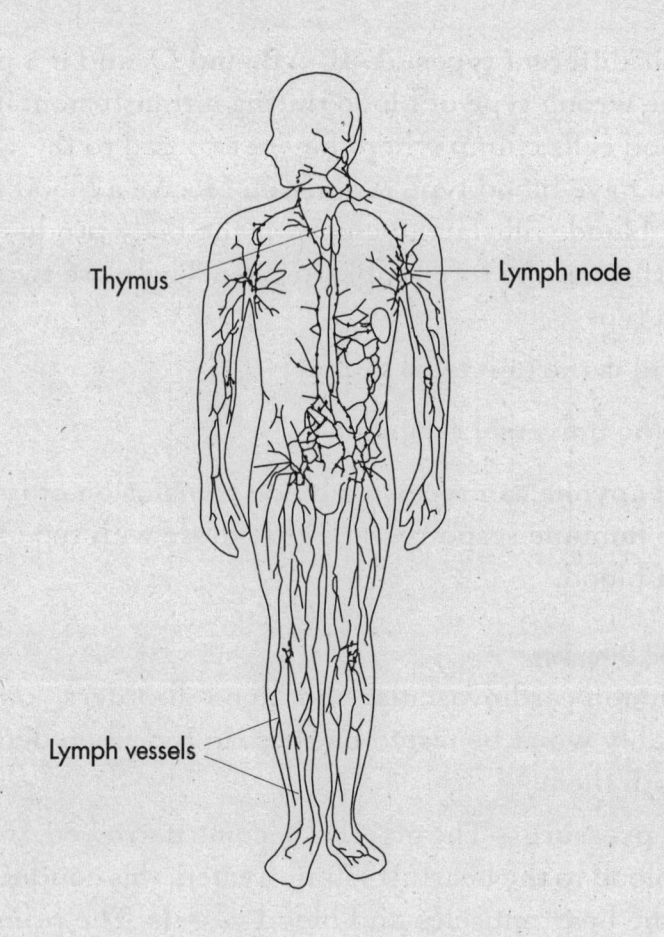

Along the lymph vessels are **lymph nodes**, which are bulges in the vessels that filter lymph; these nodes contain tissue that's filled with white blood cells. When the body is fighting an infection, the white blood cells multiply, causing the nodes to swell. Another important function of the lymphatic system is that it returns fluids and proteins (collectively called lymph) lost by the blood as it circulates through the body, to the bloodstream. Lymph diffuses through tiny lymph capillaries that are intertwined with the blood capillaries.

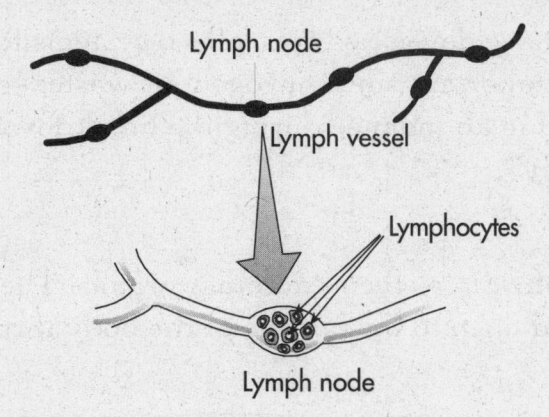

This is what your doctor is checking for when he or she feels the sides of your throat—he or she is seeing if your lymph nodes are swollen.

One final point about the immune system. The immune system provides you with **immunity** to certain diseases. For example, if you had chicken pox when you were a kid, you will most likely never get it again even if you're re-exposed to it. This is because the body now recognizes the virus that causes chicken pox. The first time your body was infected, it took the immune system a while to generate the right antibodies and tackle the invader. However, now that your body has been exposed to that viral strain, the immune system's response is incalculably faster: The moment it detects the presence of chicken pox, it remembers the virus and sends out the appropriate antibodies. This speedy response, and the protection it offers the body, is known as immunity.

Allergies

There are times, however, when the immune system doesn't function perfectly. In some cases, such common substances as dust and pollen can trigger an impressive immune response. When your body treats harmless substances as dangerous invaders, this reaction is called an **allergy**. Additionally, many people have allergies to specific foods or drugs. In these cases, the presence of the antagonistic substance can induce a runny nose, asthma, or sneezing. All of these responses are typical immune responses, which explains why the symptoms of allergies are identical to the symptoms of a cold: The body reacts the same way in both cases.

EXCRETION

As you already know, all organisms must get rid of wastes, or metabolic byproducts. Some byproducts include CO_2, salts, and nitrogenous wastes. Simple organisms, such as protists and hydra, get rid of toxic wastes through simple diffusion: wastes are released either directly into the environment or, in the case of the hydra, into a simple gastrovascular cavity and then into the environment.

LIFE FUNCTIONS ◆ 87

Higher organisms have developed specialized systems for getting rid of wastes. This is pretty important since nitrogenous wastes—products that contain nitrogen and produced in abundance during the breakdown of amino acids—are highly toxic to the body.

Earthworms

Earthworms have **nephridia** as their excretory organs. These branched tubes concentrate wastes and open to the outside of the body through tiny pores:

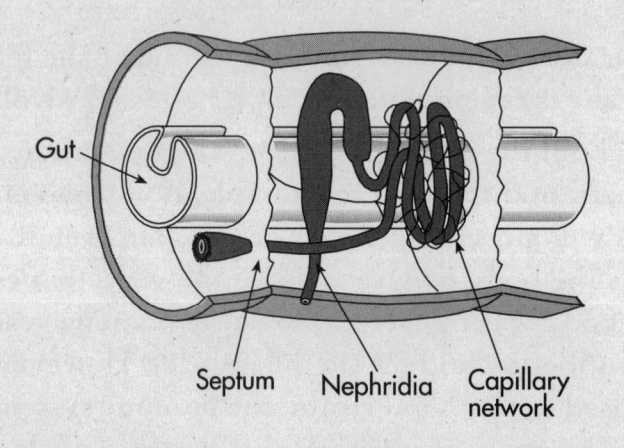

Insects

The excretory organs in insects are called **Malpighian tubules**. These tubules concentrate waste and empty into the intestine. The major waste product, **uric acid**, is excreted as a dry pellet:

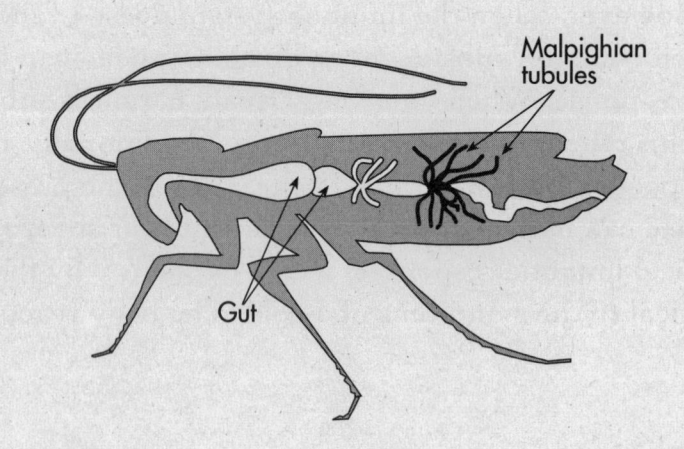

The Human Excretory System

In humans, the organs that regulate excretion are the two **kidneys**, found above the waist. Though kidneys look rather unassuming, they are fantastically complicated structures made up of millions of tiny functional units called **nephrons**.

Nephron

A nephron consists of several regions. Here's what a nephron looks like under a microscope:

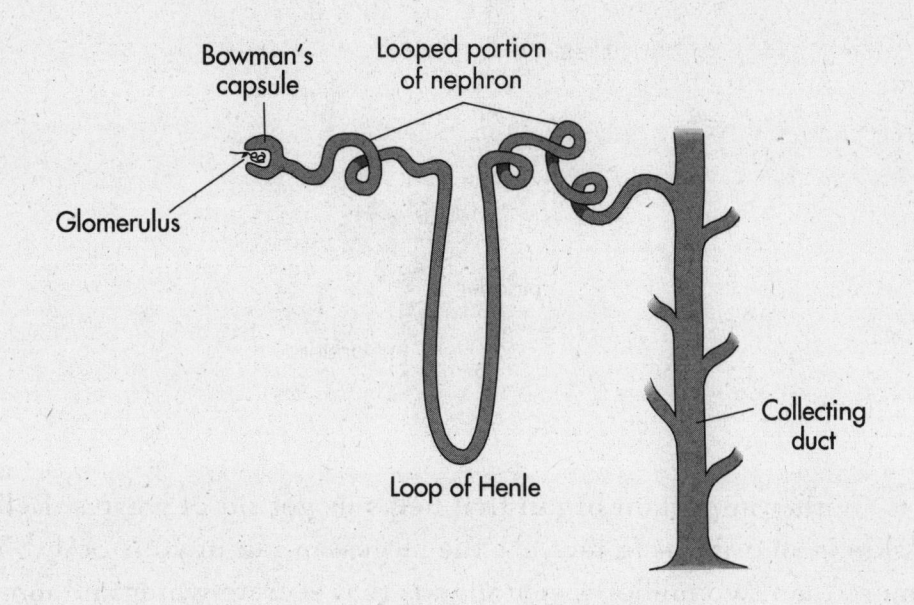

Bowman's capsule
Looped portion of nephron
Glomerulus
Loop of Henle
Collecting duct

How does a nephron work? Well, let's trace the flow of blood through a nephron. Blood vessels from the aorta lead to the kidney and branch into tiny balls of capillaries called the **glomerulus**. The glomerulus "sits" within a cup-shaped structure called the **Bowman's capsule**. Small substances in the blood such as ions, water, glucose, and amino acids easily pass through the capillary walls into the porous surface of the Bowman's capsule. The fluid collected here is called a **filtrate**.

The filtrate travels along the entire nephron, passing through its looped portion and finally into the collecting duct. As the filtrate moves through the nephron, glucose, amino acids, and salts are reabsorbed by the body, but the rest of the fluid is concentrated into urine.

This waste-concentrated urine moves from the **kidney** into the **ureter**, then into the **bladder**, and finally out through the **urethra**, a tiny tube leading from the bladder to the outside of the body.

LIFE FUNCTIONS

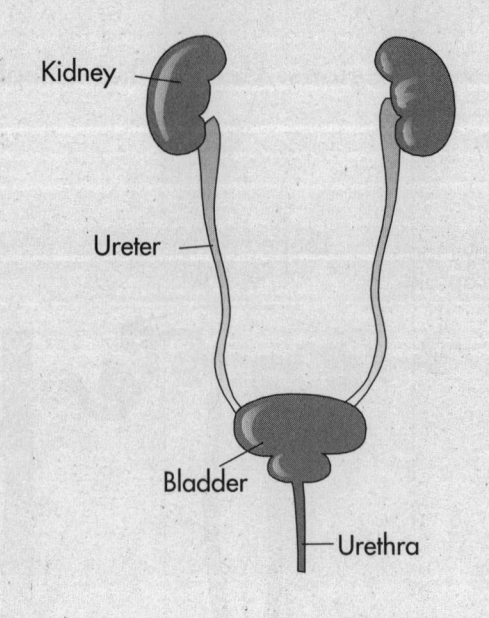

Skin

The **skin** is another important organ that helps us get rid of wastes. Believe it or not, your skin is an organ—in fact, it's the largest organ in your body! Your skin contains more than two million sweat glands that secrete water and ions. Sweat glands not only help to maintain an optimal salt balance in your body, they also help maintain body temperature:

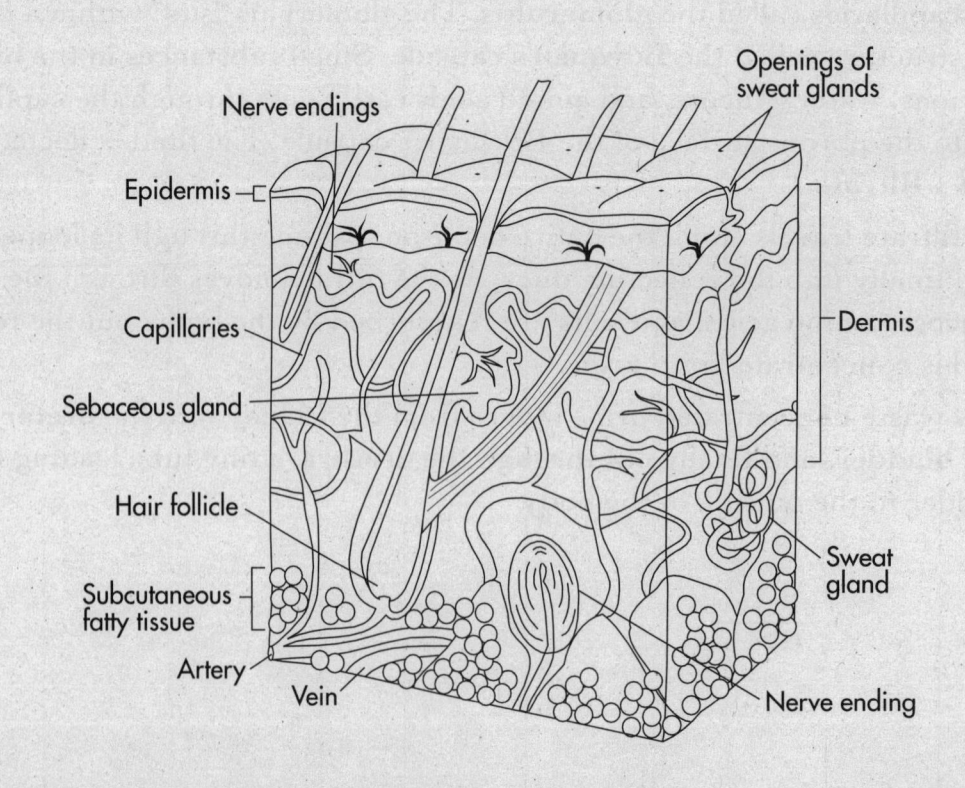

The skin is made up of three layers: the **epidermis, dermis,** and **subcutaneous tissue**. Sweat glands are found in the dermis layer, along with blood vessels, nerves, and oil (sebaceous) glands.

The Lungs and Liver

The lungs and liver also get rid of wastes in their own way. Carbon dioxide is mainly excreted by the lungs. The liver is responsible for converting amino acids into urea, the form of nitrogenous waste that is secreted. This conversion is known as **deamination**.

REGULATION

All organisms have evolved systems that allow them to adjust to changes in their external environment. The task of coordinating and processing new information, and reacting appropriately to it, falls to the **nervous system** (nerve control) and the **endocrine system** (chemical control). Let's start our discussion of regulation by taking a look at the nervous system.

The Nervous System

The basic unit of structure and function in the nervous system is a nerve cell, or a **neuron**. Neurons are specialized cells that pick up and transmit messages throughout the body. Let's take a look at your basic neuron:

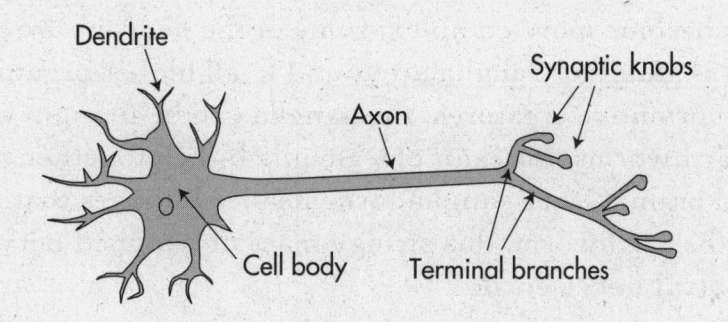

Neurons consist of a **cell body**, **dendrites** and an **axon**, with **synaptic knobs**. The cell body contains the nucleus and all the usual organelles found in the cytoplasm of a cell. The dendrites are short extensions of the cell body that receive stimuli (passed along by chemical messengers) from adjacent nerve cells. The axon is a long, slender extension of the cell body that transmits an impulse from the cell body to another neuron. Axons can be very long. For example, giraffes have single axons that span the entire length of their necks.

At the end of the axon (on the terminal branches) are thin fibers known as **synaptic knobs** that release chemical substances called **neurotransmitters**.

Neurotransmitters are chemical messengers that transmit nerve impulses from cell to cell. When a "message" arrives at a neuron's dendrites, it passes through the dendrites to the cell body, then down the axon to the terminal branches and synaptic knobs.

When an impulse reaches the end of an axon, it triggers the release of neurotransmitters into the space between the first cell's axon and the next cell's dendrites. This space is called a **synapse**. The neurotransmitter travels to the other side and binds to receptors on the dendrites of the next neuron. Now the impulse moves along the second neuron from its dendrites to its axon. It's the neurotransmitter that passes the signal to the adjacent neuron. There are many different neurotransmitters, but an important one which you should be familiar with for the exam is **acetylcholine**. Acetylcholine is one of the most common neurotransmitters in both vertebrates and invertebrates. Among other things, it is responsible for muscle contraction.

THE NERVOUS SYSTEM IN HIGHER ORGANISMS

Now that we've taken a look at the neuron, let's discuss the different types of nervous systems found in various organisms. The simplest nervous system is no more than a web of undifferentiated neurons known as a **nerve net**. The hydra has this type of nervous system, in which the neurons receive stimuli and transmit impulses in all directions.

As organisms become more complex, some of the neurons are gathered into what are known as **ganglia**. Ganglia are found in all higher organisms, including humans. In more primitive creatures, the ganglia can be thought of as rudimentary brains. In earthworms, for example, ganglia bunch together to form a simple two-lobed brain. Other ganglia form smaller bunches that run the length of the worm. In the earthworm, this stringy mass of bunched nerve cells is known as the **ventral nerve cord**:

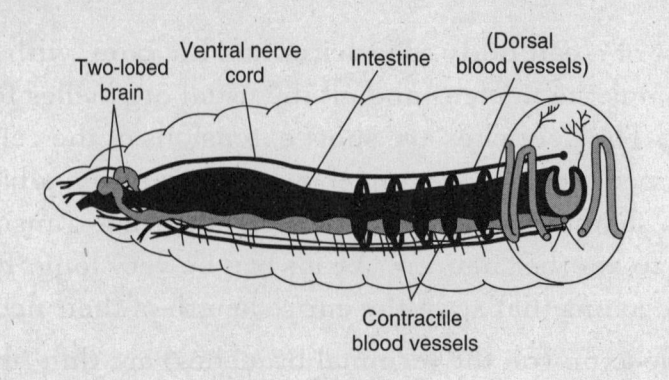

The grasshopper has a nervous system that's very similar to the earthworm's:

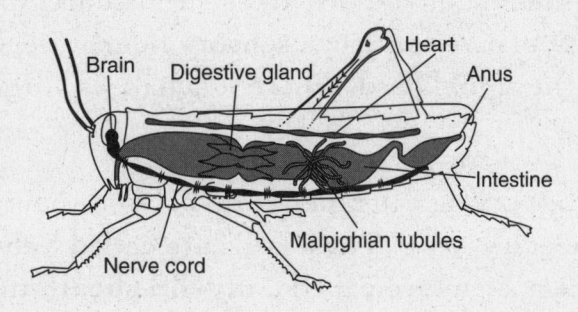

THE HUMAN NERVOUS SYSTEM

Types of Neurons

Neurons in humans are highly specialized and fall into three groups: **sensory neurons**, **motor (effector) neurons,** and **interneurons**. These three different types of neurons play distinct roles in the transmission of a nerve impulse. Let's first consider the sense of touch.

As your fingers come in contact with this page, sensory neurons pick up the "touch" impulses and transmit them toward the brain or spinal cord. Interneurons act as links between sensory neurons and are the most abundant type of neuron in the nervous system. Motor neurons are found in the brain or spinal cord; they transmit signals from the brain and spinal cord to the effector organs, which can be muscles or glands:

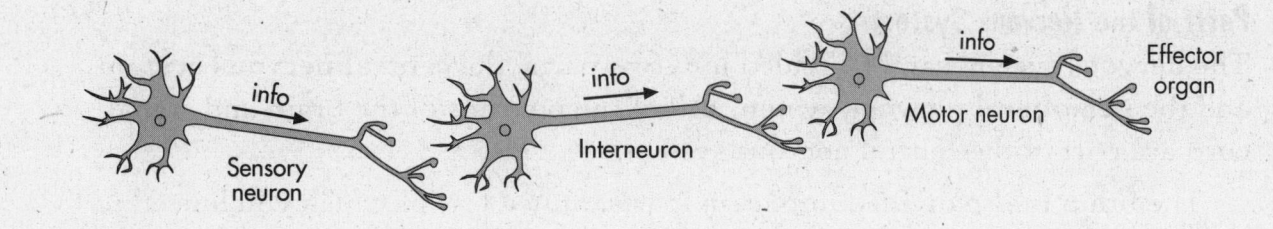

How Neurons Communicate

Before we talk about the events in the transmission of a nerve impulse, let's review how neurons interact. There are literally billions of neurons transmitting impulses throughout your body, active at all times. More often than not, several neurons are interconnected. This means that the dendrites of one neuron are adjacent to the axons of several other neurons. In the same way, the dendrites of one cell can pick up the impulses sent from axons of several other cells.

An example of nerve cell function is the **reflex arc**. When the doctor taps your knee with a hammer, he or she provokes a reflex arc. Only two neurons participate in this particular reflex arc: a sensory neuron carries information about the stimulus to the spinal cord, where it synapses with a motor neuron.

Schwann Cells

Many neurons have supporting cells that wrap around their axons like plastic insulation around an electric wire. These cells are called **Schwann cells**. Schwann cells produce a structure called a **myelin sheath** that insulates the axon. In between the sections of myelination are bare segments of the axon called the **nodes of Ranvier**:

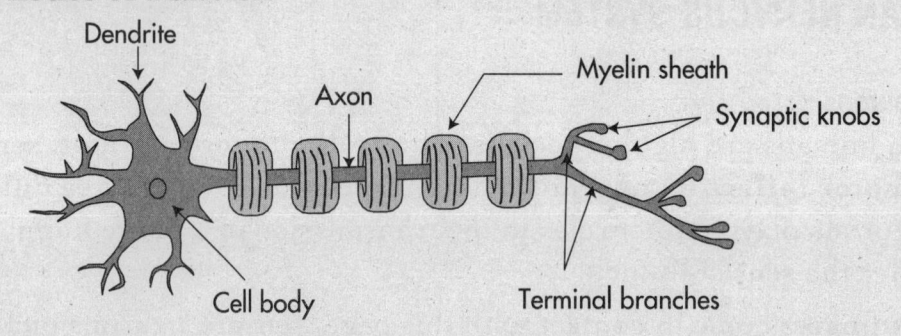

The myelin sheath enables the neuron to speed up its transmission of the impulse—the nerve impulses jump from node to node. This speeding up of the impulse allows the organism to react much more quickly to its environment.

Now that we've discussed neurons, let's see how they're organized in the nervous system itself.

Parts of the Nervous System

The nervous system can be divided into two parts: the **central nervous system** and the **peripheral nervous system**. All of the neurons of the brain and spinal cord are part of the central nervous system.

The brain is also divided into many parts, only a few of which you'll need to be familiar with. The **cerebrum** controls all voluntary activities and receives and interprets sensory information. It is the largest part of the brain. The **cerebellum** coordinates muscle activity and controls balance. The **medulla** controls involuntary actions such as peristalsis and the beating of the heart.

The **spinal cord** extends from the base of the brain to the vertebrae. It has two functions: (1) to transmit impulses to and from the brain, and (2) to control reflex activities.

All of the other neurons lying outside the brain and the spinal cord—in the skin, organs, and blood vessels—are collectively part of the **peripheral nervous**

system. Although these systems are interwoven, we still use the terms "central" and "peripheral."

The peripheral nervous system is further broken down into the **somatic nervous system** and the **autonomic nervous system**. The somatic nervous system is the part of the peripheral nervous system that controls voluntary activities. For example, the movement of your eyes across the page as you read this line is under the control of your somatic nervous system. The **autonomic nervous system** is the part that controls involuntary actions. The beating of your heart and the actions of your digestive system are both under the control of the autonomic nervous system.

The interesting thing about these two systems is that they sometimes overlap. For instance, you can control your breathing if you choose to. Yet when you sleep, you no longer need to think about it: Your somatic system hands control of your respiration over to the autonomic system.

To make matters even more complicated, your autonomic system is broken down into the **sympathetic nervous system** and the **parasympathetic nervous system**. The sympathetic system prepares your body for action, while the parasympathetic system brings the body back to homeostasis, its regular resting state.

How can you remember all this? Take a look at the flow chart below. It provides a nice overview of the different parts of the nervous system:

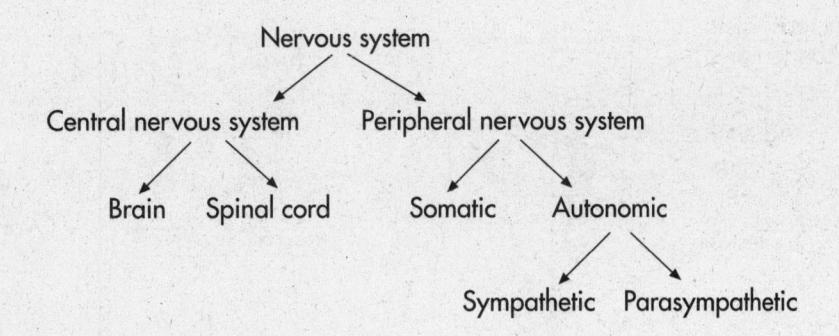

```
                    Nervous system
                   ↙            ↘
        Central nervous system   Peripheral nervous system
              ↙      ↘                ↙          ↘
           Brain   Spinal cord    Somatic      Autonomic
                                              ↙         ↘
                                       Sympathetic   Parasympathetic
```

Disorders of the Nervous System

Here's a list of some common disorders associated with the nervous system. You should recognize them as that, but you will not be tested specifically on them.

- **Meningitis**—A disease in which the connective tissue covering the brain (meninges) are infected and inflamed.

- **Cerebral palsy**—A group of motor disorders that results in a loss of muscle control (due to damage to the motor areas of the brain).

- **Stroke**—A disease in which brain tissue is destroyed because the flow of blood to the brain is blocked.

- **Polio**—A viral disease that results from the destruction of motor neurons in the spinal nerves. Polio can lead to paralysis.

Endocrine System

The endocrine system is the other major system involved in maintaining the body's internal balance, or **homeostasis**; it is closely associated with the nervous system. The **endocrine glands** (and organs in humans) depend on the signals provided by the nervous system in order to know when to release specific **hormones**. Hormones are chemical messengers produced by the endocrine glands and then released into the bloodstream to act on glands or organs in distant parts of the body.

Take a look at the endocrine glands in the human body:

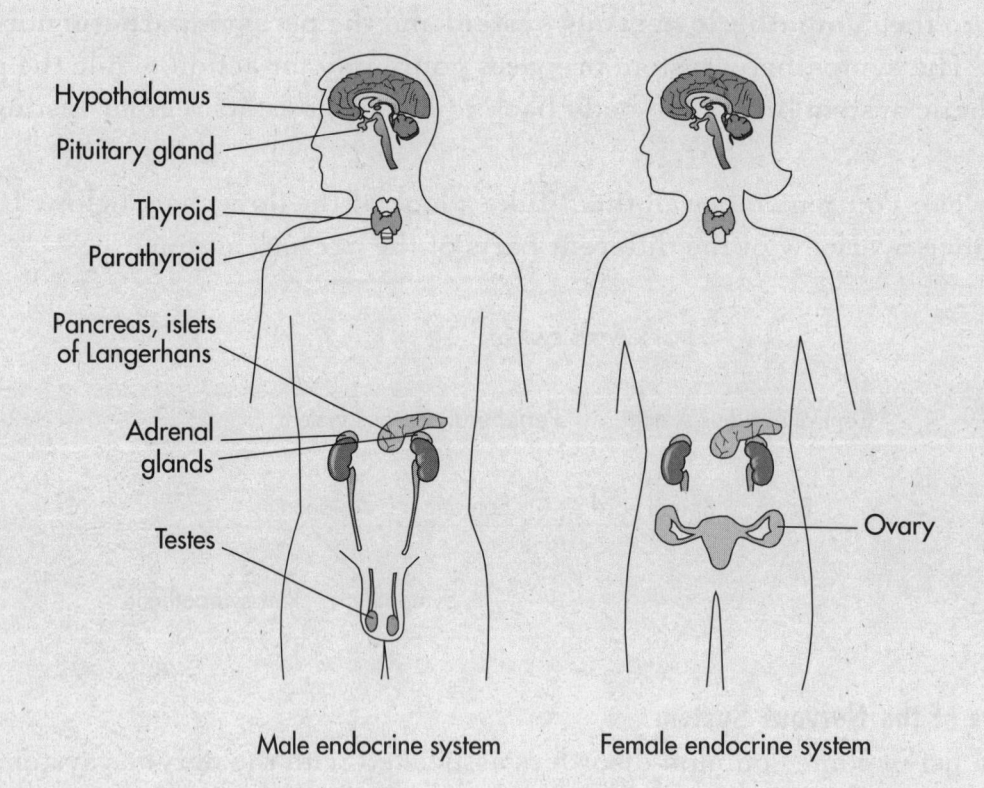

Male endocrine system — Hypothalamus, Pituitary gland, Thyroid, Parathyroid, Pancreas, islets of Langerhans, Adrenal glands, Testes

Female endocrine system — Ovary

Negative Feedback

Before we launch into a review of the different hormones in the body, let's talk about how hormones work. Although hormones flow in your blood, they are designed to affect specific cells. The cells that a hormone affects are known as its **target cells**. Suppose, for example, that gland X makes hormone Y. Hormone Y, in turn, has some effect on organ Z. We would then say that organ Z is the target organ of hormone Y.

Hormones are also regulated by a **negative feedback system**. This means that an excess of the hormone will temporarily shut down the production of that hormone. For example, when hormone Y reaches its functionally optimal level in the bloodstream, the organ that produces and secretes the hormone, gland X, is temporarily inhibited from producing hormone Y. Once the levels of hormone Y decline, the gland will resume production of the hormone.

The Pituitary: The Master Gland

Let's start by discussing the **pituitary gland**. The pituitary gland is actually made up of two lobes, one of which is the anterior pituitary, while the other is called the posterior pituitary. The pituitary used to be called the master gland because so many of its hormones regulate other endocrine functions, but it recently came to light that the pituitary receives direct hormonal orders from the hypothalamus. The pituitary secretes several hormones:

- **Follicle stimulating hormone (FSH)**, which stimulates the ovarian follicle to grow. This is an important stage in the female menstrual cycle (we'll see FSH again in chapter 9, "Reproduction.").

- **Luteinizing hormone (LH)**, which causes the release of the ovum, also during the menstrual cycle.

- **Growth-stimulating hormone (GH)**, which stimulates growth throughout the body.

- **Thyroid-stimulating hormone (TSH)**, which stimulates the thyroid to secrete its hormone (we'll discuss this shortly).

Hypothalamus

As we mentioned, the pituitary works in tandem with a part of the brain called the **hypothalamus**, and in fact, the pituitary is situated just below it:

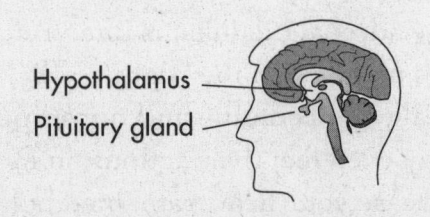

The hypothalamus secretes substances that can stimulate or inhibit the actions of the pituitary.

Pancreas

We already saw that the pancreas produces enzymes that are released into the small intestine in the chapter on digestion. But the pancreas also secretes two important hormones, **glucagon** and **insulin**. These pancreatic hormones are produced in a special cluster of cells within the pancreas called the **islet of Langerhans.** The target organs for these hormones are the liver and muscle cells. Glucagon, for example, stimulates the liver to convert **glycogen** (the stored form of glucose) into glucose. Glucagon, therefore, *increases* the levels of glucose in the blood. Insulin has the opposite effect: It stimulates the uptake of glucose by the body cells and its conversion to glycogen in the liver. Insulin therefore *lowers* the levels of glucose in the blood.

When a person's body cannot properly regulate its blood sugar levels because of a deficiency of insulin, that person is said to be **diabetic**. Diabetes is a life-threatening disorder if left untreated. Its treatment can involve alteration of diet and/or regular injections of insulin.

The Adrenal Glands

Now let's take a look at the adrenal glands. The adrenal glands are actually two endocrine glands. One is called the **adrenal medulla** (the inner region) and the other is called the **adrenal cortex** (the outer region). Although they are part of the same organ, these two endocrine glands work independently of one another.

The Adrenal Cortex

The adrenal cortex releases steroid hormones called **corticosteroids** in reaction to stress. These steroid hormones do two things: (1) they increase the blood's concentration of glucose by promoting the conversion of amino acids and fatty acids to glucose, and (2) they help the body reabsorb salt and water from the urine, in the kidneys. The effects of the adrenal cortex are slower to occur but longer in duration than those of the adrenal medulla.

The Adrenal Medulla

The other adrenal gland, the adrenal medulla, is often referred to as the "emergency gland." It releases hormones involved in the "fight-or-flight" response. These hormones (**epinephrine**, also called **adrenaline** and **norepinephrine**) kick in when you're under stress. You may even feel their actions, in fact, as you sit down to take the Biology GSE. They increase your heart rate, metabolic rate, and blood pressure, giving you a quick boost of energy; but their effects are relatively short-lived.

The Thyroid Gland
The thyroid gland is located in the neck and is stimulated by TSH to release the hormone **thyroxin** and tyrosine. Thyroxin regulates the metabolic rate in most body tissues, and makes an important contribution to the development and growth of the human body.

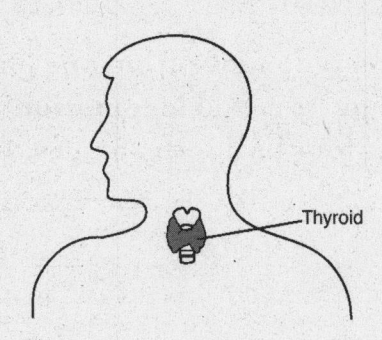

The Parathyroid Glands
The parathyroids are four little pea-shaped organs that sit on your thyroid. They secrete the hormone **parathyroid hormone**, or **PTH**, which regulates your blood calcium levels. If your body needs more calcium, PTH triggers the bones to release the calcium stored inside them. Excess calcium in the bloodstream triggers the parathyroid to stop releasing PTH (this is an example of a negative feedback loop). This, in turn, will allow the bones to uptake and store excess calcium.

The Sex Hormones
Three major hormones that are involved in human reproduction are **estrogen**, **progesterone**, and **testosterone**. Estrogen and progesterone are hormones that are released by the ovaries in women. Both hormones regulate the menstrual cycle, but estrogen also promotes female secondary sex characteristics. Testosterone is the male hormone that promotes the production of sperm. It also promotes male secondary sex characteristics. We'll take a closer look at these hormones in chapter 9.

Endocrine Disorders
Here are some principal disorders associated with the endocrine system:
- **Goiter**—A condition associated with a deficiency of thyroid hormone, which results in a horrifically enlarged thyroid. Goiter is a result of an iodine deficiency in the diet.

- **Diabetes** — As stated above, a condition in which blood sugar levels are not properly regulated by the body. It is usually due to a problem with the body's ability to produce the hormone insulin (remember that insulin is the hormone that allows the cells of the body to take up insulin).

LOCOMOTION

Most organisms have the ability to move from one place to another. In biological terms, this ability to get around is called **locomotion**. Locomotion is important to organisms because it confers four basic advantages. It makes it easier to:

1. Reproduce
2. Get food
3. Avoid predators
4. Find shelter

Needless to say, all four of these increase an organism's chances for survival.

Unicellular Organisms

Unicellular organisms such as protists use specialized structures to move about. As we saw earlier, *Amoeba* uses its pseudopodia; *Euglena*, its whip-like flagella; and *Paramecium,* its cilia. While there are other means of locomotion among microorganisms, these three appendages are among the most common.

Earthworms

Some organisms have muscles that are responsible for locomotion. For instance, earthworms have muscles that contract and relax to make their long, tube-like bodies move. They also contain short, paired bristles called **setae** that grip the soil as they inch forward.

Grasshoppers

Many organisms have a supporting skeletal system, and some wear their support on the outside. In other words, they have an **exoskeleton**—a hard covering or shell that keeps their insides from sagging toward the ground. Grasshoppers, for example, have a hard exoskeleton that's made of **chitin** (a polysaccharide). Because their muscles are attached to this exoskeleton, insects such as the grasshopper have a sturdy, effective means of locomotion. Moreover, insects have jointed appendages that are specially adapted for moving about on land, and wings that enable them to fly.

Interestingly enough, the wings of insects are not at all similar to the wings of birds or mammals (like bats), except for the fact that insects are rendered airborne by them. Biologically speaking, this means that wings in insects, birds, and bats evolved independently of one another: Each group evolved wings on its own; they did not inherit wings from a common ancestor. We'll come back to this concept in chapter 12 when we look at evolution.

Vertebrates

All vertebrates (animals with backbones) possess an **endoskeleton**—their entire skeleton is on the inside of their body. Just think of your own backbone (spine) and all your other bones—you can't see them because they're covered up by layers of muscle, nerve fibers, fat, and skin. Fish, amphibians, reptiles, birds, and mammals are vertebrates.

The Human Skeletal System

In humans, the supporting skeleton is made of both **cartilage** and **bone**. Cartilage is a flexible connective tissue found in the developing skeleton of all vertebrate embryos. It is later replaced by bone, except in such areas as the external ear and the tip of the nose.

Bones and Joints

Bone is a hard connective tissue that provides support for the body and makes locomotion possible. It is made up of calcium phosphate and collagen; tiny repeated units called **Haversian systems** make up its microscopic structure. Bones are held together by joints such as the ball-and-socket joints that can be seen where the shoulder connects to the arms. Joints are held together by tough connective tissues called **ligaments**. For the exam, just remember that ligaments attach bone to bone. The connective tissues that attach muscles to bones are called **tendons**.

Muscles

There are three kinds of muscles in the body: skeletal, smooth (visceral), and cardiac. **Skeletal muscles** control voluntary movements. You'll notice that they have stripes called **striations** and are made up of multinucleated cells.

Smooth muscles are found throughout the body—in the walls of blood vessels, the digestive tract, and internal organs. They are long and tapered, and each cell has one nucleus (mononucleated). Smooth muscles are responsible for involuntary movements. Compared to those of skeletal muscles, the contractions of smooth muscles are slow.

Cardiac muscles are found in the heart. They possess characteristics of both smooth and skeletal muscles: Cardiac muscle is striated, just like skeletal muscles, but it is under involuntary control, as is smooth muscle. Contractions in cardiac muscle are spontaneous and automatic. This simply means that the heart can beat on its own, without your willing it to beat. Both smooth muscle and cardiac muscle get their instructions from the autonomic nervous system.

One last thing you should remember about muscle contractions: They are energy-dependent. A muscle contraction requires energy in the form of ATP.

Here's a chart to help you remember the types of muscle tissues:

Types of Muscle Tissues			
	Skeletal	Smooth	Cardiac
Location	Attached to skeleton	Wall of digestive tract, inside the blood vessels	Wall of heart
Type of control	Voluntary	Involuntary	Involuntary
Striations	Yes	No	No
Multinucleated	Yes	No	No
Speed of contraction	Rapid	Slowest	Intermediate

Diseases of the Locomotive System

Here are some common diseases that can affect locomotion in humans:

- **Arthritis**—A painful inflammation of the joints.

- **Tendonitis**—A painful inflammation of the tendons. This disorder is common among athletes.

LET'S TEST WHAT YOU'VE LEARNED

1. Which sequence represents the direction of CO_2 flow as it passes out of the respiratory system into the external environment?

    1. alveoli → trachea → bronchioles → bronchi → pharynx → nasal cavity
    2. alveoli → bronchi → pharynx → bronchioles → trachea → nasal cavity
    3. alveoli → pharynx → trachea → bronchioles → bronchi → nasal cavity
    4. alveoli → bronchioles → bronchi → trachea → pharynx → nasal cavity

    Directions: (2–4): For each phrase in questions 2 through 4, select the malfunction from the list below that best describes that statement.

    Malfunctions

    A. Polio

    B. Stroke

    C. Meningitis

    D. Cerebral palsy

2. A congenital disease characterized by abnormal motor functions

3. A clot in a cerebral blood vessel that may result in brain damage

4. Inflammation of the membrane surrounding the brain and spinal cord

5. Short-tailed shrews and ruby-throated hummingbirds have high metabolic rates. As a result, these animals

    1. utilize energy rapidly.
    2. need very little food.
    3. have very few predators.
    4. hibernate in hot weather.

6. The diagram below represents a protist.

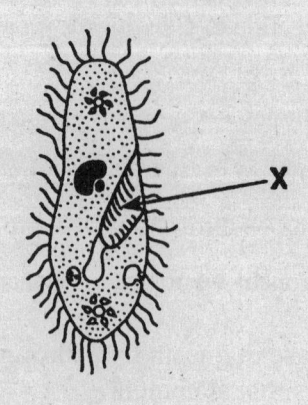

   Structure *X* is most directly involved in the process of

   1. extracellular digestion.
   2. enzymatic hydrolysis.
   3. ingestion.
   4. transpiration.

7. In an amoeba, which process is best represented by the arrows shown in the diagram below?

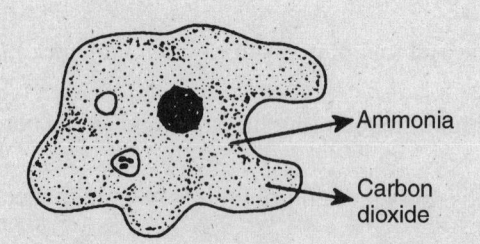

   1. Absorption by active transport
   2. Excretion by diffusion
   3. Respiratory gas exchange
   4. Egestion of digestive end products

8. Which statement describes a relationship between the human cells illustrated in the diagrams below?

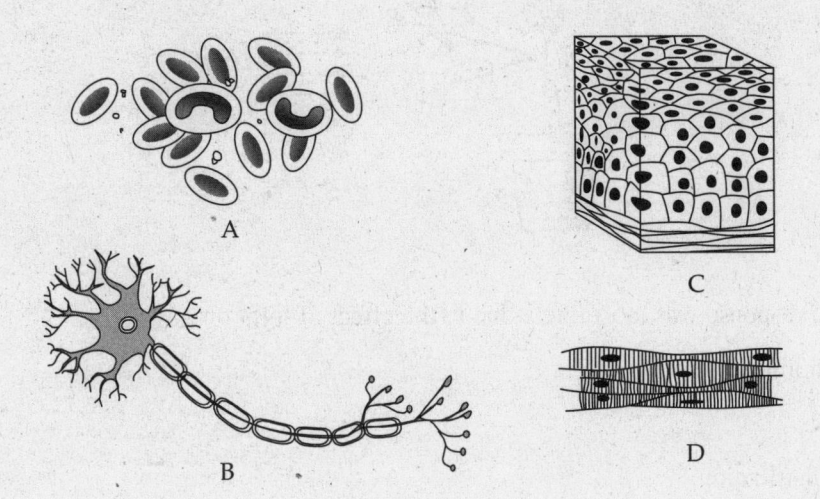

1. *B* may cause *D* to contract.
2. *A* is produced by *D*.
3. *C* transports oxygen to *A*.
4. *B* is used to repair *C*.

9. One way in which the intake of oxygen is similar in the hydra and the earthworm is that both organisms

1. absorb oxygen through a system of tubes.
2. utilize cilia to absorb oxygen.
3. use capillaries to transport oxygen.
4. absorb oxygen through their external surfaces.

10. The life function of transport in the grasshopper involves

1. an internal gas exchange surface and alveoli.
2. an open circulatory system and tracheal tubes.
3. moist outer skin and hemoglobin.
4. a dry external body surface and hemoglobin.

11. The diagram below represent a growth response in a plant.

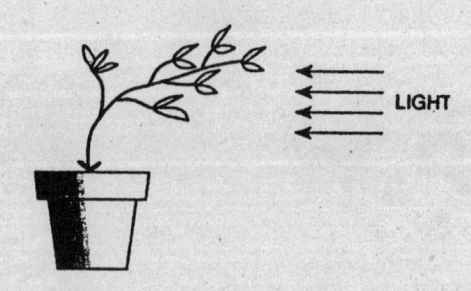

This growth response was most likely due to the effect of light on
   1. acetycholine.
   2. minerals.
   3. auxin distribution.
   4. vascular tissue.

12. The diagram below shows a longitudinal section of the human heart.

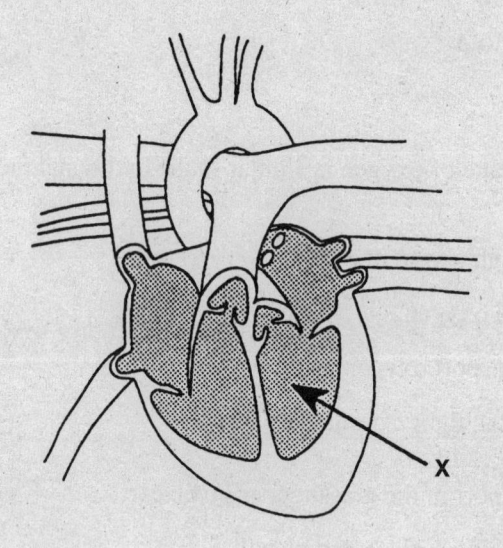

The structure labeled X is known as
   1. a ventricle.
   2. an atrium.
   3. a valve.
   4. the aorta.

13. A hawk sees a field mouse, which it then captures for food. In this activity, the eyes of the hawk function as

    1. effectors.
    2. receptors.
    3. stimuli.
    4. neurotransmitters.

14. Food is usually kept from entering the trachea by the

    1. diaphragm.
    2. epiglottis.
    3. villi.
    4. ribs.

15. The nephrons and alveoli of humans are most similar in function to the

    1. nephridia and skin of earthworms.
    2. Malpighian tubules and muscles of grasshoppers.
    3. nerve nets and gastrovascular cavities of hydras.
    4. cilia and pseudopodia of protozoa.

Chapter 9

REPRODUCTION

Reproduction in living things refers to their ability to grow and produce offspring. In this chapter, we'll take a look at both asexual and sexual reproduction. Since reproduction begins on a cellular level, let's start with the somatic (body) cell.

THE CELL CYCLE

The cells of all living things grow and multiply through a cycle that's made up of four phases. During three of these phases (G_1, S, and G_2 of interphase), the cell is growing and metabolically active, and during the fourth phase, it is undergoing division to produce two new cells (mitosis). The cell cycle has a different duration in all types of cells; for instance, some cells in the body take about 15 hours to go through a complete cycle, while for cells in our brain, the cycle can take many years. Take a look at the diagram depicting the cycle of a typical cell below:

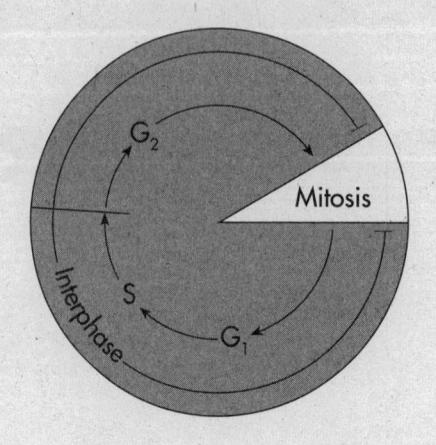

MITOSIS

Every second, thousands of cells are reproducing throughout our bodies. Body (somatic) cells are able to make identical copies of themselves at an amazing rate, thanks to a means of asexual reproduction known as **mitosis**.

It is very important that you be familiar with the process of mitosis for the Biology GSE. During mitosis, two things occur: (1) the cell duplicates its genetic material, and (2) the cell splits in half, forming two daughter cells, both of which are identical to the parent cell. The process of mitosis begins when the chromosomes in the nucleus duplicate themselves:

The original chromosome and its new twin are linked, as you can see in the figure above. These identical chromosomes are now called **sister chromatids**. The chromatids are held together by a round structure called the **centromere**:

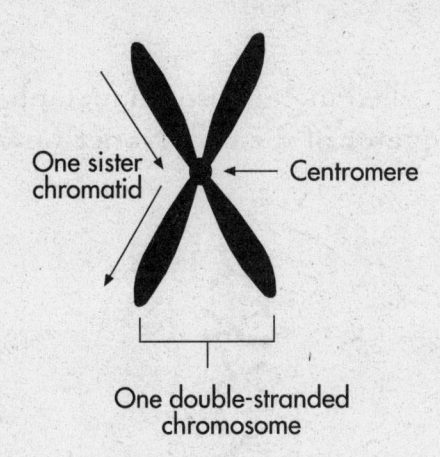

[Diagram: double-stranded chromosome with labels "One sister chromatid", "Centromere", and "One double-stranded chromosome"]

What you have going into the divisional stages of mitosis is a bunch of double-stranded chromosomes. Now let's take a close look at the steps of this important process.

The Stages of Mitosis

Mitosis consists of a linear sequence of five basic stages: **prophase**, **metaphase**, **anaphase**, **telophase**, and **cytokinesis**.

Prophase

In prophase, the newly-replicated chromosomes condense and become visible. One of the first signs of prophase is the disintegration of the nuclear membrane. During prophase, paired structures called **centrioles** start to move away from each other, toward opposite ends of the cell. Centrioles are the paired structures in animal cells that are composed of **microtubules.** (Microtubules are structural components of the cytoplasm). The centrioles spin out a system of microtubules known as the **spindle fibers** that grow toward the chromosomes:

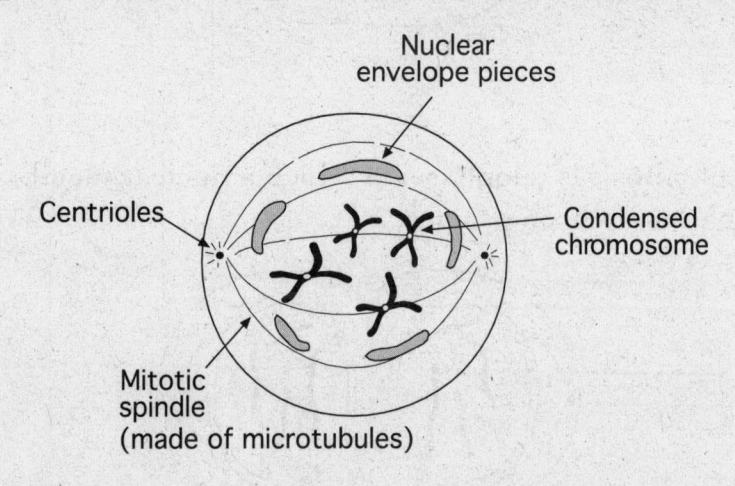

[Diagram of a cell in prophase with labels: "Nuclear envelope pieces", "Centrioles", "Condensed chromosome", "Mitotic spindle (made of microtubules)"]

Metaphase

The next stage in mitosis is called metaphase. In metaphase, the chromosomes begin to line up along the equator of the cell. Notice how nice and orderly they've become!

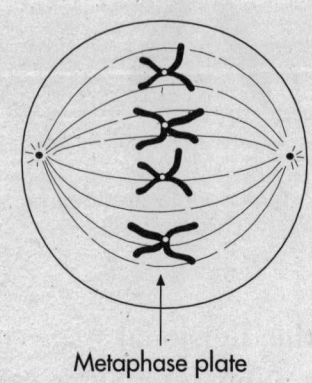

Metaphase plate

The spindle fibers are responsible for this neat arrangement: They help align the chromosomes at the middle of the cell along its equator, also known as the **metaphase plate**.

Anaphase

During anaphase, the sister chromatids of each chromosome separate at the centromere and slowly move to opposite poles. An apparent tug of war takes place as the spindle fibers pull the chromosomes apart and drag them to opposite ends of the cell:

Telophase

The next phase of mitosis is telophase, in which a nuclear membrane begins to form around each set of chromosomes.

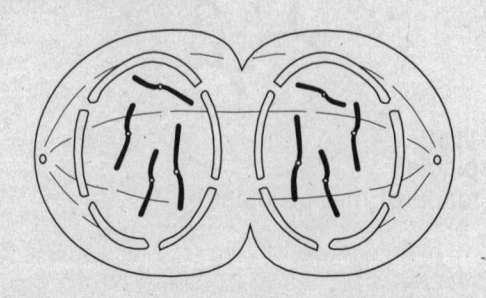

Cytokinesis

Now it's time to split the cytoplasm in cytokinesis. Look at the figure below and you'll notice that the cell membrane has begun to split along a **cleavage furrow**:

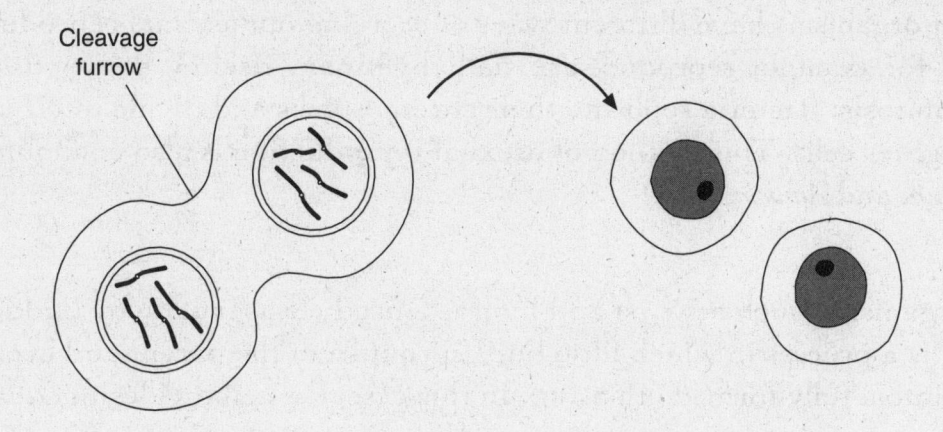

A cell membrane forms around each cell and they're split into two new daughter cells. Mitosis is complete.

We showed you how cytokinesis occurs in animal cells, but in plant cells, this final phase is slightly different. Plant cells do not form cleavage furrows. Instead, a partition called a **cell plate** forms down the middle region, separating the two daughter cells. In addition to this difference, plant cells do not contain centrioles. Otherwise, mitosis is pretty much the same in plant and animal cells.

A Mnemonic for Mitosis

Here's an easy way to remember the first four stages of mitosis. Use this mnemonic and you'll be sure to remember the major events.

PMAT

Prophase...P is for Prepare (as the cell prepares for mitosis)

Metaphase...M is for Meet (when the chromosomes meet in the middle)

Anaphase...A is for Apart (when the chromosomes draw apart)

Telophase...T is for Tear (as the cell tears in half, forming two daughter cells)

WHAT IS THE PURPOSE OF ASEXUAL REPRODUCTION?

The purpose of asexual reproduction is to produce daughter cells that are identical copies of the single parent cell. In animal cells, all cells except sex cells undergo mitosis. Just remember: *Like begets like*, so hair cells beget other hair cells; skin cells beget other skin cells, and so on.

Binary Fission

Different organisms have different ways of carrying out asexual reproduction. Bacteria, for example, reproduce asexually by **binary fission**. Binary fission is just like mitosis: Bacteria replicate their chromosomes and divide into two identical daughter cells. This method of asexual reproduction is also common in *Paramecium* and *Amoeba*.

Budding

Other organisms, such as yeast and hydra, reproduce asexually by **budding**. Budding is a process in which little buds sprout from the parent and eventually develop into a fully formed offspring. In this case, the cell divides unequally:

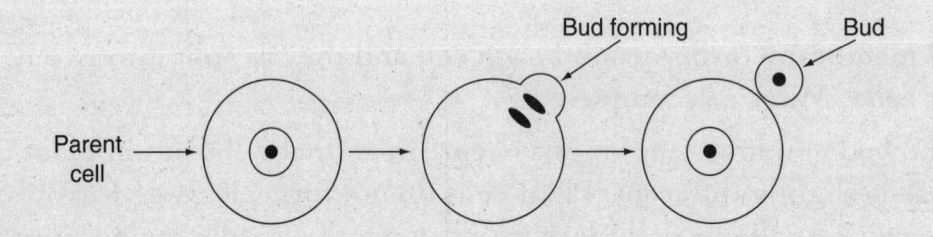

Sporulation

Another form of asexual reproduction is **sporulation**. Fungi, for example, produce **spores** (airborne cells) that are then released from the parent organism into the air:

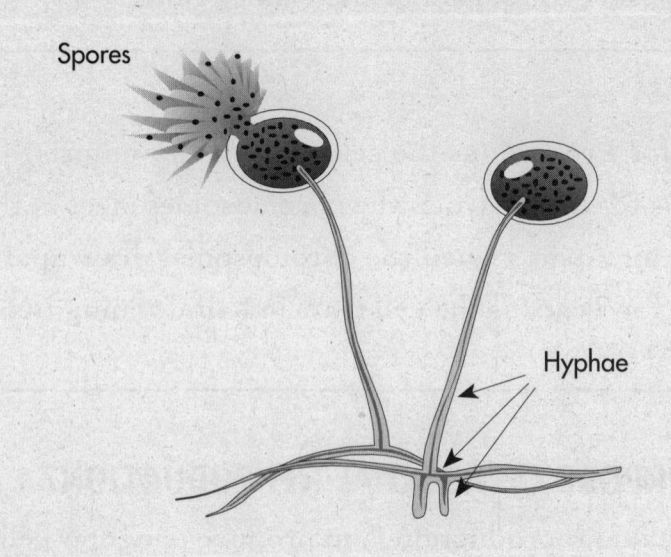

Once these tiny haploid cells land on fertile ground, they reproduce mitotically, generating other fungi. *Rhizopus*, a common bread mold, reproduces asexually by budding. As you know, if you've ever opened a week-old bag of moldy bread, sporulation is a rather effective and swift way of reproducing.

Vegetative Propagation

Although most plants reproduce by fertilization, plants can also reproduce asexually in a process called **vegetative propagation**. In vegetative propagation, some part of the parent plant—such as the root, stem, or leaf—is able to regenerate an entirely new plant. Some examples of vegetative propagation include **tubers, runners, bulbs,** and **grafting.**

For example, if you wanted to make potato plants without fertilizing them, all you'd have to do is cut out the "eyes" of a potato and plant them. Each of the eyes would then develop into a complete potato plant. The eyes are actually rudimentary tubers.

Here's a list of the different types of vegetative propagation:

TYPES OF VEGETATIVE PROPAGATION		
Types	Description	Examples
Bulbs	Short underground stems	Onions
Runners	Horizontal stems above the ground	Strawberries
Tubers	Underground stems	Potatoes
Grafting	Cut a stem and attach it to a closely related plant	Seedless oranges

Regeneration

A last form of asexual reproduction is **regeneration**, which occurs when an organism grows back a missing body part. The starfish is a perfect example. If you were to cut up a starfish and leave the severed pieces in an aquarium, each of the five limbs would regenerate an entire starfish! Such extreme examples of regeneration are relatively rare in nature.

Now that we've looked at asexual reproduction, let's move on to sexual reproduction. We'll start by discussing meiosis.

MEIOSIS

Every organism has a specific number of chromosomes. For example, fruit flies have eight chromosomes; humans have forty-six chromosomes. However, if you take a closer look at a human cell, you'll realize that we actually only possess twenty-three *different* chromosomes. So why do we have two of each?

In normal eukaryotic cells, chromosomes exist in pairs called **homologues**. When a cell has a full complement of homologues, or homologous chromosomes as they're often called, it is said to be a **diploid**. A normal diploid human cell contains forty-six chromosomes altogether, two of each kind. We can therefore say that the **diploid number** for humans is forty-six. But some cells possess only one set of chromosomes, and are called **haploid**. For instance, a haploid human cell contains a total of twenty-three chromosomes.

The terms diploid and haploid are important when we start talking about sexual reproduction. Although almost all the cells in the human body are diploid, there are special cells that are haploid. These haploid cells are called **sex cells**, or **gametes**.

Why do we have haploid cells? In human sexual reproduction, both the male and female must contribute a haploid cell, so that when their gametes join, the offspring contains the correct number of chromosomes. The problem is that each of them has a full set of chromosomes, in their regular cells. If they both threw in their full complement, the baby would have forty-six pairs of chromosomes instead of twenty-three. Within a few generations, kids would be born with 1,507,328 pairs of chromosomes! To preserve the diploid number of chromosomes in an organism, each parent must contribute only half of his or her chromosomes. **Meiosis** is the process by which the chromosomal count of sexually-reproduced organisms is maintained.

Since sexually reproducing organisms require haploid cells only for reproduction, meiosis is limited to sex cells in special sex organs called **gonads**. In males, the gonads are the **testes**, while in females they are the **ovaries**.

Meiosis actually involves two rounds of cell division: the **first meiotic division** and **second meiotic division**. As in mitosis, the chromosomes duplicate and double-stranded chromosomes are formed in interphase of the cell cycle, before cell division begins.

The First Meiotic Division

Meiosis I consists of five stages: **prophase I**, **metaphase I**, **anaphase I**, **telophase I**, and cytokinesis.

Prophase I

Prophase I is a little more complicated than mitotic prophase. As in mitosis, the nuclear membrane begins to disappear, the chromosomes become visible, and the centrioles move to opposite poles of the nucleus. But that's where the similarity ends.

In prophase I, the chromosomes line up side-by-side with their counterparts, in an event known as **synapsis**:

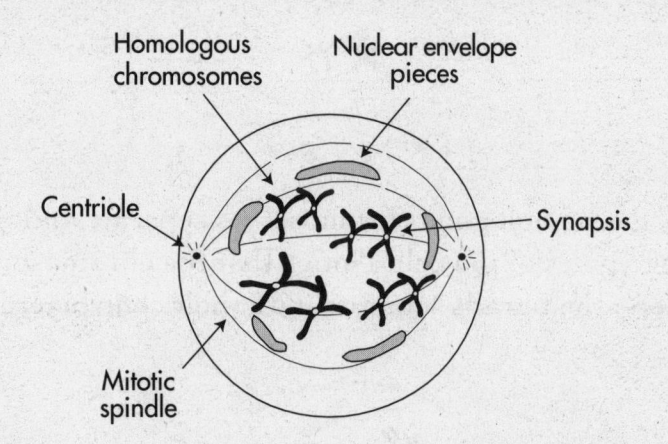

Synapsis involves two sets of chromosomes coming together to form a **tetrad**. A tetrad consists of four chromatids. Synapsis is followed by **crossing-over**, which is the exchange of segments of homologous chromosomes.

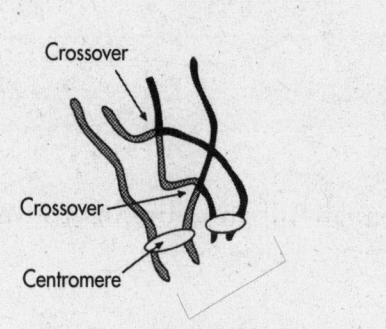

What's unique in prophase I is that pieces of homologous chromosomes are swapped between the partners in the tetrad. This is one of the ways organisms produce genetic variation.

Metaphase I
As is the case in mitosis, the chromosome pairs—the tetrads—line up at the metaphase plate in metaphase I:

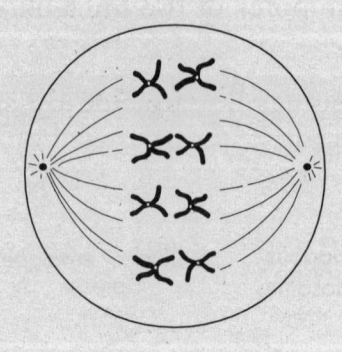

Anaphase I
During anaphase I, the homologous chromosomes separate and the chromosomes moves to the opposite poles of the cell. Notice that the chromosomes do not separate at the centromere; the tetrads separate with their centromeres intact:

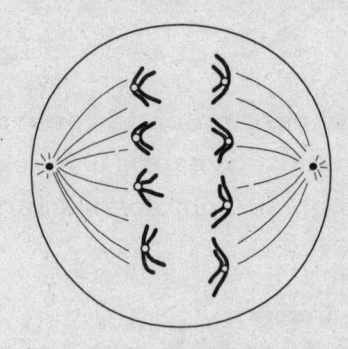

Telophase I
During telophase I, a nuclear membrane begins to form around each set of chromosomes:

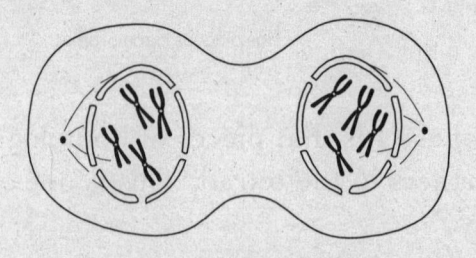

Finally, the cells undergo cytokinesis, yielding two daughter cells.

The Second Meiotic Division

The second meiotic division is virtually identical to mitosis. After a brief period, the cell undergoes a second round of cell division. During **prophase II**, the chromosomes once again condense. In **metaphase II**, the chromosomes move toward the metaphase plate. During **anaphase II**, the chromatids of each chromosome split at the centromere and move to opposite ends of the cell. During **telophase II**, a new nuclear membrane envelope begins to form around each set of chromosomes, and four new daughter cells are produced at the end of the two rounds that make up meiosis:

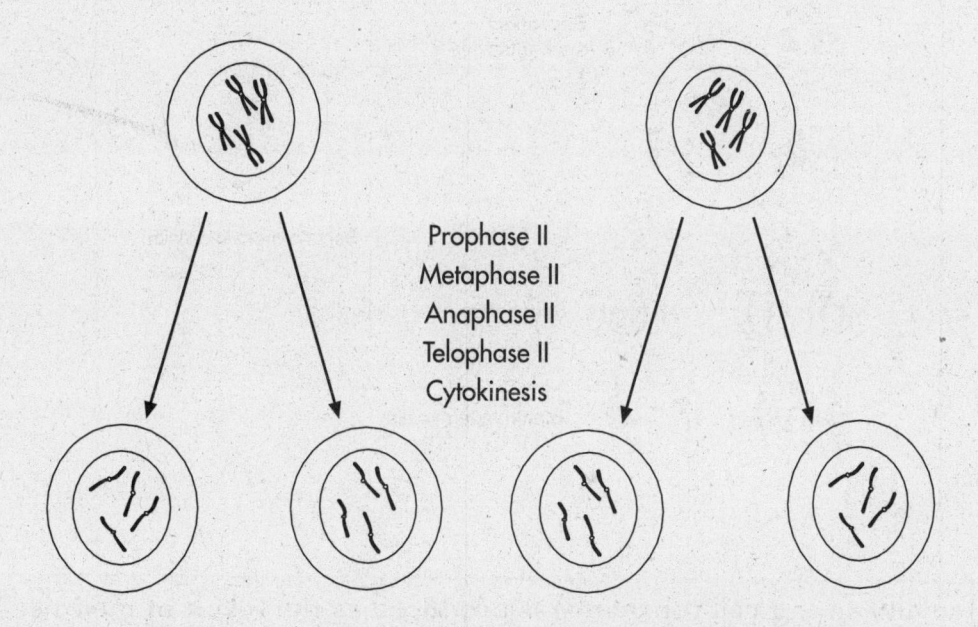

Prophase II
Metaphase II
Anaphase II
Telophase II
Cytokinesis

These resulting cells, each of which contains only half the total number of chromosomes, are haploid gametes.

Gametogenesis

Since meiosis results in the formation of gametes, it is also known as **gametogenesis**. When meiosis takes place in the male gonads, it results in the production of sperm cells. This is called **spermatogenesis**. During spermatogenesis, four sperm cells are produced from each parent cell:

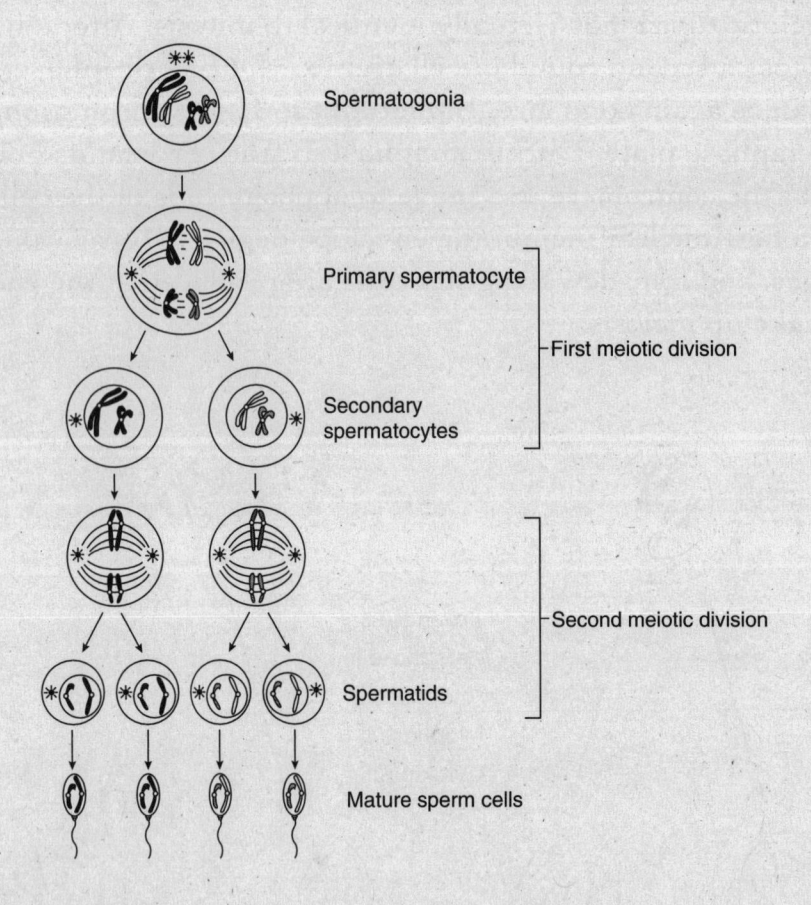

```
                    Spermatogonia

                    Primary spermatocyte  ⎤
                                          ⎥
                    Secondary             ⎥ First meiotic division
                    spermatocytes         ⎦

                                          ⎤
                                          ⎥
                                          ⎥ Second meiotic division
                    Spermatids            ⎦

                    Mature sperm cells
```

In a female, an egg cell (or ovum) is produced as the result of meiosis. This process is called **oogenesis**. Oogenesis differs slightly from spermatogenesis in that only one ovum is produced:

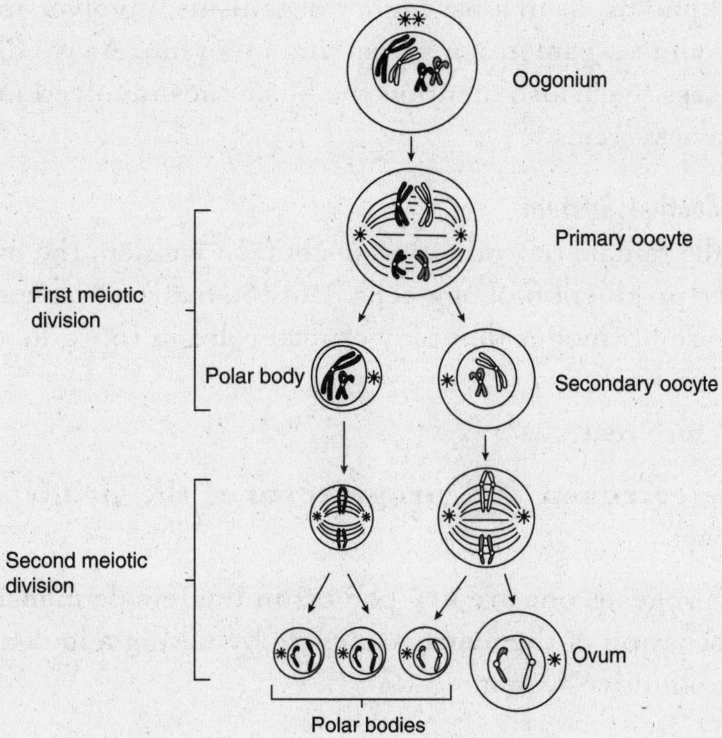
Oogonium
Primary oocyte
First meiotic division
Polar body
Secondary oocyte
Second meiotic division
Ovum
Polar bodies

The other three cells, called **polar bodies**, will eventually degenerate. Why do women produce only one ovum? Well, because the female wants to conserve as much cytoplasm as possible to nurture the surviving gamete. This means the ovum contains lots of stored nutrients.

Here's a summary of the major differences between mitosis and meiosis:

Mitosis:	Meiosis:
• Occurs in somatic (body) cells	• Occurs in germ (sex) cells
• Produces identical cells	• Produces gametes
• Diploid cell → diploid cells	• Diploid cell → haploid cells

THE HUMAN REPRODUCTIVE SYSTEM

Reproduction in humans, as in most higher organisms, involves the formation of new organisms from two gametes, a sperm and an ovum. As we discuss the reproductive process, we'll also mention the hormones involved in the male and female reproductive systems.

The Female Reproductive System

Let's begin with the female reproductive system. In women, the ovaries are responsible for the production of egg cells. But the ovaries also act as endocrine glands: They release hormones that play crucial roles in reproduction. The two main roles of the ovaries are:

1. to manufacture **ova**
2. to secrete **estrogen** and **progesterone**, the principal female sex hormones.

Estrogen and progesterone are key players in the female menstrual cycle. Let's start our discussion of the menstrual cycle by taking a look at this diagram of the female reproductive system:

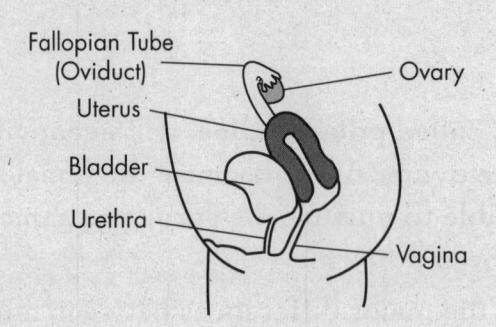

The Menstrual Cycle: The Follicle Stage

In the first phase, the anterior pituitary (remember that gland from our discussion of the endocrine system?) secretes two hormones, **follicle-stimulating hormone (FSH)** and **luteinizing hormone (LH)**. Follicle-stimulating hormone stimulates several follicles in the ovaries to grow. One of these follicles eventually gains the lead, and this halts the growth of the others.

Throughout the period of its growth, the follicle churns out estrogen. Estrogen eventually causes the pituitary to release a surge of LH; in fact, this quick release of LH is known as a **luteal surge**. The luteal surge triggers **ovulation**, which is the release of the follicle from the ovaries.

Here's a quick summary of the hormones associated with the follicle stage:

1. follicle-stimulating hormone, or FSH,
2. estrogen (which originates in the follicle) and
3. luteinizing hormone, or LH (which originates in the anterior pituitary gland).

The luteal surge causes the follicle to burst and release the ovum. The ovum then begins its journey into the **fallopian tube**, also known as the **oviduct**. The release of the ovum marks the end of the follicle stage, which lasts about 12 days.

The Menstrual Cycle: The Corpus Luteum Stage

By the end of the follicle stage, the ovum has moved into the fallopian tube and the follicle has been ruptured and left behind in the ovary. The ruptured follicle (a fluid-filled sac) now condenses into a little yellow blob called the **corpus luteum**, which is Latin for "yellow body."

The corpus luteum continues to secrete estrogen. In addition, it starts to produce the other main hormone involved in female reproduction, progesterone. Progesterone is responsible for readying the body for pregnancy. It does this by preparing the uterine lining for implantation of the egg cell. Without progesterone, a fertilized ovum cannot implant into the uterus and develop into an embryo.

If fertilization and implantation have not occurred after about 13 to 15 days, the corpus luteum shuts down. Once the corpus luteum turns off, the uterus can no longer maintain its thickened walls and reabsorbs most of the tissue that progesterone has encouraged to grow. However, since there is too much for it to reabsorb, a certain amount is shed. This sloughing off, or apparent bleeding, is known as **menstruation**.

At the end of menstruation, the cycle starts all over again. Here's a graph of the concentration of the various female reproductive hormones during the menstrual cycle of female humans:

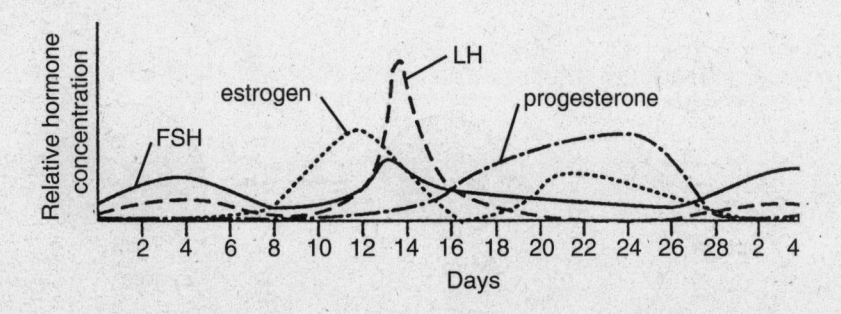

The Male Reproductive System

Now let's discuss the male reproductive system. In human beings, sperm cells are produced in paired gonads called **testes**. The testes are contained within the **scrotum**, a skin-covered sac. The main sex hormone in males is **testosterone**, which is responsible for the development of the sex organs and secondary sex characteristics. In addition to the deepening of the voice, these sex characteristics include the growth of body hair, muscle growth, and facial hair, all of which indicate the onset of **puberty**.

Once sperm cells are produced, they are transported through conducting tubes and mix with secretions from accessory glands. The sperm and added fluids leave the body via the urethra. The structure that delivers the sperm into the female reproductive tract is the penis.

Here's a side view of the male reproductive system:

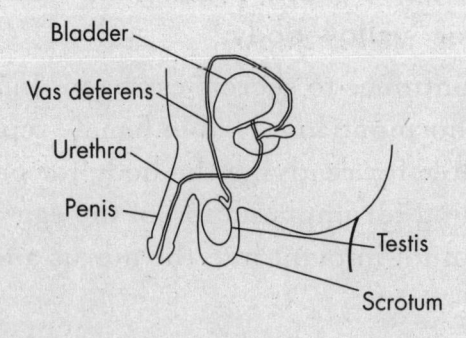

EMBRYONIC DEVELOPMENT

How does a tiny, single-celled egg eventually become a complex, multicellular organism? By growing, of course. The study of how the original minuscule cell develops into the great variety of specialized tissues found in organisms is called **developmental biology**.

In order to understand some of the early steps of development, let's go right back to the beginning when the ovum and sperm cell first meet. This meeting is called **fertilization**, and it results in a diploid cell called a **zygote**.

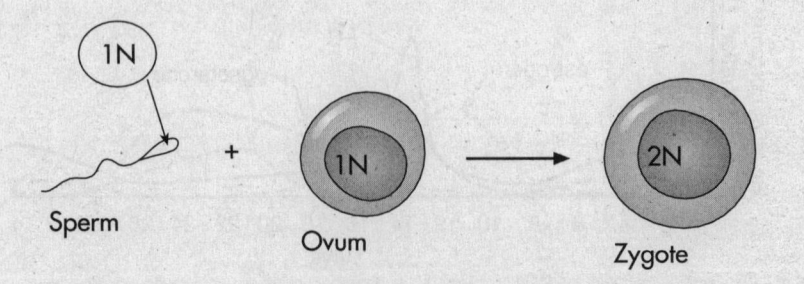

Fertilization can occur externally (outside of the female organism) or internally (inside of the female organism). External fertilization usually occurs among aquatic animals such as fish and amphibians. In more complex terrestrial organisms, fertilization occurs internally.

Here's one more thing you should remember for the big exam: The sex of the organism is usually determined by the *sperm cell* involved in fertilization. This is because sperm cells carry either an X or a Y sex chromosome. If the offspring receives an X chromosome from its father, it will be a female. If it receives a Y, it will be a male. The female gametes do not play a role in sex determination because females have two X chromosomes. (This will be reviewed in the next chapter.)

Cleavage

Fertilization triggers the zygote to undergo a series of rapid cell divisions called **cleavage**. At this stage, the cells keep dividing until they form a solid, undifferentiated ball called a **morula**. When we say that it is an undifferentiated ball of cells, we basically mean that the cells that make up the ball are not specialized to carry out unique functions—they are all the same type of cell.

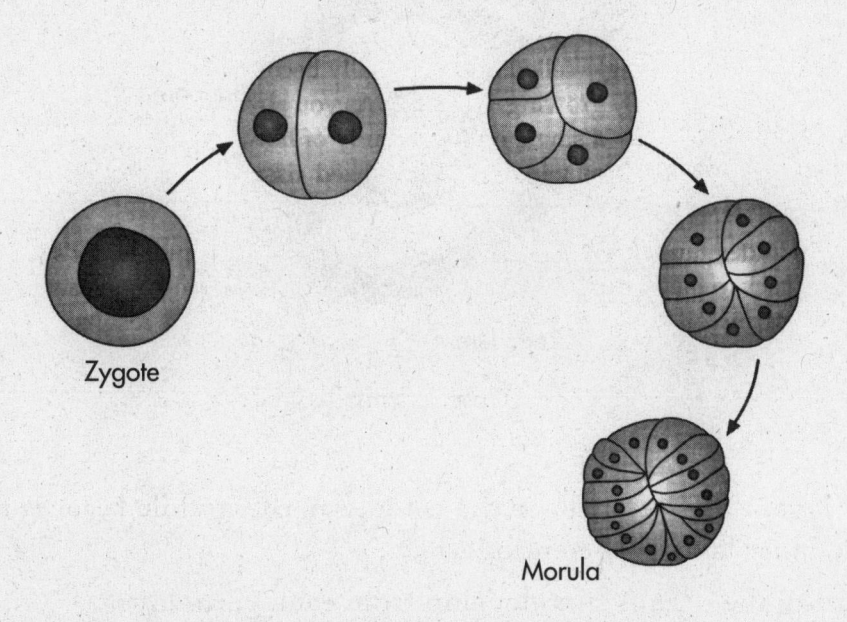

Blastula

In the next stage, the morula becomes a **blastula**. As the cells continue to divide they "press" against each other and produce a hollow ball of cells:

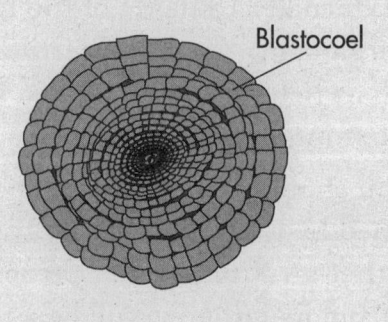

Blastula (cross-section)

Gastrula

During **gastrulation**, the blastula begins to change its shape. Cells now migrate into the **blastocoel** (the hollow center) to form three layers of cells called **germ layers**. These three layers will eventually give rise to all of the different tissues in the body. The three germ layers are the **ectoderm**, **mesoderm**, and **endoderm**.

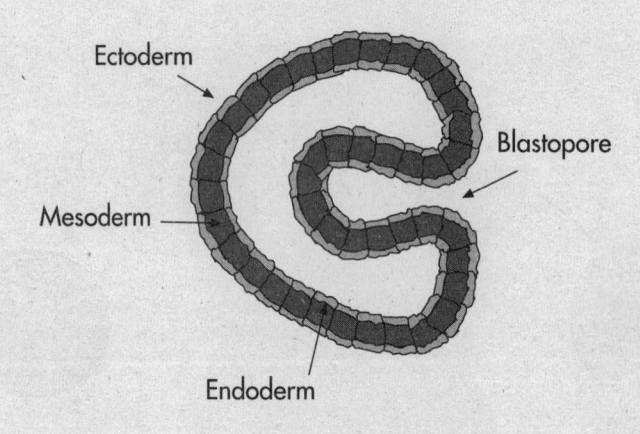

Gastrula (cross-section)

The outer layer of the gastrula is the ectoderm, the middle layer is the mesoderm, and the inner layer is the endoderm.

Here's a list of the organs that develop from each germ layer.

Cell Layer	Tissues
Ectoderm	Skin, eyes, and nervous system
Endoderm	Lining of the digestive and respiratory tracts, pancreas, gall bladder, and liver

Mesoderm	Bones, muscles, gonads, excretory, circulatory and reproductive systems

Differentiation

Over time, the cells in the various germ layers differentiate, or *specialize*, developing into the organs and tissues listed above. To sum up, the order of the stages within embryonic development run like this:

$$\text{Zygote} \to \text{Cleavage} \to \text{Blastula} \to \text{Gastrula} \to \text{Differentiation}$$

That'll do it for embryonic development.

CHICK EMBRYOS

One ever-popular embryo that you should be familiar with for the GSE is the chick embryo. In addition to the three primary germ layers, many birds (such as chickens) have extraembryonic membranes. There are basically four extraembryonic membranes: the **yolk sac**, **amnion**, **chorion**, and **allantois**.

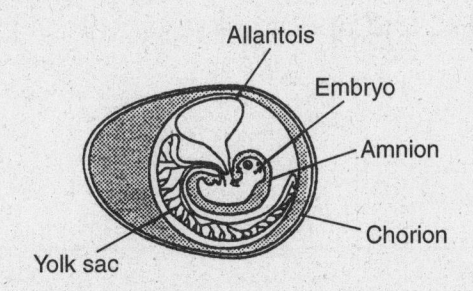

These extraembryonic membranes are somewhat common in terrestrial animals. Here's a list of the membranes and their functions:

Functions of Extraembryonic Membranes	
Extraembryonic membrane	Function
Yolk sac	Provides food for the embryo
Amnion	Forms a fluid-filled sac that protects the embryo
Allantois	Membrane involved in gas exchange
Chorion	Outermost membrane that surrounds all the other extraembryonic membranes

One difference between chicks and humans, however, is that birds like chickens develop inside hard nonporous shells called eggs, while humans develop in the uterus of the female. For this reason, the egg needs to contain all of the nutrients necessary for development of a new bird, while a human embryo receives a constant supply of nutrients from the body of its mother in a special structure called a placenta.

Placental and Nonplacental Mammals

As we mentioned above, many mammals have a **placenta**, which is a structure formed in the uterus from the uterine lining and embryonic membranes. The placenta joins the embryo to the mother and provides the fetus with the mother's blood supply. This is how the embryos of mammals such as humans receive nutrients and eliminate wastes.

Marsupials mammals, on the other hand, don't have a placenta. The developing embryos receive very little nourishment from the mother in the uterus. Marsupials nourish their young with milk provided through nipples inside a pouch in the abdominal region. Marsupial fetuses pop out about 8 days after fertilization but continue their maturation in their mother's pouch. Examples of marsupials are kangaroos, koalas, and opossums.

LET'S TEST WHAT YOU'VE LEARNED

1. The diagrams below represent stages of a cellular process.

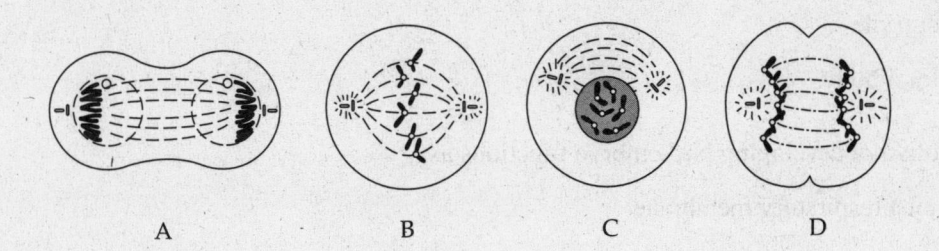

   A   B   C   D

   Which is the correct sequence of these stages?

   1. A → B → C → D
   2. B → D → C → A
   3. C → B → D → A
   4. D → B → A → C

2. Which statement best describes the division of the cytoplasm and the nucleus in budding?

   1. Both the cytoplasm and the nucleus divide equally.
   2. The cytoplasm divides unequally, but the nucleus divides equally.
   3. The cytoplasm divides equally, but the nucleus divides unequally.
   4. Both the cytoplasm and the nucleus divide unequally.

3. *Rhizopus*, a bread mold, usually reproduces asexually by

   1. budding.
   2. sporulation.
   3. regeneration.
   4. fission.

4. Which statement is true regarding plants produced by vegetative propagation?

   1. They normally exhibit only dominant characteristics.
   2. They normally have the monoploid number of chromosomes.
   3. They normally obtain most of their nourishment from the seed.
   4. They are normally genetically identical to the parent.

5. The chromatids of a double-stranded chromosome are held together at a region known as the
    1. polar body.
    2. centromere.
    3. centriole.
    4. Golgi body.

6. The yolk of a developing bird embryo functions as a
    1. moist respiratory membrane.
    2. storage site for waste.
    3. food source.
    4. fluid environment.

7. In humans, the fertilization of two eggs at the same time usually results in
    1. chromosomal abnormalities.
    2. gene mutations.
    3. identical twins.
    4. fraternal twins.

8. Which situation is a result of crossing-over during meiosis?
    1. Genes are duplicated exactly, ensuring that offspring will be identical to the parents.
    2. Chromatids thicken and align themselves, helping to ensure genetic continuity.
    3. Genes are rearranged, increasing the variability of offspring.
    4. Chromatids fail to sort independently, creating abnormal chromosome numbers.

9. The diagrams below represent the gametes and zygotes associated with two separate fertilizations in a particular species

The abnormal zygote is most likely the result of

1. polyploidy.
2. nondisjunction.
3. chromosome breakage.
4. gene linkage.

10. Which statement is true about the process of fertilization in both tracheophytes and mammals?

1. It normally results in the production of monoploid offspring.
2. It occurs externally in a watery environment.
3. It is followed by yolk production.
4. It occurs within female reproductive organs.

11. In sexually reproducing species, doubling of the chromosome number from generation to generation is prevented by events that take place during the process of

    1. gametogenesis.

    2. cleavage.

    3. nondisjunction.

    4. fertilization.

12. In a rabbit, the embryo normally develops within the

    1. placenta.

    2. uterus.

    3. yolk sac.

    4. umbilical cord.

13. The production of large number of eggs is necessary to ensure the survival of most

    1. mammals.
    2. molds.
    3. fish.
    4. yeasts.

Chapter 10

GENETICS

Genetics is the study of heredity, a study of how certain characteristics are passed on from parents to children. The basic principles of heredity were first discovered by Gregor Mendel, a monk who lived in the nineteenth century. Since then, the field of genetics has expanded greatly. In order to discuss Mendel's work, we'll first need to review some genetics vocabulary. You should be familiar with the following words for the GSE, because you will most likely see a question on Mendelian genetics.

- **Genes:** Each trait—or expressed characteristic—is produced by a pair of hereditary factors collectively known as **genes**. Within a chromosome, there are many genes, each of which controls the inheritance of a particular trait. A gene is a segment of a chromosome that produces a particular trait. For example, in pea plants, there's a gene on the chromosome that codes for seed coat. The position of a gene on a chromosomes is called its **locus**.

- **Alleles:** A gene usually consists of a *pair* of hereditary factors called **alleles**. Each organism carries two alleles for a particular trait. Another way to say this is that alleles make up a gene, which in turn produces a particular trait. Alleles are alternate forms of the same trait. For example, if we're talking about the height of a pea plant, there's an allele for tall and an allele for short. The two alleles are alternate forms of the gene for height.

- **Dominant and Recessive Alleles:** An allele can be **dominant** or **recessive**. In simple cases, an organism expresses either the dominant or recessive trait. For example, a plant can be tall or short. The convention is to assign a capital and a lowercase of the same letter for the two alleles: The dominant allele receives the capital letter, while the recessive allele receives the lowercase. For instance, if tallness is dominant in pea plants, we might give the dominant allele a "T" for tall, and the short, recessive allele a "t." We'll later see some examples of why this is useful.

- **Phenotype and Genotype:** When discussing the physical appearance of an organism, we refer to its **phenotype**. The phenotype tells us what the organism looks like. When talking about the genetic makeup of an organism, are referring to its **genotype**. The genotype tells us which alleles the organism possesses.

- **Homozygous and Heterozygous:** When an organism has two identical alleles for a given trait, we say that the organism is **homozygous**. For instance, TT and tt would both represent the genotype of homozygous organisms, one homozygous dominant and the other homozygous recessive. If an organism has two different alleles for a given trait, that organism is **heterozygous**.

- **Parent and Filial Generations:** The first generation is always called the **parent** or P1 generation. The offspring of the P1 generation are called the **filial** or F1 generation, and the offspring of the F1 generation are the F2 generation.

MENDELIAN GENETICS

One of Mendel's most famous studies explored the effects of cross-breeding on different strains of pea plants. Mendel worked exclusively with true-breeder pea plants. This means that the plants he used were genetically pure and consistently produced the same traits in their offspring (the F1 generation). Tall plants always produced tall plants, and short plants always produced short plants. By crossing hundreds and hundreds of pea plants for many years, he came up with two principles: the **law of segregation** and the **law of independent assortment**.

Before we get into these laws, let's examine one type of experiment that Mendel performed that applies both the concept of dominance the Punnett square. Mendel crossed two true-breeding plants that had contrasting traits: a tall pea plant and a short pea plant. This type of cross is called a **monohybrid cross**—it constitutes a study of only one trait. In this case, the trait is height.

To his surprise, when Mendel mated these plants, the characteristics didn't blend to produce plants of average height. Instead, all of the offspring were tall:

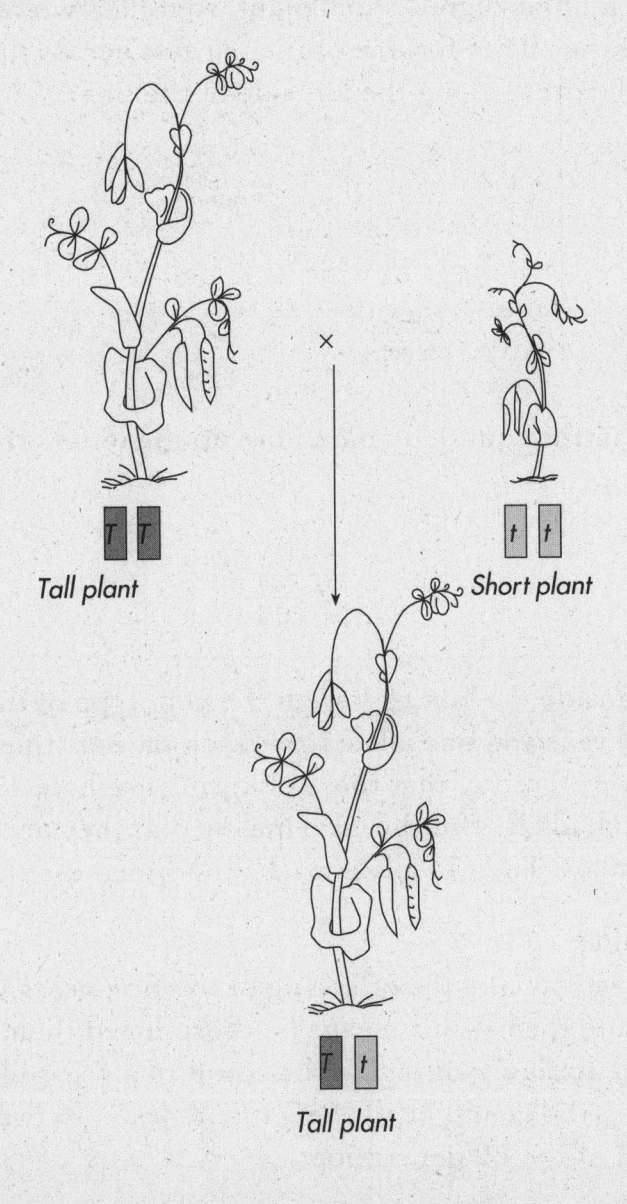

Tall plant × Short plant

Tall plant

He recognized that the trait of the tall plant somehow masked the trait of the short plant. Mendel called this phenomenon **dominance**. The dominant tall allele, T, somehow masked the presence of the recessive short allele, t. Consequently the plant needed only one tall allele in order to make it tall.

Crosses Using the Punnett Square

A simple way to represent a cross is to set up a Punnett square. Let's construct one in order to predict the results of a cross between a homozygous tall and homozygous short pea plant.

Since one parent is a homozygous tall plant, it has two dominant alleles (TT). The other parent is a homozygous short plant, so it has two recessive alleles (tt). We start by putting the alleles for one of the parents across the top of the box and the alleles for the other along the left side of the box:

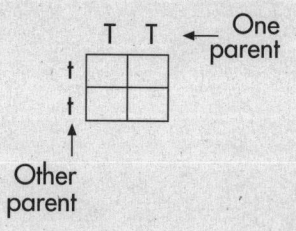

```
       T  T  ← One
              parent
    t ┌──┬──┐
      │  │  │
    t ├──┼──┤
      │  │  │
      └──┴──┘
       ↑
     Other
     parent
```

Now we can fill in the square by matching up the letters. Here are the results of the F1 generation:

```
       T   T
    t│ Tt │ Tt │
    t│ Tt │ Tt │
```

The individuals inside the box represent the genotype of the offspring, and as you can see, they all received one allele from each parent (they've got one T and one t). We would therefore say that these offspring are heterozygous: they all have one copy of each allele. But this also means that they are all tall, since tallness (T) is dominant. The (T) allele masks the shortness (t) allele.

F2: The Next Generation

Mendel's next step was to take the offspring of the first cross (the F1 generation) and self-pollinate them—this means he reproduced them asexually. Let's use a Punnett square to figure out what the result of a cross like this would be. This time we're using the genotype of the F1 generation to predict the phenotype (and genotype) of the F2 generation:

	T	t
T	TT	Tt
t	Tt	tt

F2 Generation

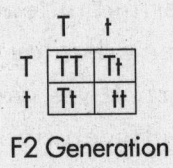

You can see that one of the offspring has the genotype tt, which means that since it has no T allele, it is short. The shortness trait reappeared in the F2 generation, but how did that happen? Once again, the alleles separated and recombined to produce a new combination. The cross resulted in one homozygous short plant (tt) plus two heterozygous tall plants (Tt) and one homozygous tall plant (TT).

Although all of the F1 plants were tall, the alleles separated and recombined during the cross to produce one short plant in the F2 generation. This is an example of the **law of segregation**, which states that allele pairs separate (or segregate) when gametes are formed (remember that each gamete receives half of the chromosome count from its parent cell during meiosis), and are paired again when gametes fuse at fertilization:

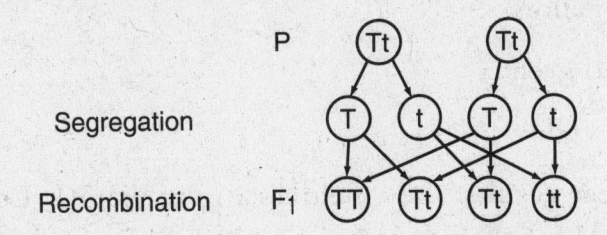

P (Tt) (Tt)

Segregation (T) (t) (T) (t)

Recombination F1 (TT) (Tt) (Tt) (tt)

We can summarize the results from the last cross in a ratio form:

The phenotype is **3:1**   Three tall: one short

The genotype is **1:2:1**   One TT: two Tt: one tt

The Law of Independent Assortment

So far, we have looked at the two alleles for one characteristic—height in pea plants. But what happens when we study two traits at the same time? The two traits will still segregate randomly. This is known as **independent assortment**. Now let's take a look at height and color in pea plants at the same time.

As we've already seen, a pea plant can be either tall or short. When it comes to color, let's say that pea plants can also be either green or yellow. We'll say that green is dominant, using (G) for the allele for green and (g) for the allele for yellow.

GENETICS ◆ 137

Remember that each trait is inherited independently of the others. For example, a plant that's tall can be either green or yellow. In the same way, a plant that's green can be either tall or short. If we were to figure out all the genotypes of all possible outcomes of a cross between two true breeding parent plants, this would mean we would start with plants with genotypes TTGG and ttgg, which would produce the gametes TG and tg. These would fuse during fertilization to produce offspring with the genotype TtGg. If we did a cross between two of these F1 generation plants to produce an F2 generation, it would like this:

	TG	Tg	tG	tg
TG	TG TG	Tg TG	tG TG	tg TG
Tg	TG Tg	Tg Tg	tG Tg	tg Tg
tG	TG tG	Tg tG	tG tG	tg tG
tg	TG tg	Tg tg	tG tg	tg tg

For the sixteen offspring shown above there are:
- nine tall and green
- three tall and yellow
- three short and green
- one short and yellow

If we combine these results, they yield a ratio of 9:3:3:1. Let's summarize the rules we learned for Mendelian genetics:

SUMMARY OF MENDEL'S LAW	
Laws	**Definition**
Dominance	One trait masks the effects of another trait.
Law of Segregation	Alleles can segregate and recombine.
Law of Independent Assortment	Traits can segregate and recombine independently of other traits.

It wasn't until the mid-1900s that scientists became aware that Mendel's hereditary factors—now called **genes**—were carried on chromosomes. This theory is called the **gene-chromosome theory** and nicely correlates to Mendel's law of segregation.

BEYOND MENDELIAN GENETICS

Not all patterns of inheritance obey the principles of Mendelian genetics. In fact, many traits occur due to a combined expression of alleles. Here are a couple of examples of non-Mendelian forms of inheritance:

- **Intermediate inheritance:** In some cases, traits will *blend*. For example, a white snapdragon plant (dominant) and a red snapdragon plant (recessive) will produce a pink snapdragon plant; this phenomenon is called **incomplete dominance**. In incomplete dominance, the F1 generation has a phenotype that's somewhere in between that of its parents.

- **Codominance:** Sometimes you'll see an equal expression of both alleles. One example is the roan-colored coat in cattle. If one parent has an entirely red coat (RR) and the other parent has a white coat (WW), the offspring will have a roan coat (mottled red and white coat). Both alleles are expressed (RW).

- **Multiple alleles:** Sometimes the expression of a single trait involves more than two alleles. For example, two genes are involved in the expression of the AB blood group. The combination of genes determines the blood types in an individual. The possible blood types are A, B, AB, and O. In this case, both alleles are equally expressed in a single trait.

Sex Determination

As we mentioned, humans contain twenty-three pairs of chromosomes. Twenty-two of the pairs are called **autosomes** and they code for many different traits. The other pair is the **sex chromosomes**. As we said in the previous chapter, this pair determines the sex of the individual. A female has two X chromosomes, while a male has one X and one Y chromosome—the X is from his mother and the Y is from his father.

Sex Linkage

Some traits are carried on these sex chromosomes. **Color blindness** and **hemophilia**, for example, are two disorders whose causative alleles are carried on the X chromosome; these conditions are said to be **sex-linked traits**.

You should know that the human X chromosome is much larger than the Y chromosome, which means that there are many more X-linked traits than Y-linked ones. This also means that many of the X-linked traits have no homologous loci on the Y-chromosome.

What happens if a male has a defective X chromosome, meaning an X chromosome that contains an allele that may be recessive but causes an aberration in phenotype? Unfortunately, because there is no homologous loci on the Y chromosome, he'll express the **sex-linked trait**. However, if a female has only one defective X chromosome (and it's recessive), she won't express the sex-linked trait. In order for her to express the trait, she has to inherit two defective X chromosomes. A female with one defective X is called a **carrier**. Although she appears normal, she can still pass the trait on to her children, especially if one of her children is a boy.

Punnett squares can be used to figure out the results of crosses involving sex-linked traits, but you need to work with the sex chromosomes. Here's an example: A male who is normal for color vision marries a woman who is a carrier for color blindness. How many of their children will be color blind? Let's check out the possibilities with a Punnett square. We'll indicate the presence of the gene for color blindness by placing a bar above Xs that carry the defective allele. Take a look:

$$\begin{array}{c|c|c|} & X & \overline{X} \\ \hline X & XX & X\overline{X} \\ \hline Y & XY & \overline{X}Y \\ \hline \end{array}$$

Father → (rows X, Y); Mother → (columns X, $\overline{X}$)

$\overline{X}$ = diseased X

According to our square, the couple could have one son who is colorblind, a normal son, a daughter who is a carrier, or a normal daughter. Notice that in our cross, the affected child is a son. With the parents we used, the only child who could possibly be color blind is the son.

LET'S TEST WHAT YOU'VE LEARNED

1. Traits that are controlled by genes found on an X chromosome are said to be

    1. dominant
    2. recessive
    3. codominant
    4. sex-linked

2. In raccoons, a dark mask is dominant over a bleached face mask. Several crosses were made between raccoons that were heterozygous for dark face mask and raccoons that were homozygous for bleached face mask. What percentage of the offspring would be expected to have a dark face mask?

    1. 0%
    2. 50%
    3. 75%
    4. 100%

3. Mendel developed his basic principles of heredity by

    1. microscopic study of chromosomes and genes
    2. breeding experiments with *Drosophila*
    3. mathematical analysis of the offspring of pea plants
    4. ultracentrifugation studies of cell organelles

4. In screech owls, red feathers are dominant over gray feathers. If two heterozygous red-feathered owls are mated, what percentage of their offspring would be expected to have red feathers?

    1. 25%
    2. 50%
    3. 75%
    4. 100%

5. In humans, normal color vision (N) is dominant over color blindness (n). A man and woman with normal color vision produced two color blind sons and two daughters with normal color vision. The parental genotypes must be

    1. X^NY and X^NX^N
    2. X^nY and X^NX^N
    3. X^NY and X^NX^n
    4. X^nY and X^nX^n

6. Although genetic mutations may occur spontaneously in organisms, the incidence of such mutation may be increased by

   1. radioactive substances in the environment
   2. lack of vitamins in the diet
   3. long exposure to humid climates
   4. a short exposure to freezing temperatures

Chapter 11

MODERN GENETICS

DNA: THE BLUEPRINT OF LIFE

DNA can be thought of as the hereditary blueprint of the cell. The DNA of a cell is contained in structures we've already talked quite a bit about, called **chromosomes**. The chromosomes are basically enormous coils of DNA and associated proteins called **histones**. Found in the nucleus, chromosomes direct and control all the activities necessary for life, including passing their information on to future generations.

The Structure of DNA

The DNA molecule consists of two long, connected strands in the shape of a twisted ladder called a **double helix.** The structure of DNA was first determined in 1956 by two scientists named Watson and Crick.

Each strand of DNA is made up of repeating subunits called **nucleotides**. Each nucleotide consists of a **sugar**, a **phosphate**, and a **nitrogenous base**. Take a look at the very simplified schematic of a nucleotide below:

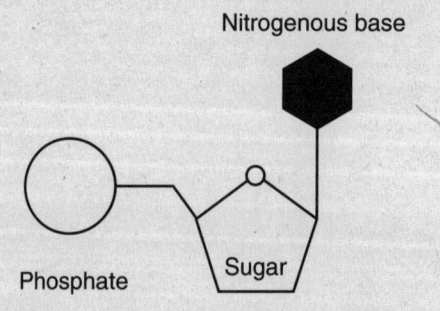

The name of the five-carbon sugar in DNA is **deoxyribose**, which is where the name *deoxyribo*nucleic acid comes from. Notice that the sugar is linked to two things: a phosphate group and a base. A nucleotide in DNA can be attached to one of four different bases:

- adenine
- guanine
- cytosine
- thymine

Any of these four bases can attach to the sugar. The good news is that you will not need to recognize the structures of these bases for the GSE.

A Single Strand

Now The nucleotides link in a single strand of DNA through their phosphate groups. Here's a very simple drawing of a small section of a DNA strand:

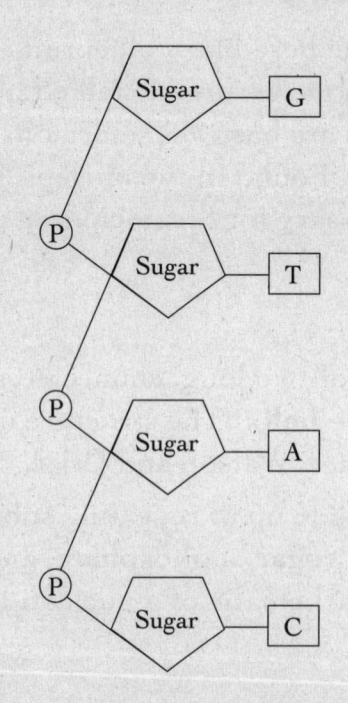

The Double Strand

Now let's look at the way in which two DNA strands are joined to form the double helix. As we mentioned, you can think of DNA as a ladder. The sides of the ladder consist of alternating sugar and phosphate groups, while the rungs of the ladder consist of pairs of nitrogenous bases joined by hydrogen bonds. **Hydrogen bonds** are not really bonds at all; they are just strong intermolecular forces.

You'll notice from the diagram above that the nitrogenous bases pair up in a particular way. Adenine in one strand always binds to thymine in the other strand. Similarly, guanine always binds to cytosine. This specific matching of the bases is known as **base pairing**, and because of this predictable matching of bases, the two strands are said to be **complementary**. If you know the sequence of the bases in one strand, you know the sequence of the bases in the other strand. For example, if the base sequence in one strand is A-T-C, the base sequence in the complementary strand will be T-A-G. One more thing to keep in mind: Two hydrogen bonds join each adenine and thymine base pair, and three join each guanine and cytosine base pair. This is shown in the art above.

DNA Replication

Chromosomes are capable of replicating (duplicating) themselves, as we mentioned in the chapter about mitosis. In fact, you may even remember that they do this during interphase. Since the DNA molecule is twisted in its double helix conformation, the first step in DNA replication is the unwinding of the double

MODERN GENETICS ◆ 145

helix and the breaking of the hydrogen bonds between the strands. Now each strand can serve as a **template**, or a blueprint, for the synthesis of a new strand.

One important thing to remember for the GSE is that DNA replication occurs in the nucleus of the cell. Free-floating DNA nucleotides are added one after the other to each strand. These new bases match correctly with the bases contained in the template strand. For example, adenine nucleotides will attach to thymine nucleotides, and guanine attaches to cytosine; the new strands are complementary to the template strands. These new stretches of nucleotides are joined by hydrogen bonds to produce a continuous strand, and two new strands of DNA are created.

Now that we've had a very brief review of how DNA is replicated, let's take a look at how the genetic code is expressed.

PROTEINS AND THE GENETIC CODE

DNA is crucial to the day-to-day operations of the cell. Without it, the cell would not be able to direct the production of proteins that regulate all the activities of the cell. However, DNA does not directly manufacture proteins. This job falls to an intermediate known as **ribonucleic acid (RNA)**.

RNA carries out the instructions of DNA, so the order of events looks like this:

$$\text{DNA} \xrightarrow{\text{(transcription)}} \text{RNA} \xrightarrow{\text{(translation)}} \text{proteins}$$

The above is referred to as the central dogma of molecular biology. Information is passed from DNA to RNA, which then handles the production of polypeptides (don't forget that "polypeptide" is simply a fancy name for proteins. We'll see why in just a bit). But before we discuss the way in which RNA makes proteins, let's talk about its structure. RNA differs from DNA in three principal ways:

1. RNA is single-stranded, not double-stranded.

2. The five-carbon sugar in RNA is **ribose**, not deoxyribose.

3. The nitrogenous bases in RNA are adenine, guanine, cytosine, and **uracil**. Uracil replaces thymine in RNA.

Here's a table to help you memorize the differences between DNA and RNA:

Differences between DNA and RNA		
	DNA (double stranded)	RNA (single stranded)
Sugar	deoxyribose	ribose
Bases:	adenine guanine cytosine thymine	adenine guanine cytosine uracil

Types of RNA

There are three types of RNA: **messenger RNA (mRNA), ribosomal RNA (rRNA)** and **transfer RNA (tRNA)**. All three types of RNA are key players in the synthesis of proteins. Messenger RNA carries the information from the DNA after the process of transcription, which we'll get to in a minute. Ribosomal RNA makes up the ribosomes, the primary sites of protein synthesis in the cytoplasm. Transfer RNA shuttles amino acids around the cell, bringing them into place at the ribosome. With this information, let's move on to transcription.

Transcription, the Synthesis of mRNA

As we've said, DNA transcribes its information into RNA, which travels out of the nucleus (into the cytoplasm) to undergo translation to a polypeptide. As is the case with DNA replication, the strand of DNA must first split, and transcription begins—the nucleotides that make up the new RNA molecule take their places one at a time along the template, forming temporary hydrogen bonds with DNA. But in mRNA synthesis, only one strand of DNA acts as a template. When transcription is complete, the new mRNA strand peels away from the DNA template, which allows the DNA to rezip as its hydrogen bonds are formed again. Don't forget—uracil takes the place of thymine in RNA!

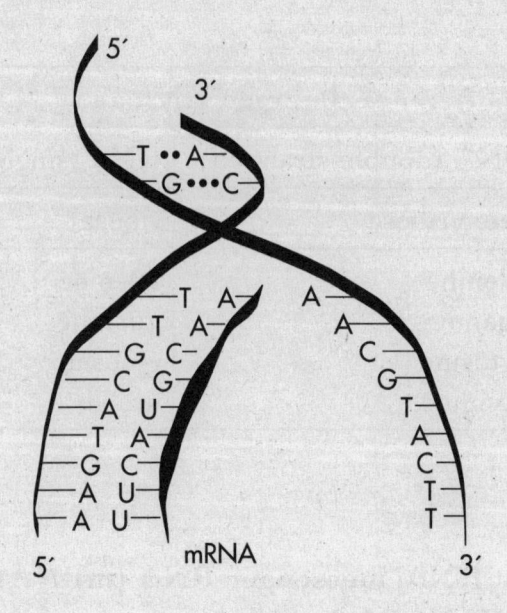

Translation, Protein Synthesis

At this point, mRNA travels out of the nucleus into the cytoplasm. The mRNA molecule carries the message from DNA in the form of **codons**, which are groups of three bases, each of which corresponds to one of 20 amino acids. Codons are very specific. For example, the sequence A-U-G found on an mRNA molecule corresponds to the amino acid methionine.

The mRNA finds a ribosome in the cytoplasm and attaches itself to wait for the appropriate amino acid to pass by. This is where tRNA comes in. One end of the tRNA binds to an amino acid. The other end, called an **anticodon**, has three nitrogenous bases that pair up with the bases contained in the codon.

Transfer RNA molecules are the "go-betweens" in protein synthesis. Each tRNA molecule picks up an amino acid in the cell's cytoplasm and shuttles it to the ribosome. For example, the tRNA with the anticodon U-A-C is methionine's personal shuttle: It carries no other amino acid. This way, every time mRNA shows a codon of A-U-G, it is certain to pick up only methionine.

But Where's the Protein?

Remember that the mRNA contains many thousands of codons, or "triplets," of nucleotide bases. As each amino acid is brought to the mRNA, it is linked up by the formation of a peptide bond (remember this from chapter 3?). And when many amino acids link up, a **polypeptide** is formed.

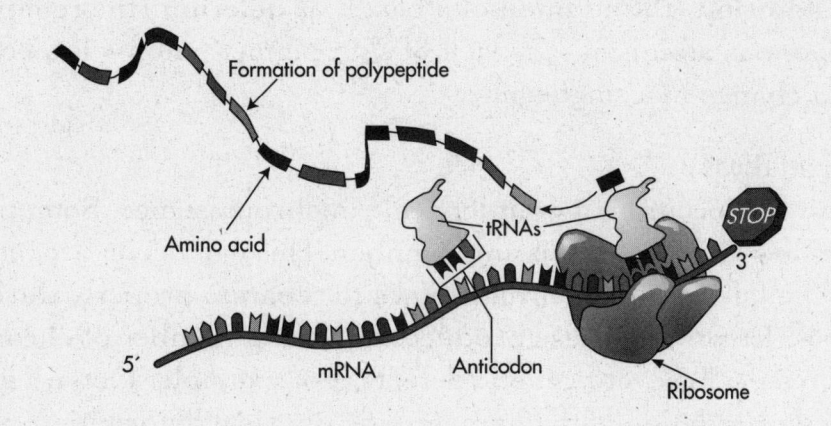

The One Gene-One Polypeptide Hypothesis

Originally, we've said that a gene is a region of the chromosome that codes for a particular trait. Now that we've discussed protein synthesis and the role of proteins in the cell, we can make our definition of a gene slightly more specific. We just saw that proteins direct the processes of the cell. We can therefore say that a gene is a region of DNA that codes for a single polypeptide.

This is known as the **one gene-one polypeptide hypothesis** and it comes a little nearer to the true definition of a gene. As we saw earlier, to define genes simply in terms of traits leads to some confusion. We said that some traits are the consequence of the interaction of several genes. However, when we define a gene as a region of the genetic code that codes for a specific polypeptide, it's much easier for us to pinpoint where one gene begins and where the other ends.

Mutations

A cell uses some 20 amino acids to construct its proteins. However, errors occasionally occur during DNA replication that cause the amino acids to be attached in the incorrect order. For example, suppose a short segment of a template DNA strand has the sequence T-A-C. The complementary DNA segment should be A-T-G. If for some reason another thymine is inserted in the last position instead of guanine, the new strand of DNA would read A-T-T, and this would lead to the insertion of the wrong amino acid in the protein. One error of this sort is enough to inactivate the entire protein!

A change in one or more of the nucleotide bases is called a **mutation**. Mutations can occur when DNA is exposed to radiation (X rays and ultraviolet light) or chemical agents.

There are many types of gene mutations. If an error results from a change in a single base, it may produce a **base substitution** (the exchange of one base for

MODERN GENETICS ◆ 149

another), an **addition** (the addition of a base), or **deletion** (the removal of a base). For example, albinism—the lack of skin pigmentation—is a condition that results from a change in a single gene.

Chromosome Mutations

Mutations can also occur on a grander scale in chromosomes. Sometimes a set of chromosomes has an extra or missing member. This can occur because of **nondisjunction**, the failure of the chromosomes to separate properly during crossing over in meiosis. Errors like these produce the wrong number of chromosomes in a cell, which results in severe genetic defects. For example, Down's syndrome, a form of mental retardation with characteristic physical deformities, results from the presence of an extra twenty-first chromosome. An individual afflicted with Down's syndrome has *three* rather than two copies of this single chromosome.

Chromosomal abnormalities also occur when a segment of a chromosome breaks. The most common examples are **translocation** (when a segment of a chromosome moves to another chromosome), **inversion** (when a segment of a chromosome is inserted in the reverse orientation), and **deletion** (when a segment of a chromosome is lost).

Manipulating the Code

Modern technology allows scientists to manipulate genetic information either indirectly by **artificial selection** or directly by **genetic engineering**.

There are a number of techniques that can indirectly manipulate the inheritance of genes in plants and animals. In artificial selection, desirable characteristics are bred into populations. This is accomplished by allowing only those organisms with the desired characteristics to interbreed. For example, by hand-pollinating flowers, rose breeders have produced thousands of new roses. Other breeding techniques include **hybridization** (in which animals are crossbred to maximize the favorable traits of both varieties of a given species) and **inbreeding** (to produce pure breeds). Examples of these breeding patterns are found in corn, flowers, fruits, cattle, and dogs, among others.

Scientists have found new ways of altering organisms through the *transfer* of individual genes from one organism to another in a process known as genetic engineering. In genetic engineering, DNA is cut out of one gene and transferred to another. The host DNA is now called **recombinant DNA**. When the cell undergoes protein synthesis, it will read the inserted portion of DNA as if it were its own, and this leads to the production of specific proteins.

This technique has resulted in the successful production of large amounts of proteins such as insulin and growth hormone. For example, the DNA that instructs a human cell to make insulin can be transferred to a bacterium. As this bacterium divides, it passes the gene for insulin to its offspring. Pretty soon you've got millions upon millions of bacteria churning out insulin. Once it's isolated from the solution in which the bacteria are raised, the insulin can be used by diabetics to help regulate their blood sugar.

Looking for Defects

Many genetic defects are detectable even before an organism is born. Researchers and doctors use several techniques to identify such defects. You should be familiar with these terms just in case one of them pops up in a question on the exam:

- **Genetic screening**—A technique used to identify abnormal conditions by detecting the presence or absence of certain chemicals in the blood or urine.

- **Amniocentesis**—A technique in which a sample of amniotic fluid is taken from the mother's womb. In the amniotic fluid is an abundance of fetal cells. By examining the fetal cells, doctors can detect severe disorders that might pose a risk to the fetus.

- **Karyotyping**—A technique in which paired chromosomes are arranged based on their shape and size. The chromosomes below are organized into a human karyotype:

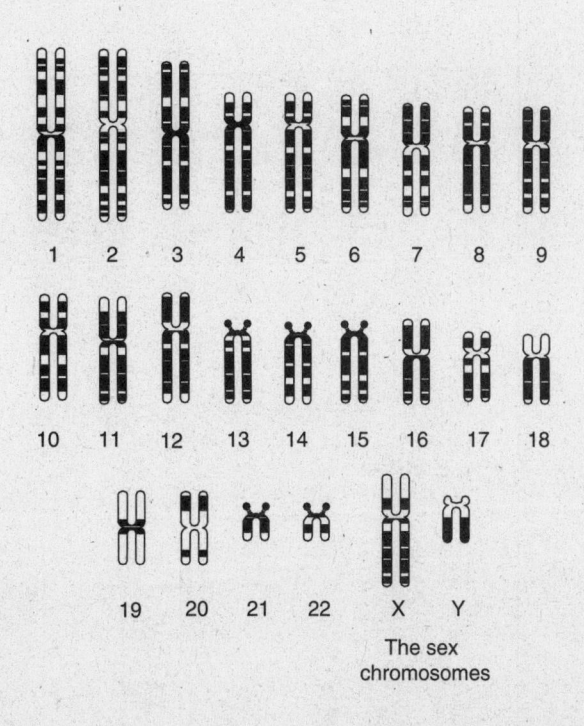

This procedure helps to identify such chromosomal abnormalities as extra or missing chromosomes.

GENETIC DISORDERS

Here's a list of some genetic disorders you should also be aware of:

- **Phenylketonuria (PKU)**—A genetic disorder in which the body is unable to metabolize the amino acid phenylalanine. This condition may lead to mental retardation.

- **Sickle-cell anemia**—A genetic disorder in which red blood cells are abnormally shaped and have trouble traveling through the capillary beds.

- **Tay-Sachs disease**—A genetic disorder in which the nervous system malfunctions due to the accumulation of fat in the brain.

LET'S TEST WHAT YOU'VE LEARNED

1. Deoxyribonucleic acid molecules (DNA) serve as a template for the synthesis of molecules of
    1. amino acids
    2. carbohydrates
    3. messenger RNA
    4. lipids

2. What is the role of DNA in controlling cellular activity?
    1. DNA provides energy for all cell activities.
    2. DNA determines which enzymes are produced by a cell.
    3. DNA is used by cells for the excretion of nitrogenous wastes.
    4. DNA provides nucleotides for the construction of plasma membrane.

3. In addition to a phosphate group, a DNA nucleotide could contain
    1. thymine and deoxyribose
    2. uracil and deoxyribose
    3. thymine and ribose
    4. uracil and ribose

4. Which of the following molecules is found in RNA molecules but not in DNA molecules?
    1. phosphorus
    2. adenine
    3. uracil
    4. thymine

5. Although genetic mutations can occur spontaneously in organisms, the incidence of such mutations can be increased by
    1. radioactive substances in the environment
    2. lack of vitamins in the diet
    3. long exposure to humid climates
    4. a short exposure to freezing temperatures

Chapter 12

EVOLUTION

Most organisms that exist today arose from earlier organisms in a process known as **evolution**. One definition of evolution could be a gradual change in the gene pool of a population over time. (The term **gene pool** refers to the total aggregate of genes in a population at any one time.) Much of what we now know about evolution is based on the work of **Charles Darwin**. Darwin was a nineteenth-century British naturalist who sailed the world in a ship called the *HMS Beagle*. Darwin developed his theory of evolution after studying animals in the Galapagos Islands off the western coast of South America. From his observations, Darwin deduced that different populations of animals must have once belonged to the same species (among other things).

Darwin came to this conclusion on the basis of two very simple facts: (1) different groups of animals had similar traits, and (2) different groups of animals had dissimilar traits. There's nothing necessarily surprising in animals having similar and dissimilar traits. But what Darwin found most striking was that the differences among these animals were well-suited to their environments. For example, tortoises living on islands on which low vegetation was scarce had very long necks, so that they could reach vegetation that was higher up. Without long necks, these tortoises would have starved to death. Tortoises on other islands where low vegetation was abundant had shorter necks.

Darwin believed that these differences were evidence of **natural selection**, the driving force of evolution. By natural selection, Darwin meant the process by which nature chooses which organisms will survive. Which ones are they? They're the ones best suited to their environment. To take the example of our tortoises, on an island with only high-growing vegetation, tortoises with longer necks are simply more likely to survive because they'll be able to eat more. As a consequence, they will outlive those tortoises with shorter necks and produce more offspring. Over time, this pattern of competition and extinction (as the short-necked tortoises die off) will result in the formation of new species.

To summarize, these were Darwin's key observations:

- Each species produces more offspring than can survive.

- These offspring compete with each other for the limited resources available to them.

- In every population, different organisms have different traits.

- The offspring with the most favorable traits are the ones most likely to survive and produce offspring.

Taken together, these observations led him to conclude that natural selection is the driving force of evolution.

LAMARCK'S INFAMOUS GIRAFFES

Darwin was not the first to propose a theory that explained the variety of life on earth. One of the most widely accepted theories of evolution in Darwin's day was that proposed by **Jean-Baptiste de Lamarck**.

In the eighteenth century, Lamarck proposed traits acquired by an organism through its lifetime could be passed on to the organism's offspring. For example, he thought that giraffes got long necks because they were constantly reaching for higher leaves to feed, and that giraffes with the longest necks survived and had more offspring. This theory is referred to as the "law of use and disuse."

We know now that Lamarck's theory is wrong. Think about it this way: If you were to lose one of your fingers, your children would not inherit this trait.

EVIDENCE FOR EVOLUTION

Today we find support for the theory of evolution in several areas:

- **Geological or fossil records**—The study of fossils has revealed the major lines of evolution to us. Scientists study the fossilized remains of now extinct organisms in order to gain some sense of the path of evolution. Such famous examples as *Archaeopteryx*—a winged, feathered reptile from the age of the dinosaurs—have helped scientists trace the development of life on earth. *Archaeopteryx* has led biologists to conclude that birds are in fact distant descendants of the great dinosaurs.

- **Comparative embryology**—The study of the development of various organisms. If you look at the early stages in vertebrate development, the embryos of fish, amphibians, birds, and even humans all look similar—the embryos of all vertebrates even have gill slits!

- **Comparative anatomy**—The study of the anatomy of various animals. Scientists have discovered that some animals have similar structures that serve different functions. For example, a bat's wing, a whale's fin, and a human's arm are all appendages that have evolved to serve different purposes. These structures, called **homologous structures,** point to common ancestors.

- **Comparative biochemistry**—The study of the polypeptides of various organisms. Scientists look at the DNA sequences and the proteins from different organisms in order to identify similarities at the biochemical level. They've found that organisms that are closely related have a greater proportion of polypeptides in common than do distantly related species.

SPECIES

A housecat and a butterfly obviously cannot create offspring together. We would therefore say that they belong to different **species**. However, a tabby (striped housecat) and an angora (those big, furry housecats) *could* reproduce. They are not of different species; they are merely of different breeds. **Speciation**, or origin of new species in the course of evolution, occurs when organisms that were once members of the same species can no longer interbreed. It is this emergence of a new species that marks an "evolutionary stage," or a step in evolution.

Two factors lead to the process of speciation: **geographic isolation** and **reproductive isolation**. In geographic isolation, a geographic barrier separates two groups of organisms. One example of this would be an earthquake thrusting a mountain up between two different groups of squirrels. At this point, the squirrels are geographically isolated. They are still of the same species, the two groups are just cut off from one another.

Over time, however, environmental pressures may lead to drastic changes in these two groups of squirrels. For example, let's say that the mountain catches all the moisture on its western slope, turning its eastern slope into a desert. The only squirrels that would survive on its eastern slope would be those least susceptible to desiccation because of traits like feeding habits, color, or size. Over eons, this group of squirrels evolve to become so different from the original group that the two would no longer be able to interbreed. At this point, we would say that a new species of squirrel had evolved in the process of speciation.

However, a new species might also arise due to **reproductive isolation**. Imagine that erosion eventually flattens our mountain, leaving our two groups of squirrels free to interact once again. Even if the squirrels haven't evolved into two totally separate species, they might still not be able to interbreed because of behavioral differences. For instance, one group may breed in the summer, when it's warm and moist, while the desert squirrels may breed only in the winter, when it's cool enough to seek out a mate. Such a factor is a specific type of reproductive isolation called **temporal isolation**. Over time, these two would eventually become totally separate species, incapable of interbreeding even if they could synchronize their mating seasons. Other types of reproductive isolation are: **ecological isolation**, which occurs when two species live in different habitats so that they encounter each other too rarely to interbreed; **behavioral isolation**, which occurs because of evolved behavioral differences that affect mating; and **mechanical isolation**, which occurs when closely related species attempt to mate but fail because of their anatomical differences.

You won't need to know all these terms for the exam, but you should be familiar with the many reasons for speciation.

EVOLUTION: FAST OR SLOW?

Scientists have long debated whether evolution occurs gradually or suddenly. Some believe that evolution is a gradual process. This view is known as **gradualism**. Proponents of this theory believe that large changes such as speciation happen only because of many small changes that occur over very long stretches of time.

Other scientists believe in **punctuated equilibrium**. According to punctuated equilibrium, there are long stretches of time where essentially nothing happens, and although organisms are constantly reproducing, competing for resources and dying, they are not *evolving*. Evolution only occurs, according to this view, under extreme environmental stress. For example, if a massive comet had not struck the earth, wiping out the dinosaurs (as many contend), mammals would not have had room to evolve and become the predominant life form (or so we like to think of ourselves). Mammals did exist during the age of the dinosaurs, but they were mostly small, scurrying creatures much like today's rodents.

Here's a graph that illustrates the difference between the two theories:

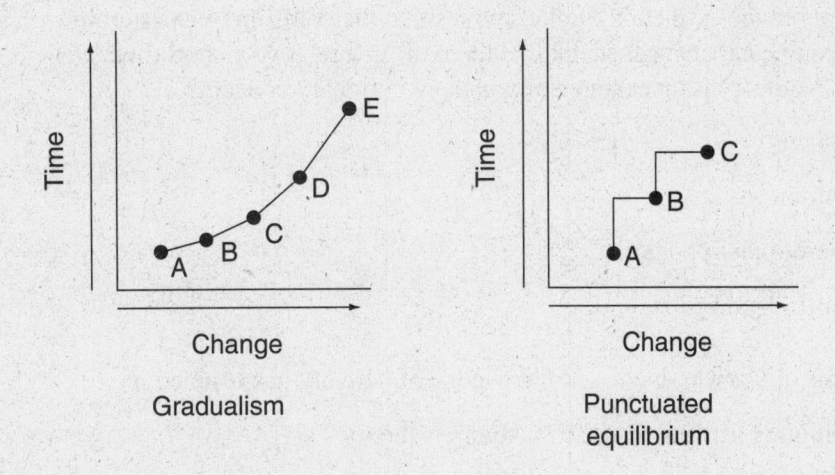

Gradualism

Punctuated equilibrium

THE HETEROTROPH HYPOTHESIS

One issue that is still hotly debated among scientists is the origin of life. Most scientists believe that the earliest precursors of life were nonliving matter—basically gases—in the primitive oceans of the earth. This theory was developed in the 1920s. Two scientists, Oparin and Haldane, proposed that the primitive atmosphere contained the following gases: methane (CH_4), ammonia (NH_3), hydrogen (H_2), and water (H_2O). Interestingly enough, there was almost no free oxygen (O_2) in this early atmosphere. The mixture of gases formed a sort of "primordial soup" in which gases collided, participating in chemical reactions that eventually led to the organic molecules we know today.

Oparin and Haldane's theory didn't receive any substantial support until 1953. In that year, Stanley Miller and Harold Urey simulated the conditions of primitive earth in a laboratory. They put the gases together in a flask, struck them with electrical charges in order to mimic lightning, and organic compounds similar to amino acids appeared!

It's been a long journey from these basic amino acids to the unbelievable complexity of modern-day organisms, but scientists speculate that the earliest forms of life were heterotrophs. Do you remember what a heterotroph is? It's an organism that obtains nutrients from ingesting other organisms or their by-products. In any event, the idea that the first living organisms were heterotrophs is known as the **heterotroph hypothesis**.

By "consuming" organic molecules in the primordial soup, these earliest organisms acquired the energy necessary for life. It was only much, much later that autotrophs—organisms capable of making their own food—appeared on Earth, filling the atmosphere with oxygen gas.

LET'S TEST WHAT YOU'VE LEARNED

1. One theory about the extinction of dinosaurs is that the collision of an asteroid with the Earth caused environmental changes that killed them off in a relatively short time, changing the course of evolution. This theory is an example of which evolutionary concept?

    1. Gradualism
    2. Competition
    3. The heterotroph hypothesis
    4. Punctuated equilibrium

2. Since the time of Darwin, increased knowledge of heredity has resulted in

    1. the addition of use and disuse to Lamarck's theory
    2. the elimination of all previous evolutionary theories
    3. increased support for the theory of natural selection
    4. disagreement with Mendel's discoveries

3. Which phrase best defines evolution?

    1. An adaptation of an organism to its environment
    2. A sudden replacement of one community by another
    3. A geographic or reproductive isolation of organisms
    4. A process of change in organisms over a period of time

4. Which statement would most likely be in agreement with Lamarck's theory of evolution?

    1. Black moths have evolved in a area because they were better adapted to the environment and had high rates of survival and reproduction.
    2. Geographic barriers may lead to reproductive isolation and the production of new species.
    3. Giraffes have long necks because their ancestors stretched their necks reaching for food.
    4. Most variations in animals and plants are due to random chromosomal and gene mutations.

5. How does natural selection operate to cause change in a population?

    1. The members of a population are equally able to survive any environmental change.

    2. The members of the population differ so that only some survive when the environment changes.

    3. The members of the population do no adapt to environmental changes.

    4. All the members of the population adapt to environmental changes.

Chapter 13

THE DIVERSITY OF LIVING THINGS

TAXONOMY

People have long been aware of the diversity of life, but figuring out exactly how organisms are related to one another has taken an incredible amount of work, and all of the evolutionary relationships have yet to be determined. But from the very beginning, naturalists could spot similarities among many organisms. For example, they knew that dogs and wolves were closely related. After all, they resemble one another and behave in very similar ways. But what about birds and bats? Or sharks and dolphins? Sharks and dolphins also look nearly identical, with their fins and tails, and they both live in the sea. Wouldn't it seem perfectly reasonable to lump them together as being closely related?

As you can imagine, figuring out the best way to classify all the creatures on the planet is no easy task. Interestingly, just like those earliest scientists, we now place organisms into different groups on the basis of shared characteristics or traits. Yet while these first biologists classified organisms solely on the basis of appearance and habitat, we now classify living things on the basis of evolutionary relatedness.

From this perspective, sharks and dolphins are not closely related. As you might know, sharks breathe with gills, whereas dolphins possess lungs. These two very different traits, acquired over the long process of evolution, would lead us to conclude that sharks and dolphins split off somewhere way back on the evolutionary tree. Consequently, although they both live in the sea, they are no more than very distant relations. As we also now know, sharks are fish, while dolphins are mammals. To a student of biology, this comes as no surprise. But as little as two hundred years ago, if you had proposed that dolphins were more closely related to humans than to sharks, you would have been laughed out of the classroom!

Let's take a look at the ways in which we currently classify living things. The science of classifying organisms according to their traits is known as **taxonomy**.

HOW CLASSIFICATION WORKS

The simplest way to think about taxonomy is to remember that organisms are classified on the basis of shared characteristics. The order of classification is: **kingdom, phylum, class, order, family, genus**, and **species**. As you move from kingdom to species, organisms share more and more traits in common. The kingdom is the largest category; each kingdom contains some organisms that share very few traits. The species is the smallest grouping, and its members have the most traits in common.

Classification

Let's take a closer look at how organisms are actually ordered into various levels. We'll start with the highest level, the kingdom. All organisms belong to one of five kingdoms: **Monera**, **Protista**, **Fungi**, **Plantae**, and **Animalia**. A quick summary of the five kingdoms appears below. You'll notice that the kingdoms are further broken down into phyla and classes, and some of the main characteristics particular to each are mentioned. While you don't have to know all of the classes, you should be familiar with at least the major phyla. We will list some phylums and characteristics of Fungi and Animalia.

5 Kingdoms	Characteristics	Ecological Role
1. Monera	Prokaryotes (lack distinct nuclei and other membranous organelles); single-celled; microscopic.	
Bacteria	Cell walls composed of peptidoglycan (a substance derived from amino acids and sugars). Cells may be spherical (cocci), rod-shaped (bacilli), or coiled (spirilla).	Decomposers; some chemosynthetic autotrophs; important in recycling nitrogen and other elements. A few are photosynthetic, usually employing hydrogen sulfide as hydrogen source. Some pathogenic (cause disease).
Cyanobacteria	Photosynthetic; previously known as blue-green algae.	Producers; blooms (population explosion) associated with water polution.
2. Protista	Eukaryotes; mainly unicellular or colonial.	
Protozoa	Microscopic; unicellular; depend upon diffusion to support many of their metabolic activities.	Important part of zooplankton; near base of many food chains.
Eukaryotic algae	Some are difficult to differentiate from the protozoa. Some have brown pigment in addition to chlorophyll.	Very important producers, especially in marine and fresh-water ecosystems.
Slime molds	Protozoan characteristics during part of life cycle; fungal traits during remainder.	
3. Fungi	Eukaryotes; plantlike but lack chlorophyll and cannot carry on photosynthesis.	Decomposers, probably to an even greater extent than bacteria. Some are pathogenic (e.g., athlete's foot is caused by a fungus).
Molds, yeasts, mildew, mushrooms	Body composed of threadlike hyphae; rarely discrete cells.	Some used on food (yeast is used in making bread and alchoholic beverages); responsible for much spoilage and crop loss.
4. Plantae	Multicellular eukaryotes; adapted for photosynthesis; photosynthetic cells have chloroplasts. All plants have reproductive tissues or organs and pass through distinct developmental stages and alterations of generations. Cell walls of cellulose; cells often have large central vacuole.	Other organisms depend upon plants to produce foodstuffs and molecular oxygen.
5. Animalia	Multicellular eukaryotic heterotrophs, many of which exhibit advanced tissue differentiation and complex organ systems. Lack cell walls. Extremely and quickly responsive to stimuli, with specialized nervous tissue to coordinate responses; determinate growth.	Almost the sole consuming organisms in the biosphere, some being specialized herbivores, carnivores, and detrivores (eating dead organisms or organic material such as dead leaves).

CLASSIFICATION OF FUNGI

Phylum	Characteristics	Examples	
Fungi	Lack chlorophyll; produce spores	Molds, yeast, mushrooms	

CLASSIFICATION OF ANIMALS

Phylum	Characteristics	Examples	
1. Porifera	Two layers of cells with pores	Sponge	
2. Coelenterata	Two layers of cells; hollow digestive cavity with tentacles	Hydra, jellyfish	
3. Platyhelminthes (Flatworms)	Three layers of cells; flat; bilateral symmetry	Tapeworm, planaria, fluke	
4. Nematoda (Roundworms)	Digestive system with a mouth and anus; round	Hookworm	
5. Rotifera	Digestive system	Rotifer	
6. Annelida (Segmented worms)	Long, segmented body; digestive system; closed circulatory system	Earthworm	
7. Mollusca	Soft bodies; hard shell	Clam, snail	
8. Arthropoda	Segmented body; jointed legs; exoskeleton		
Class Crustacea	Gills for breathing; jointed legs	Crab, lobster	
Insecta	Three body parts; one pair of antennae; six legs; tracheal breathing system	Bee, grasshopper	
Arachnida	Two body parts; eight legs	Spider	
Chilopoda	One pair of legs per segment	Centipede	
Diplopoda	Two pairs of legs per segment	Millipede	
9. Echinodermata (Spiny-skinned)	Spiny exoskeleton; complete digestive system	Starfish, sea urchin, sea cucumber	

CLASSIFICATION OF ANIMALS (Continued)

Phylum	Characteristics	Examples
10. Chordata	Notochord; dorsal nerve cord; gill slits	
Subphylum Vertebrate	Backbone	
Class Pisces (fish)	Gills; scales; two-chambered heart	Salmon
Amphibia	Breathe through gills, lungs and thin, moist skin; three-chambered heart	Frog
Reptilia	Eggs with a chitinous covering; cold-blooded; scales; three-chambered heart	Snake
Aves	Warm-blooded; four-chambered heart; eggs with shell; wings	Owl
Mammalia	Warm-blooded; hair; produce milk to feed young	Human, kangaroo

CLASSIFICATION OF PLANTS

Phylum	Characteristics	Examples
1. Bryophyta	No true roots and stems; produce spores	Liverworts
		Mosses
2. Tracheophyta	True roots, stems, leaves; contain a vascular system	Flowering plants

THE DIVERSITY OF LIVING THINGS

Monera includes bacteria, the smallest and most primitive of all living organisms. As we saw in chapter 4, monerans lack a nuclear membrane, mitochondria, and several other organelles. Organisms in this kingdom are prokaryotes, but all other organisms whose cells have a nuclear membrane are called eukaryotes.

All organisms are given scientific names consisting of a species name and genus name. This classification scheme, called the **binomial classification system**, was developed by Carolus Linnaeus. For example, we humans are called *Homo sapiens*. *Homo* is our genus name and *sapiens* is our species names. *Homo* means "man" and *sapiens* means "wise."

LET'S TEST WHAT YOU'VE LEARNED

1. A fungus is classified as a heterotroph rather than an autotroph because it

    1. grows by mitosis

    2. absorbs food from the environment

    3. manufactures its own food

    4. transforms light energy into chemical energy

2. Which is the most specific term used to classify humans?

    1. *sapiens*

    2. Animals

    3. *Homo*

    4. fungi

3. In which group do all the organisms belong to the same kingdom?

    1. yeast, mushroom, maple tree

    2. paramecium, amoeba, euglena

    3. bacteria, amoeba, euglena

    4. bacteria, moss, geranium

4. In modern classification, blue-green algae, plants, and algae are known as

    1. heterotrophs

    2. autotrophs

    3. animals

    4. plants

5. Which of the following terms includes the other three?

    1. genus

    2. species

    3. kingdom

    4. phylum

Chapter 14

ECOLOGY

So far we've spent most of our time discussing individual organisms, but one important concept that will be tested on the GSE is ecology. **Ecology** can be defined as the study of the interactions between living things and their physical environment.

The best way for us to understand the various levels of ecology is to start with the big picture, the biosphere, and work our way down to the smallest ecologic unit, the population. First let's define some terms:

- **Biosphere**—The entire part of the earth where living things exist. This includes abiotic (nonliving) factors such as soil, water, light, and air. In comparison to the overall mass of the earth, the biosphere is relatively small. If you think of the earth as being the size of a basketball, the biosphere is equivalent to a coat of paint over its surface.

- **Ecosystem**—All of the living organisms in a given area, along with the abiotic factors with which they interact.

- **Community**—A group of different organisms that live in the same area.

- **Population**—A group of individuals that belong to the same species.

BIOSPHERE

The biosphere can be divided into large regions called **biomes**. Biomes are massive areas that are classified mostly on the basis of their climate and plant life. Because of the different climates and terrains on the earth, the types and distribution of living organisms varies. It's important for you to be familiar with both the names of the different biomes and their characteristic **flora** (plant life) and **fauna** (animal life).

Here's a summary of the major **terrestrial** (land) biomes.

Tundra
Regions—northernmost regions
Plant life—few, if any, trees; primarily grasses and flowers
Characteristics—contains permafrost (a layer of permanently frozen soil); has a short growing season.
Animal life—includes lemmings, arctic foxes, snowy owls, caribou, and reindeer

Taiga
Region—northernmost regions
Plant life—wind-blown conifers (evergreens), stunted in growth, possess modified spikes for leaves
Characteristics—very cold, long winters
Animal life—includes caribou, wolves, moose, bear, rabbits, and lynx

Temperate Deciduous Forest
Regions—northeast and middle eastern United States, western Europe
Plant life—deciduous trees which drop their leaves in winter
Characteristics—moderate precipitation; warm summers, cold winters
Animal life—includes deer, wolves, bear, small mammals, birds

Grasslands
Regions—American Midwest, Eurasia, Africa, South America
Plant life—grasses
Characteristics—hot summers, cold winters; unpredictable rainfall
Animal life—includes prairie dogs, bison, foxes, ferrets, grouse, snakes and lizards

Deserts
Regions—western North America, Arctic
Plant life—sparse, includes cacti, drought-resistant plants
Characteristics—arid, low rainfall; extreme diurnal temperature shifts
Animal life—includes jackrabbits (in North America), owls, kangaroo rats, lizards, snakes, tortoises

Tropical Rain Forests
Regions—South America, Colombia
Plant life—high biomass; diverse types
Characteristics—high rainfall and temperature; impoverished soil
Animal life—includes sloths, snakes, monkeys, birds, leopards, and insects

Remember that the biomes tend to be arranged along particular latitudes. For instance, if you hiked from Alaska to Kansas, you'd pass through the following biomes: tundra, taiga, temperate deciduous forests, and grasslands.

Biomes can also be arranged along particular altitudes. For instance, if you hiked from the bottom to the top of a snow-capped mountain in South America, you'd pass through the following biomes: tropical rain forest, temperate deciduous forests, taiga, and tundra.

ECOSYSTEM

Ecosystems are self-contained regions that include both living and nonliving components. For example, a lake, the land that surrounds it, the atmosphere above it, and all the organisms that live in or feed off the lake would be considered a complete ecosystem. As you probably know, there is an exchange of materials between the components of an ecosystem. Take a look the flow of substances through a typical ecosystem:

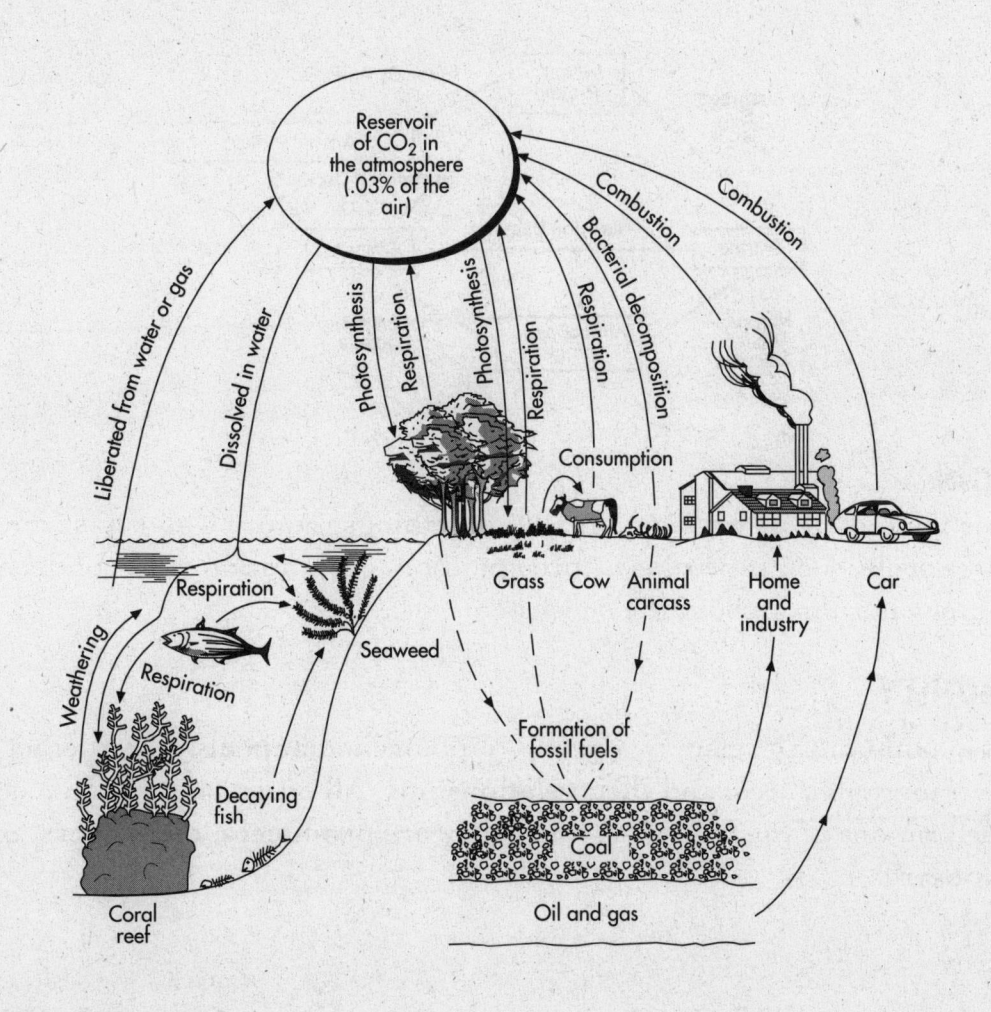

You'll notice that carbon, hydrogen, and oxygen are cycled throughout the ecosystem. For instance, in photosynthesis, plants use carbon dioxide and water to make glucose, releasing oxygen in the process. Consumers then use this oxygen to access the energy stored in glucose, releasing carbon dioxide and water back into the environment. Other examples of ecologic cycles are the **nitrogen cycle** and the **water cycle**.

Nitrogen Cycle

Plants need nitrogen to survive and to make plant proteins. However, in most places, the soil is relatively poor in nitrogen. Although the atmosphere is rich in nitrogen, the nitrogen in the air is not in a usable form. Fortunately for plants that live in nitrogen-poor soil, there are bacteria that are able to use or "fix" this atmospheric nitrogen. **Nitrogen-fixing bacteria** are associated with the roots of legumes and convert atmospheric nitrogen to a useable form called **nitrates**. Nitrates are then used to make plant proteins. Here's a diagram of the nitrogen cycle:

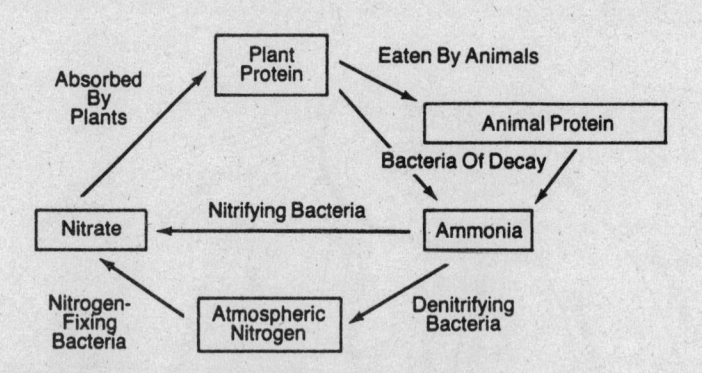

Water Cycle

Water is vital to life as we know it; all living things require water to survive. In the water cycle, such processes as precipitation, evaporation, and condensation distribute water throughout the ecosystem.

COMMUNITY

The term **community** refers to a group of plants and animals that interact in a specific geographic area, and their relationships. All organisms within a community perform one of the following roles: they are **producers, consumers,** or **decomposers**.

Producers

Producers have the ability to make their own food; they are **autotrophs**. Think about your average houseplant. Sure, it needs a square foot of soil from which it extracts some base nutrients, but for the most part, it does just fine with air, sunlight, and a little water. Your houseplant is a typical producer. From water and the gases that abound in the atmosphere, and with the aid of the sun's energy, these autotrophs convert light energy to chemical energy. As we saw in chapter 6, they accomplish this through photosynthesis.

Consumers

Consumers, or heterotrophs, are forced to find their energy sources in the outside world. Basically, heterotrophs are the eaters and autotrophs are the eaten (though plenty of consumers also get eaten). Heterotrophs digest the carbohydrates of their prey into carbon, hydrogen, and oxygen, and use these molecules to make organic substances. Examples of heterotrophs are **herbivores** (organisms that eat plants), **carnivores** (organisms that eat animals), **omnivores** (organisms that eat plants and animals), and **saprophytes** (organisms that eat decaying organic matter).

Decomposers

All organisms at some point yield to **decomposers**. Decomposers are the organisms that break down organic matter. Generally, fungi and bacteria are the decomposers.

THE FOOD CHAIN

Each organism has its own **niche**—its position or function in a community, and each heterotrophic organism must rely on other organisms for sustenance. Connections between trophic (feeding) levels are shown in the **food chain**. A food chain describes the ways in which different organisms depend on one another for food. There are basically four levels to the food chain: **producers**, **primary consumers**, **secondary consumers**, and **tertiary consumers**.

Autotrophs produce all of the available food. They make up the first trophic (feeding) level. They also possess the largest **biomass** (the total mass of all the organisms in an area) and exist in the greatest numbers. Did you know that plants make up about 99% of the Earth's total biomass?

Primary consumers, (herbivores) are organisms that feed directly on producers. A good example of an herbivore is a cow. Cows belong to the second trophic level. The energy flow, biomass, and numbers for members within an ecosystem can be represented in an **pyramid**. Organisms that are "higher up" on the pyramid are less numerous and have less biomass:

```
           Tertiary
           consumers
          /         \
         / Secondary \
        /  consumers  \
       /---------------\
      /    Primary      \
     /    consumers      \
    /---------------------\
   /       Producers       \
  /_____\
```

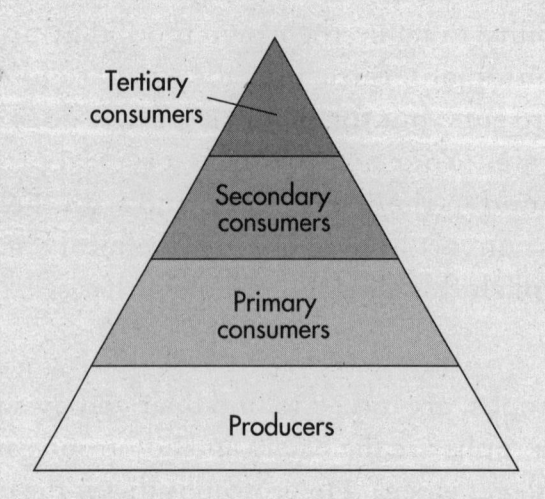

This diagram simply tells us that primary consumers have less biomass than producers, and secondary consumers have less biomass than primary ones, etc. At the top of the pyramid are the tertiary consumers who eat just about everything. In total we have:

- producers that make their own food
- primary consumers (herbivores) that eat producers
- secondary consumers (heterotrophs and carnivores) that eat primary consumers
- tertiary consumers (heterotrophs and omnivores) that eat all of the above.

But what about decomposers? Where do they fit on the food chain? They don't—they are not considered part of the food chain. Decomposers are usually placed just below the food chain to show that they can decompose any organism.

SYMBIOTIC RELATIONSHIPS

We've already mentioned that organisms interact with each other, and many organisms even coexist in what we call **symbiotic relationships**. One example of this type of organism is remoras, or sucker fish, which attach themselves to the backs of sharks in order to more easily obtain food.

Overall, there are three basic types of symbiotic relationships:

1. **mutualism**, in which both organisms profit from the relationship
2. **commensalism**, in which one organism benefits from the relationship and the other one is neither helped nor harmed.

3. **parasitism**, in which one organism benefits while the other is harmed in the relationship.

Make sure you're clear on the difference between these three for the test. Here's a simple (if slightly goofy) summary of the benefits or harm derived by different organisms in symbiotic relationships:

Relationship	Organism I	Organism II
Mutualism	:)	:)
Commensalism	:|	:)
Parasitism	:(	:)

ECOLOGICAL SUCCESSION

Communities of organisms don't just spring up on their own; they develop gradually over time. **Ecological succession** refers to a predictable procession of plant communities over a relatively short period of time (decades or centuries). Centuries may not seem like a short time to us, but if you consider that evolution occurs over millions of years, you'll see that it is relatively very short. Ecological succession begins with pioneer organisms.

Pioneers

How does an abandoned area full of rocks and dirt eventually turn into a field filled with grass and flowers? Well, the toughest part of the job usually falls to a community of **lichens**. Lichens are hardy organisms that can invade an area, land on bare rocks, and erode the rocks' surfaces, turning them into soil. Lichens are considered **pioneer organisms**. While they resemble mosses or simple plants, however, they are actually symbiotic associations of millions of algal cells and fungal hyphae.

Once lichens have rendered an area more habitable, other organisms can settle in. Communities establish themselves in an orderly fashion. Lichens are replaced by mosses and ferns, which in turn are replaced by tough grasses, then low shrubs, then deciduous trees, and finally evergreen trees. Why are lichens replaced and, in fact, what is the driving force behind ecological succession? Well, lichens are replaced because the introduction of taller plants causes them to lose the battle for sunlight and other nutrients they need in order to survive.

ECOLOGY ◆ 177

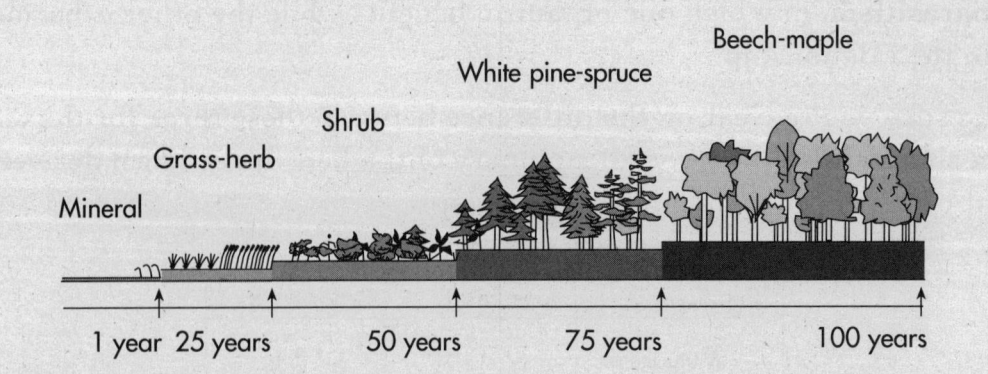

Succession occurs until a final, most stable community is reached; this final community is called the **climax community**. In our example, the beech-maple trees are members of the climax community.

HUMANS AND THE ENVIRONMENT

Before the 1850s, the human population was low because it was kept relatively in check by limiting factors such as disease and food shortages. Since the mid-nineteenth century, however, human population growth has increased at a rapid rate. Our population is now increasing by about 200,000 individuals per day!

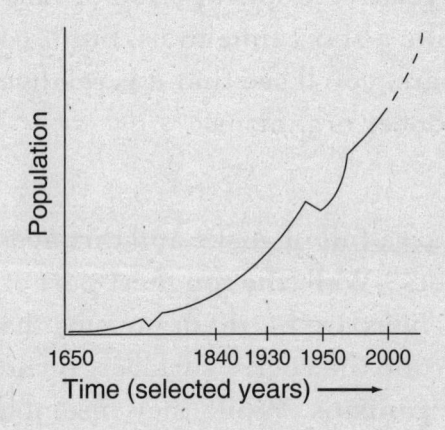

This population growth has put a lot of stress on the environment. As if overpopulation weren't bad enough, we've also managed to harm our environment in many other ways. Take a look:

- **Overhunting**—Many species have been hunted into extinction, some for food, others merely for sport.

- **Exploitation of organisms**—Many exotic plants and animals are killed for commercial trade. For example, the white rhino is routinely slaughtered simply for its horn.

- **Poor land-use management** — Land has been abused through overfarming and unchecked development.

- **Technological oversight** — New technologies have been used without consideration of their effects on the environment. These technologies have often polluted our air and water supply. For example, **biocide use** — the use of chemicals such as pesticides and herbicides to control pests — often damages the soil and increases water and land pollution.

However bad the situation may be at this point, in recent years, we've begun to make an effort to remedy some of these problems. Here is a list of some of the ways we're working to improve our environment:

- **Population control** — People are now encouraged to practice family planning.

- **Conservation of resources** — People are now practicing reforestation and water conservation to help protect the soil.

- **Species preservation** — Wildlife refuges and international bans on hunting have been enacted in order to protect endangered species.

- **Biological controls** — Natural enemies are often used to control pests instead of dangerous chemicals.

- **Environmental laws** — Various laws are passed to preserve and protect the environment, including new, widespread recycling laws.

LET'S TEST WHAT YOU'VE LEARNED

1. Which is an example of an ecosystem?
    1. A population of monarch butterflies
    2. The interdependent biotic and abiotic components of a pond
    3. All the abiotic factors found in a field
    4. All the mammals that live in the Atlantic Ocean

2. In the nitrogen cycle, plants use nitrogen compounds to produce
    1. glucose
    2. starch
    3. lipids
    4. proteins

3. A flea in the fur of a mouse benefits at the mouse's expense. This type of relationship is known as
    1. commensalism
    2. parasitism
    3. saprophytism
    4. mutualism

Base your answer to questions 4 and 5 on the diagram below and on your knowledge of biology.

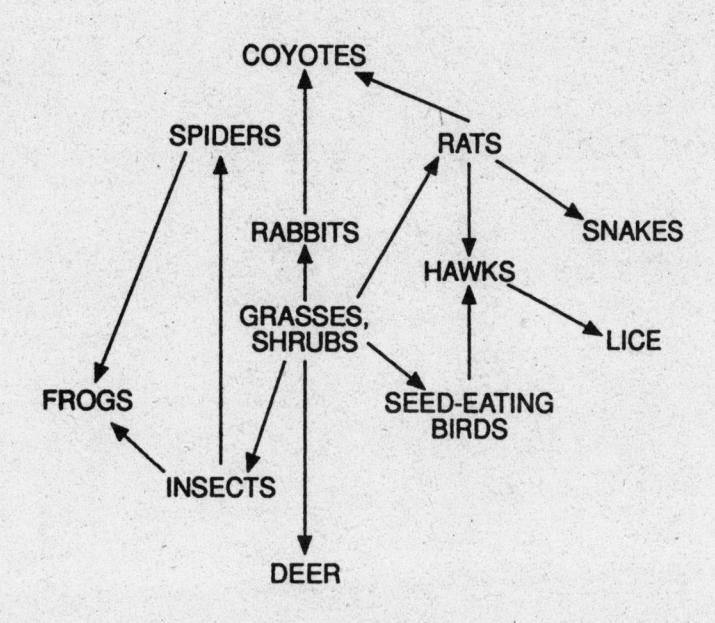

```
                        COYOTES
                         ↑   ↖
           SPIDERS    RATS
              ↑      ↗  ↓  ↘
            RABBITS      SNAKES
              ↑      HAWKS
           GRASSES,    ↑    ↘
           SHRUBS           LICE
        ↙    ↓    ↘
    FROGS        SEED-EATING
      ↑            BIRDS
    INSECTS
       ↕
      DEER
```

4. Which organisms would contain the greatest amount of available energy?

    1. Rabbits and deer

    2. Grasses and shrubs

    3. Lice

    4. Hawks

5. The primary consumers include

    1. rabbits and snakes

    2. insects and seed-eating birds

    3. rats and frogs

    4. spiders and coyotes

Chapter 15

LABORATORY SKILLS

On the GSE, the lab sections usually test two things: (1) how well you understand the key concepts in biology, and (2) how well you think analytically. For instance, can you design experiments, manipulate data, and draw conclusions from experiments?

THE SCIENTIFIC METHOD

Let's begin by discussing the **scientific method**. It's just a fancy name for the steps an investigator takes in conducting an experiment. One of the key steps in conducting an experiment is to state the **problem** to be studied. The problem is the dilemma or mystery the experiment intends to explain. For example, an experiment may be designed to study the effect of pH on enzyme activity. The problem here can be phrased as a simple question: How does pH affect the activity of a given enzyme?

The expected results in a study are then presented in the form of a **hypothesis**. A hypothesis is a possible explanation for the observable facts. For example, a hypothesis for the effect of pH on enzyme activity might be that enzymes are designed to work at specific pH levels.

The Variables

Next, a student should be able to identify the **variables** in the study. The variables are the parts of the experiment that are altered in order to obtain results. Let's take the problem mentioned above. If we were to conduct an experiment to test our hypothesis, we would have to test the rate of an enzyme-assisted reaction as a function of one or more variables. In this case, our principal variable would be the pH of the solution in which we place our enzyme.

By altering the pH and keeping careful track of the effect this variation has on the enzyme, we come up with a bunch of data. These data are called the **results**.

Results

Once we've compiled our results, we can organize them into a chart or graph. Let's look at a typical coordinate graph. The coordinate graph has a horizontal axis (x-axis) and a vertical axis (y-axis):

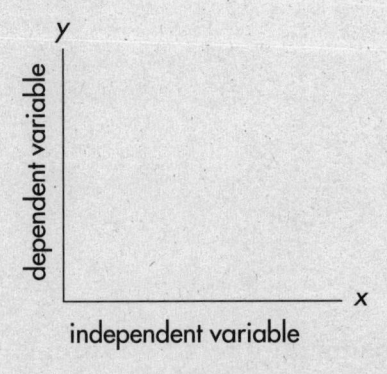

The x-axis usually contains the **independent variable**, the component being manipulated. The y-axis contains the **dependent variable**, the component affected when the independent variable is changed.

Now let's look at what happens when we place our data on the graph. Every point on the graph represents both an independent variable and a dependent variable:

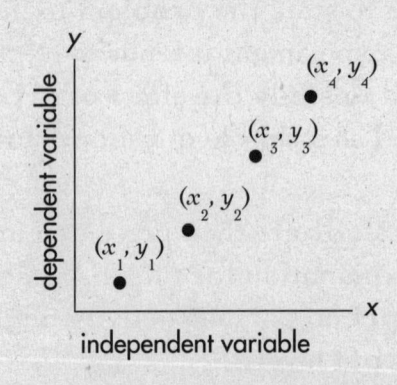

To make a graph, draw both axes and label the axes with the independent and dependent variable. Then you can begin to plot the points on the graph. The graph below shows how the rate of our reaction changed as pH increased:

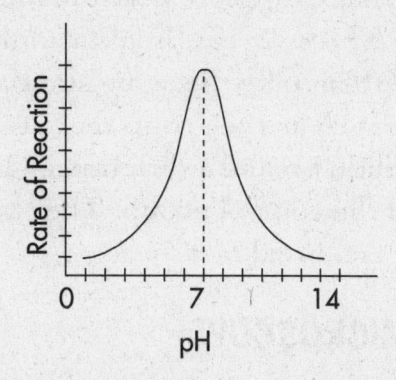

Notice how the dots were connected to form a curved line. The graph shows that the rate of the reaction is greatest at a pH of 7.

Once the data has been collected and presented in a readable form, we can make **conclusions** and draw **inferences** (conclusions based on the facts). The conclusion is the final statement based on the findings in the study. For our particular study, our conclusion might be that pH does in fact exert an effect on enzyme activity. In the case of the enzyme we examined, a pH of 7 turned out to be optimal.

Generalization

Based on the results, you should now be able to make a **generalization** or broad conclusion based on the study. In our example, the generalization would be that pH has a definite effect on enzyme activity. The best way to confirm these results is to repeat the study several times.

Controls

Almost every experiment will have at least one variable that remains constant throughout the study. This variable is called the **control**. A control is simply a standard of comparison. It enables the investigator to be certain that the outcome of the study is due to the changes in the independent variable and nothing else.

Let's look at an example. Let's say the principal of your school thinks that students who eat breakfast do better on standardized tests than those who don't eat breakfast. He takes a group of ten students from your class and gives them free breakfast every day for a year. When the school year is over, he administers a standardized test and they all score brilliantly!

Did they do well because they ate breakfast every day? We don't know for sure. Maybe the principal picked only the smartest kids in the class to participate in the study.

The best way to be sure that eating breakfast made a difference is this case is to pick students in the class who *never* eat breakfast and follow them for a year. At the end of the year, have them take the same standardized test and see how they score. It they do just as well as the group that ate breakfast, then we'll know that eating breakfast didn't make a difference. The group of students that didn't eat breakfast is called the control group. They were not "exposed" to the variable of interest, in this case, breakfast.

THE COMPOUND LIGHT MICROSCOPE

One of the most common tools used to study tiny structures is the **compound light microscope**. A compound microscope magnifies the size of a specimen. The main components of the microscope are the **eyepiece lens, objective lens, stage, diaphragm, coarse-adjustment knob**, and **fine-adjustment knob**. Let's review the parts of a light microscope and how they work:

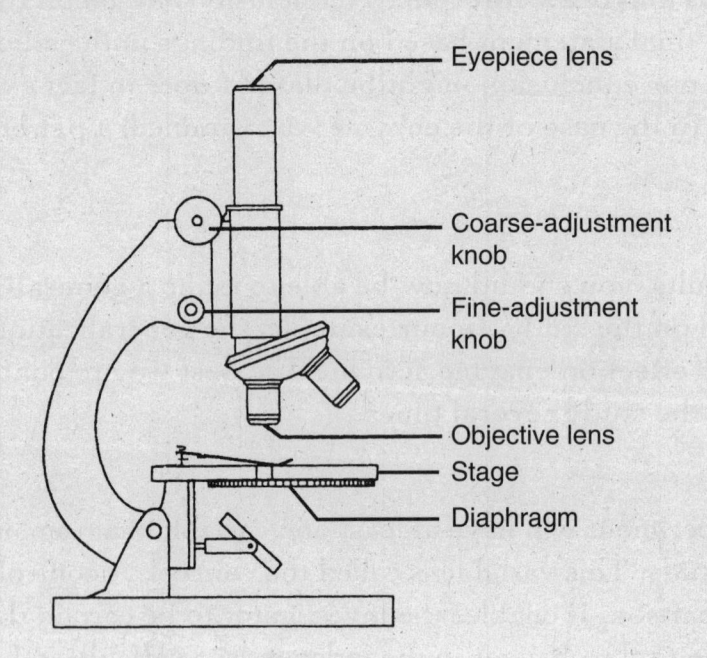

- **Eyepiece (ocular) lens** — The lens through which the image is observed directly.

- **Objective lens** — The lens closest to the specimen.

- **Stage** — The platform on which the specimen is placed in order to be viewed.

- **Coarse-adjustment knob** — Brings the image into rough focus.
- **Fine-adjustment knob** — Brings the image into sharp focus.
- **Light source** — The object which provides the light used to illuminate the specimen.
- **Diaphragm** — Controls the amount of light trained on the specimen.
- **Magnification** — The apparent enlargement of the specimen.
- **Resolution** — The degree to which the microscope distinguishes detail.

To find the total magnification, multiply the power of the eyepiece by the power of the objective lens. For example, if the eyepiece power is 10x and the objective lens is 40x, then the total magnification is 10 times 40, which equals 400x. This means the specimen studied under high power will be magnified 400 times.

Here's one more thing you should remember: The object is not only magnified but also reversed and inverted.

To view structures under a light microscope, you need to provide contrast between cells and their cell structures. This is accomplished through staining techniques. The two most common stains are **iodine** and **methylene blue**.

OTHER INSTRUMENTS

We can obtain additional information about cells using the other instruments listed below:

- **Electron microscope** — Uses a beam of electrons to increase the magnification in excess of 100,000 times. Only nonliving things can be observed.
- **Dissecting microscope** — A low-power microscope which gives us a three-dimensional image of the specimen.
- **Ultracentrifuge** — Spins cells in a machine and separates them according to their densities.
- **Microdissection instrument** — A tool used to dissect or transfer tiny structures.

OTHER LAB TECHNIQUES

Measuring The Length Of Cells

Cells, which are extremely small, are usually measured in micrometers (μm). For example, most cells are approximately 10 mm in size. One micrometer (μm) is equal to 1,000 millimeters (μm).

Indicators

An indicator is a substance that is used to determine the chemical characteristics of a sample or solution. The most common indicators are:

- **pH paper**—Measures the acidity of a solution. pH paper turns red in an acidic solution and blue in a basic solution.

- **Bromthymol blue**—Used to detect the presence of carbon dioxide in a solution.

- **Benedict's (Fehling's) solution**—Used to detect the presence of simple sugars in a solution. When a solution containing sugar and Benedict's solution is heated, the sample turns colors ranging from yellow to red, depending on the concentration of the sugar.

- **Iodine (Lugol's) solution**—Used to detect the presence of starch in a solution. It turns blue-black when added to a sample that contains starch.

ANSWERS TO LET'S TEST WHAT YOU'VE LEARNED

Chapter 3
1) 1
2) 2
3) 2
4) 4
5) 3

Chapter 4
1) 3
2) 3
3) 4
4) 3
5) 2

Chapter 5
1) 2
2) 1
3) 3
4) 4
5) 2

Chapter 6
1) 4
2) 1
3) 1
4) 2
5) 1

Chapter 7
1) 4
2) 4
3) 2
4) 1
5) 1

Chapter 8
1) 4
2) 4
3) 2
4) 3
5) 1
6) 3
7) 2
8) 1
9) 4
10) 2
11) 3
12) 1
13) 2
14) 2
15) 1

Chapter 9
1) 3
2) 2
3) 2
4) 4
5) 2
6) 3
7) 4
8) 3
9) 2
10) 4
11) 1
12) 2
13) 3

Chapter 10
1) 4
2) 2
3) 3
4) 3
5) 3
6) 1

Chapter 11
1) 3
2) 2
3) 1
4) 3
5) 1

Chapter 12
1) 4
2) 3
3) 4
4) 3
5) 2

Chapter 13
1) 2
2) 1
3) 2
4) 2
5) 3

Chapter 14
1) 2
2) 4
3) 2
4) 2
5) 2

Part III

The Princeton Review GSE Biology Practice Tests

Chapter 16

THE PRINCETON REVIEW PRACTICE TEST I: SESSION I

MULTIPLE-CHOICE QUESTIONS

Directions: The multiple-choice portion of the examination will give you an opportunity to demonstrate your knowledge of biology. You will answer 30 multiple-choice questions in 45 minutes. Allow yourself enough time to complete all 30 questions. Choose one of the four options for each answer.

1. The diagram below represents three steps of a chemical reaction:

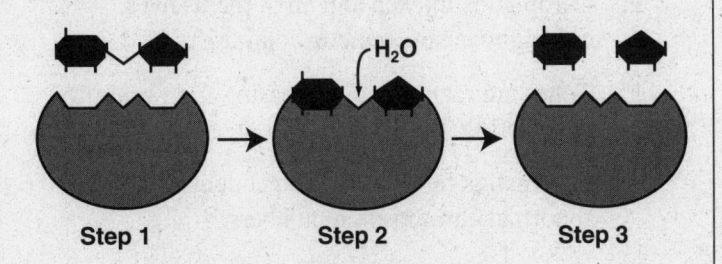

   Step 1   Step 2   Step 3

   This diagram best illustrates the
   1. synthesis of a polypeptide
   2. emulsification of a fat
   3. synthesis of a polysaccharide
   4. hydrolysis of a carbohydrate

2. The structural formula below represents urea:

   This structural formula indicates that urea is
   1. an organic compound
   2. an inorganic compound
   3. a carbohydrate
   4. a nucleic acid

3. Which of the following is *not* characteristic of an animal cell?
   1. It contains ribosomes.
   2. It has a membrane-bound nucleus.
   3. It contains a cell wall.
   4. It contains chloroplasts.

4. What is a direct result of aerobic respiration?
   1. The potential energy of glucose is transferred to ATP molecules.
   2. The enzymes for aerobic respiration are produced by lysosomes.
   3. Lactic acid is produced in muscle tissue.
   4. Alcohol is produced by yeast and bacteria.

5. Which of the following is a product of glycolysis?
   1. Pyruvic acid
   2. Lactic acid
   3. Alcoholic fermentation
   4. Water

6. Which of the following equations represents the overall reaction for photosynthesis?

   1. $6 O_2 + 12 H_2O \rightarrow C_6H_{12}O_6 + 6 O_2 + 6 H_2O$
   2. $C_6H_{12}O_6 + 6O_2 + 6H_2O \rightarrow 6 CO_2 + 12 H_2O$
   3. $6 CO_2 + 12 H_2O \xrightarrow{\text{sunlight}} C_6H_{12}O_6 + 6 O_2 + 6 H_2O$
   4. $6 O_2 + 12 H_2O \xrightarrow{\text{sunlight}} C_6H_{12}O_6 + 6 O_2 + 6 H_2O$

7. In the branch of a cherry tree, gases are exchanged between the environment and the cells through

   1. lenticels
   2. cambium
   3. xylem
   4. phloem

8. The diagrams below represent stages of a cellular process:

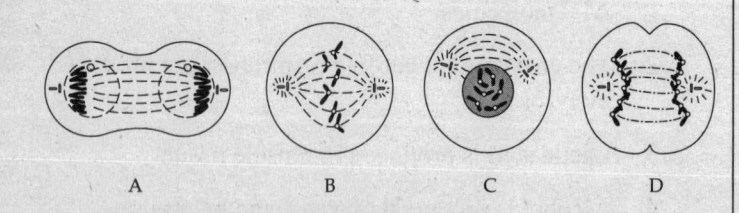

   A   B   C   D

   Which is the correct sequence of these stages?

   1. A → B → C → D
   2. B → D → C → A
   3. C → B → D → A
   4. D → B → A → C

9. Which statement best describes the division of the cytoplasm and the nucleus in budding?

   1. Both the cytoplasm and the nucleus divide equally.
   2. The cytoplasm divides unequally, but the nucleus divides equally.
   3. The cytoplasm divides equally, but the nucleus divides unequally.
   4. Both the cytoplasm and the nucleus divide unequally.

10. The yolk of a developing bird embryo functions as a

    1. moist respiratory membrane
    2. storage site for waste
    3. food source
    4. fluid environment

11. Which situation is a result of crossing-over during meiosis?

    1. Genes are duplicated exactly, ensuring that offspring will be identical to the parents.
    2. Chromatids thicken and align themselves, helping to ensure genetic continuity.
    3. Genes are rearranged, increasing the variability of offspring.
    4. Chromatids fail to sort independently, creating abnormal chromosome numbers.

12. In sexually reproducing species, doubling of the chromosome number from generation to generation is prevented by events that take place during the process of

    1. gametogenesis
    2. cleavage
    3. nondisjunction
    4. fertilization

13. Which event is not part of the process of DNA replication?

    1. Nitrogenous base pairs are formed.
    2. Hydrogen bonds are broken.
    3. A double-stranded molecule unwinds.
    4. Ribosomes are synthesized.

14. Which statement best describes an energy pyramid?

    1. There is more energy at the consumer level than at the producer level.
    2. There is more energy at the producer level than at the consumer level.
    3. There is more energy at the secondary consumer level than at the primary consumer level.
    4. There is more energy at the decomposer level than at the consumer level.

15. Which indicators could be used to test for the presence of simple sugar and starch in a fluid solution?

    1. Benedict's solution and Lugol's iodine
    2. Bromthymol blue solution and pH paper
    3. Fehling's solution and bromthymol blue
    4. pH paper and Lugol's iodine

16. Which of the following act as coenzymes?

    1. Lipids
    2. Peptides
    3. Vitamins
    4. Minerals

17. Which of the following correctly lists the order in which blood travels through the heart?

    1. Aorta, capillaries, arterioles, left ventricle, venules, veins, right ventricle, right atrium, lungs, right atrium
    2. Right atrium, right ventricle, arterioles, capillaries, aorta, venules, veins, left atrium, left ventricle, lungs
    3. Left atrium, left ventricle, aorta, arterioles, capillaries, venules, veins, right atrium, right ventricle, lungs
    4. Left atrium, left ventricle, lungs, aorta, arterioles, capillaries, venules, veins, right atrium, left ventricle

18. Which of the following take place in the nephron?

    1. Filtration only
    2. Reabsorption only
    3. Both filtration and re-absorption
    4. Neither filtration nor re-absorption

19. Where is bile stored?

    1. In the liver
    2. In the pancreas
    3. In the gall bladder
    4. In the small intestine

20. Which of the following enzymes is secreted by the salivary glands of the mouth?

    1. Amylase
    2. Pepsin
    3. Lipase
    4. Maltase

21. All of the following are smooth muscles EXCEPT

    1. those in the digestive tract
    2. those in the uterus
    3. those in the diaphragm
    4. those in the heart

22. All of the following are producers EXCEPT

    1. cacti
    2. pea plants
    3. blue-green algae
    4. mushrooms

23. A bear foraging for food first swipes open a honeycomb to get at the honey, then feasts on some blueberry bushes, ambles over to a rotten log to search for grubs, and ends up by a stream, eating a salmon it just caught. Based on its consumption, the bear is a(n)

    1. omnivore
    2. herbivore
    3. carnivore
    4. saprophyte

24. Which of the following is NOT found in a molecule of DNA?

    1. Adenine
    2. Deoxyribose
    3. Phosphorus
    4. Uracil

25. A population of a single species of birds is divided by natural disaster and the two populations are subjected to different environmental conditions. After a period of 6,000,000 years it is most likely that the descendants of the two populations, if brought together, would

    1. occupy the same niche
    2. have identical mating seasons
    3. be in competition for identical resources
    4. be unable to mate together

26. A principal effect of insulin produced by the pancreas is to

    1. stimulate metabolism
    2. increase blood glucose levels
    3. decrease blood glucose levels
    4. regulate secondary sex characteristics

27. Which of the following biomes has flora consisting mainly of lichen, mosses, and grasses?

    1. Tundra
    2. Taiga
    3. Desert
    4. Temperate deciduous forest

Questions 28 and 29 refer to an experiment in which investigators probed the response of four plant seedlings to various conditions of sunlight deprivation over a period of four days. Each seedling was 6 inches tall and seedlings one through four were capped in various ways with a flexible material.

As shown below, seedling one was capped at its bottom and the remainder of the plant was exposed to sunlight. Seedling two was capped at its tip and the remainder of the plant was exposed to sunlight. Seedling three was capped near its tip but both the tip and the lower portion of the plant remained exposed to sunlight. Seedling four was capped at its tip and the cap covered the majority of the plant's body. It was found that on day one seedlings one and three began to bend in their growth and continued in this bending pattern through day four. Seedlings two and four exhibited no bending.

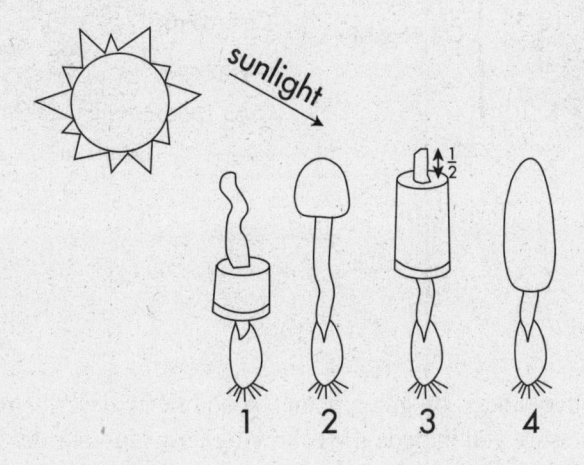

28. It is most likely that seedlings one and three bend
    1. away from the source of sunlight
    2. toward the source of the sunlight
    3. toward the center of the earth
    4. only during the night

29. The bending of seedlings one and three is an example of
    1. phototropism
    2. geotropism
    3. hydrotropism
    4. autotropism

30. Members of which of the following phyla contain a chitin exoskeleton, one or two body parts, and four pairs of jointed appendages?
    1. Arthropoda
    2. Coelenterata
    3. Annelida
    4. Porifera

WRITTEN-RESPONSE QUESTION

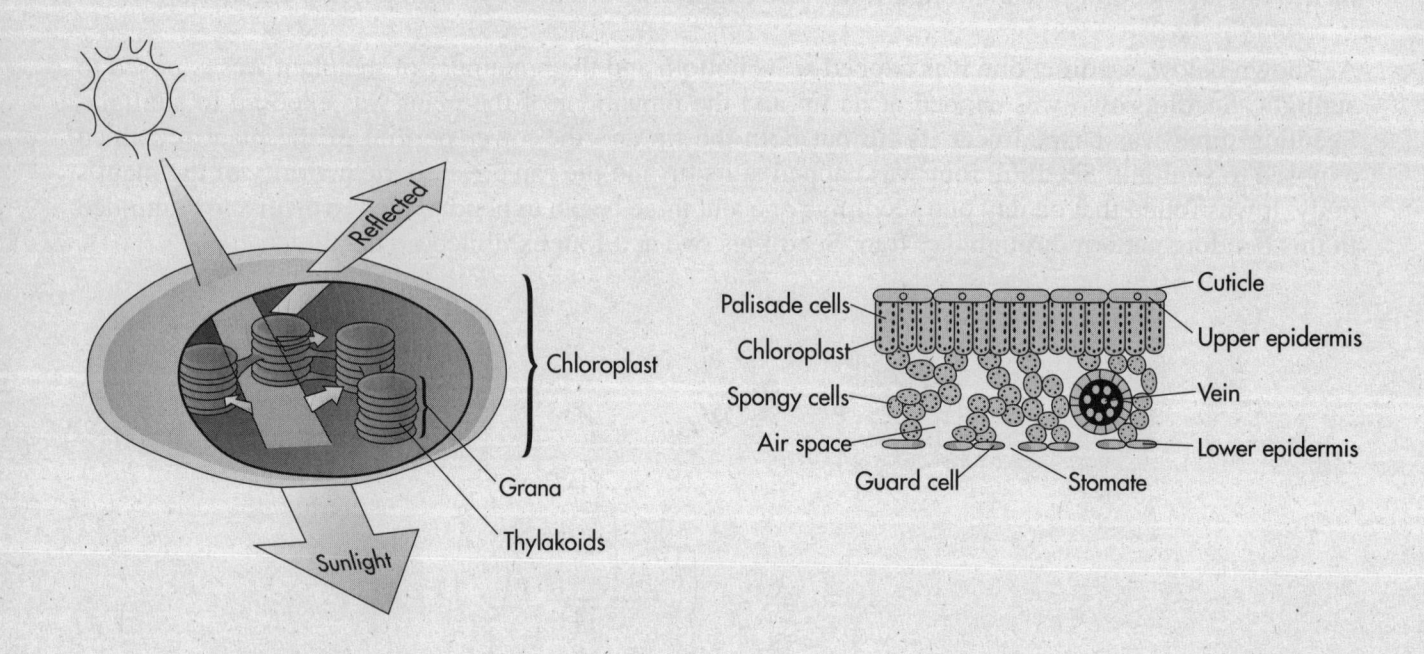

a. State the major product of photosynthesis by green plants. Also briefly describe the reactions that take place in the leftmost structure, above. Make sure you include the following terms in your description: light reactions, dark reactions, stroma, photons, carbon dioxide.

b. Describe the function of the guard cells, shown on the right above, in gas exchange. Then state how the process of photosynthesis is a major contributor to the existence of humans.

c. Describe the greenhouse effect and global warming.

ANSWERS AND EXPLANATIONS

1. Choice 4 is the correct answer. Notice the ringed compound attached to the enzyme is a disaccharide. The addition of water breaks the disaccharide into two monosaccharides in a process called hydrolysis.
2. Choice 3 is the correct answer. Maltose is a disaccharide that's formed when two monosaccharides are joined via dehydration synthesis. This means that water is removed as the bond is formed.
3. Choice 1 is the correct answer. The structural formula of urea is given in this question. Fortunately, you don't need to know anything about urea except that it contains carbon, hydrogen, and nitrogen. This means that it's an organic compound.
4. Choice 1 is the correct answer. During aerobic respiration, the energy-rich bonds within a glucose molecule are used to make ATP.
5. Choice 4 is the correct answer. Water is produced in the final stage of aerobic respiration.
6. Choice 3 is the correct answer. Use the process of elimination. Because photosynthesis requires sunlight, we can eliminate answer choices 1 and 2. The starting materials for photosynthesis are CO_2 (in carbon fixation) and water (in photolysis), not O_2 (oxygen) and water.
7. Choice 1 is the correct answer. Lenticels are small pores on woody stems and facilitate gas exchange.
8. Choice 3 is the correct answer. The correct sequence of mitosis is prophase, metaphase, anaphase, and telophase. During prophase (C), the centrioles move to opposite ends of the cell. During metaphase, (B), the chromosomes line up in the middle of the cell. During anaphase (D), the chromosomes separate. During telophase, (A), two daugher cells are formed.
9. Choice 2 is the correct answer. In budding, the nucleus divides evenly, but the cytoplasm divides unequally.
10. Choice 3 is the correct answer. The yolk of a bird is an extraembryonic sac that provides food (nutrients) for the animal during its development.
11. Choice 3 is the correct answer. Crossing over is the exchange of segments of chromosomes during meiosis. This process leads to the rearrangement of chromosomal segments and genetic variability.
12. Choice 1 is the correct answer. Gametogenesis refers to the formation of gametes. During this process, the diploid number of chromosomes is reduced to the haploid or monoploid number. This prevents the chromosome number from increasing exponentially over time.
13. Choice 4 is the correct answer. This question tests your knowledge of DNA replication. We know that during DNA replication, the double-stranded molecule un-

winds (3), the hydrogen bonds are then broken (2), and the nitrogenous base pairs are linked (1). Ribosomes are not synthesized during DNA replication.

14. Choice 2 is the correct answer. The distribution of energy in a community can be pictured as a pyramid, with the first trophic level (the producers) at the base, and the last level (the consumers) at the top. Energy decreases as you move up the pyramid. Consequently, there is more energy at the producer level than at the consumer level.

15. Choice 1 is the correct answer. Benedict's (Fehling's) solution is an indicator that tests for simple sugars. Lugol's iodine is an indicator that tests for the presence of starch.

16. Choice 3 is the correct answer. As we learned in chapter 3, vitamins are an example of organic coenzymes; enzymes need them in order to catalyze biological reactions. Inorganic enzyme helpers are known as cofactors.

17. Choice 3 is the correct answer. Go back to chapter 8 if you can't figure this one out. Blood travels from the left atrium to the left ventricle, then out the aorta to the body (systemic circulation). It returns via the right atrium, flows into the right ventricle, and leaves again to head for the lungs and pulmonary circulation.

18. Choice 3 is the correct answer. Remember that nephrons are the functional units of the kidney. Blood is filtered as it flows by the Bowman's capsule, and as the filtrate moves along the remaining section of the nephron, glucose, amino acids, and salts are reabsorbed by the body.

19. Choice 3 is the correct answer. You learned in chapter 8 that bile is an emulsifier that cuts up fats into small droplets during digestion. You also learned that bile is made in the liver and stored in the gall bladder.

20. Choice 1 is the correct answer. Saliva is secreted by the salivary glands in the mouth and contains salivary amylase, which begins the digestion of starches into maltose.

21. Choice 4 is the correct answer. Smooth muscles are involuntary muscles; they're found throughout the body, in the blood vessels, digestive tract, and internal organs. Their contractions are relatively slow. Cardiac muscle is found in the heart, and skeletal muscle is voluntary muscle.

22. Choice 4 is the correct answer. Producers can make their own food through the carbon-fixing reactions of photosynthesis. Green plants are the main category of producers, but blue-green algae also qualify. Mushrooms are in the Fungi kingdom and are not producers.

23. Choice 1 is the correct answer. Omnivores eat both plants and animals, while herbivores eat only plants, carnivores eat only animals, and saprophytes eat decaying organic matter.

24. Choice 4 is the correct answer. When you take the GSE Biology, remember this key difference between RNA and DNA: RNA has uracil instead of thymine as a base.

25. Choice 4 is correct. This question concerns one of evolution's fundamental tenets. If populations of the same species are separated and subjected for long periods to different conditions, they will adapt to the altered conditions. This will result in drastic changes to their genomes over time, which will make it impossible for them to breed together—they will have become different species.
26. Choice 3 is correct. Insulin is a hormone produced by the pancreas. It allows the uptake of blood glucose by cells. For the purposes of the GSE in Biology, just remember that the pancreas secretes insulin, and insulin lowers blood glucose levels.
27. Choice 1 is correct. The tundra is located in the northern parts of North America, Europe, and Asia. Soil is frozen year-round, and plant life consists of lichen, mosses, wildflowers, and grasses. Remember that trees generally do not grow in the tundra.
28. Choice 2 is correct. Auxins are plant hormones located at the plant's tips; they respond to sunlight, and cause the plant to grow toward the sun. This type of bending is known as phototropism, "photo-" for light and "trop-" for growth.
29. Choice 1 is the correct answer. Auxins cause plants to grow toward the sun in phototropism. Geotropism refers to a bending toward or away from the ground. Hydrotropism means growing toward a water source. Autotropism has nothing to do with a plant's hormonal response.
30. Choice 1 is the correct answer. Review the classification list in chapter 13. Arthropods have a chitinous exoskeleton, jointed appendages, and several body parts.

WRITTEN-RESPONSE ANSWERS

A. The major product of photosynthesis by plants is glucose. The main reactions of photosynthesis are the light reactions and dark reactions. The light reactions take place in the thylakoid membranes of the stacks of grana, while the dark reactions take place in the stroma. In the light reactions, photons of light are converted into chemical energy, in the form of ATP and NADPH. The light reactions also split a molecule of water into protons and diatomic oxygen. In the dark reactions, ATP and carbon dioxide are used to make glucose.

B. The guard cells surround each stomate, which are openings in the epidermal layer of the leaf that allow for gas exchange, and regulate the opening and closing of the stomates. The guard cells open when photosynthesis begins. They open in order to take in carbon dioxide and expel oxygen, a product of the photosynthetic reactions. Because oxygen is a byproduct of photosynthesis and is expelled through the stomates, plants render Earth's atmosphere habitable for humans, which need oxygen to breathe.

C. The greenhouse effect refers to the existence of greenhouse gases (which trap heat) in our atmosphere. Carbon dioxide is the main greenhouse gas, and without it, the earth would be too cold for us to live on. Global warming refers to the rising global temperature. The temperature is rising because of the increase in greenhouse gases in the atmosphere.

Chapter 17

THE PRINCETON REVIEW PRACTICE TEST I: SESSION II

All right, we've already said that it would be impossible for us to simulate a lab setting in order to get you ready for the big exam. But we've decided to do the next best thing—in the following chapters you'll find a traditional lab exercise, the likes of which you could see on the exam. You should read through each of the lab sections and become familiar with the chemicals and equipment used, as well as the procedures and techniques.

In the latter two lab sections, we provide you with data and a chance to graph and interpret it. You should practice on these graphs because you will almost certainly be asked to do some graphing on the biology GSE.

So, without further ado...

THE EFFECTS OF SALT CONCENTRATIONS ON CELLS

On the table in front of you, you will find the following:

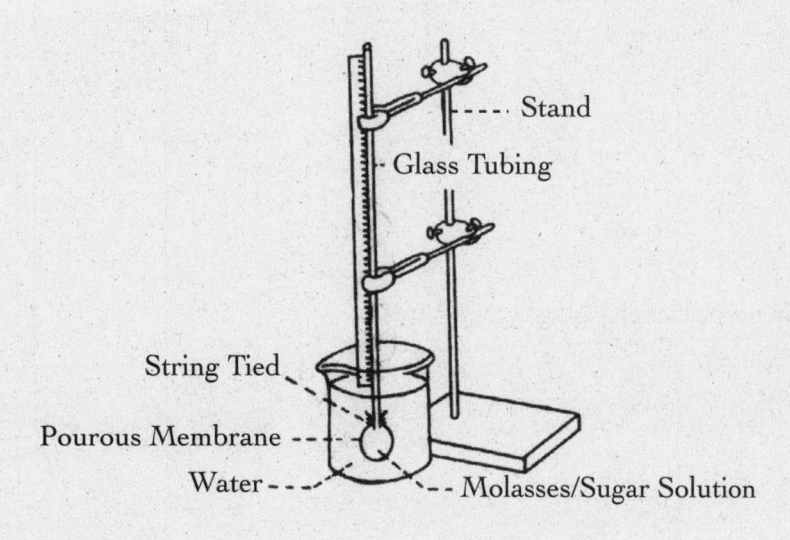

Osmometer

Read and follow the steps in the order given.

Record all observations, results, and answers to the questions as directed.

Immediately notify the proctor of spills or other problems.

Make your answers as complete as possible to demonstrate fully your knowledge of scientific principles and how to apply them.

1. Osmosis.

All molecules are constantly in motion, and the higher the temperature (the greater the kinetic energy), the faster the molecules will move. Diffusion is the process in which molecules move from regions of higher concentration to those of lower concentration. Take a look at the osmometer before you. It consists of a long piece of tubing that's closed at one end, and the other end is attached to a piece of glass tubing. The cellophane bag contained within the long tubing is filled with molasses and immersed in a beaker of water.

At this point, the sugar solution and the water are separated by a thin membrane that will allow water molecules to pass through, but not the large sugar molecules. Because of the difference in concentration of water on both sides of the membrane, water will diffuse across the membrane.

Please describe what occurs to the solution that's in the long glass tubing of the osmometer. Explain why this occurs.

ANSWER:

Is the water in the beaker changing color? Why?

ANSWER:

2. Rate of Osmosis

In this section of the experiment, we will study the rate of osmosis by filling dialysis bags with sucrose solutions and regular tap water, and then measuring the weight change in the bags, at intervals of 7 minutes.

For this experiment, you will need five pieces of dialysis tubing, each of which should be 15 cm in length. Open the pieces of tubing by wetting them and then rubbing them between your fingers. Knot one end of each of the pieces of dialysis tubing. Fill the bags in the following way:

Bag 1—15 ml of tap water

Bag 2—15 ml of 20% sucrose solution

Bag 3—15 ml of 40% sucrose solution

Bag 4—15 ml of 60% sucrose solution

Bag 5—15 ml of tap water

Close each bag and knot them. Then weigh each bag separately and record their weights in Table 1 (we've done this for you with probable data).

Now place each bag in a separate beaker and cover bags 1, 2, 3, and 4 with tap water. Cover bag 5 with 60% sucrose solution.

Every 7 minutes, remove the bags from the beakers, and weigh each one. Record their weights in Table 1.

Please write your conclusions in the spaces below the data, in Table 1.

Time (minutes)	1	2	3	4	5
beginning	~15	15.12	15.20	15.35	15.00
7	~15	15.24	15.30	15.65	14.80
14	~15	15.40	15.51	15.90	14.63
21	~15	15.48	15.74	16.19	14.52
grams lost or gained over 21 minutes	0	+.36	+.54	+.84	−.48
		water diffused inwards	water diffused inwards	water diffused inwards	water diffused inwards

3. Movement through the semipermeable membranes of the living cell.

In this section of the laboratory, plant cells will be exposed to different salt concentrations and the effects of the trials will be observed.

Take a red onion and, with a sharp razor, make a very small cut in the onion. The slice of onion should be so thin as to nearly be invisible. Place the onion on a slide, and add two drops of water, then cover it with a cover slip. Under low power, find a spot in which the cells that contain the red pigment are visible. The cell wall of these plant cells should be translucent. Draw one of the cells in the space below:

Now add one drop of 15% NaCl to the edge of the cover slip, and touch a piece of paper towel to a different edge of the cover slip. This will cause the salt solution to surround the cells. Please record the appearance of the cells after they've been exposed to the NaCl solution, and in the Conclusions section, state the reasons for these changes in cell appearance.

ANSWER 1:

Water travels, because of osmosis, from regions of higher concentration, to those of lower concentration. In this case, water will travel across the membrane, to dilute the molasses.

ANSWER 2:

The water in the beaker should not change color—as the setup indicated, the sugar molecules cannot diffuse across the membrane, so although water can diffuse into the molasses sack, molasses cannot diffuse out to alter the color of the water.

Chapter 18

THE PRINCETON REVIEW PRACTICE TEST II: SESSION I

MULTIPLE-CHOICE QUESTIONS

Directions: The multiple-choice portion of the examination will give you an opportunity to demonstrate your knowledge of biology. You will answer 30 multiple-choice questions in 45 minutes. Allow yourself enough time to complete all 30 questions. Choose one of the four options for each answer.

1. Which of the following is a feature of prokaryotic cells?
   1. They lack a plasma membrane.
   2. They contain organelles.
   3. They lack DNA.
   4. They lack a membrane-bound nucleus.

2. When a geranium plant is placed in a horizontal position, auxins accumulate on the side of the stem closest to the ground. As a result, what will most likely occur in the stem of the geranium?
   1. Stomates will close.
   2. Leaves will develop.
   3. The plant will begin to grow up toward the sky.
   4. Cell growth will stop.

3. Which activity would not be carried out by an organism in order to maintain a stable internal environment?
   1. Removal of metabolic waste products
   2. Transport of organic and inorganic compounds
   3. Production of offspring by the organism
   4. Regulation of physiological processes

4. According to the heterotroph hypothesis, which event immediately preceded the evolution of aerobes?
   1. The production of oxygen by autotrophs
   2. The production of ammonia by heterotrophs
   3. The production of carbon dioxide by autotrophs
   4. The production of carbon dioxide by heterotrophs

5. Organisms with favorable variations reproduce more successfully than organisms with less favorable variations. This statement best describes the concept of
   1. overproduction
   2. use and disuse
   3. inheritance of acquired characteristics
   4. survival of the fittest

6. The concept that evolution is the result of long period of stability interrupted by geologically brief periods of significant change is known as
   1. gradualism
   2. natural selection
   3. geographic isolation
   4. punctuated equilibrium

7. Which of the following processes yields a net total of 2 ATP?
   I. Anaerobic respiration
   II. Electron transport and oxidative phosphorylation
   III. The Krebs cycle
   1. I only
   2. II only
   3. I and II only
   4. I and III only

8. What is the function of the guard cells of a plant?

   1. To release a toxin when the plant is approached by a predator
   2. To provide a seal against mechanical abrasions
   3. To conduct photosynthesis in the presence of sunlight
   4. To regulate the opening and closing of the stomates

9. The plant in the diagram above is exhibiting what kind of tropism due to what plant hormone?

   1. Gravitropism due to auxins
   2. Phototropism due to giberellins
   3. Phototropism due to auxins
   4. Gravitropism due to giberellins

10. Transfer RNA, also called tRNA, functions in translation in which of the following ways?

    1. It acts as the site of protein synthesis.
    2. It carries a series of nucleotide sequences that dictate the order in which amino acids will be arranged to form a polypeptide.
    3. It supplies the peptide bonds that join individual amino acids into a polypeptide.
    4. It transports specific amino acids that correspond to a sequence of nucleotides on mRNA.

11. During metaphase of mitosis

    1. the nuclear envelope disintegrates
    2. sister chromatids line up at the equator of the cell
    3. sister chromatids condense
    4. sister chromatids move to opposite poles of the cell

12. Which of the following structures derives from the ectoderm?

    1. The blood vessels
    2. The eye
    3. The inner lining of the digestive tract
    4. The muscles

13. In which digestive structure is protein initially broken down?

    1. The mouth
    2. The esophagus
    3. The stomach
    4. The small intestine

14. Chemical messengers released by an organism that regulate homeostasis are known as

    1. auxins
    2. hormones
    3. pheromones
    4. enzymes

214 ◆ CRACKING THE GOLDEN STATE EXAMINATION: BIOLOGY

15. Which of the following is true regarding symbiosis?

    1. It involves a pairing of organisms of the same species.
    2. Two organisms form a short-lived partnership.
    3. At least one member of the pair always suffers.
    4. At least one member of the pair always benefits.

16. Commensalism is a symbiotic association in which

    1. one partner is injured and the other benefits
    2. both partners benefit
    3. both partners are injured
    4. one partner benefits and the other is neither helped nor harmed

17. What life form is the most likely to colonize bare rock?

    1. Lichen
    2. Algae
    3. Grasses
    4. Shrubs

18. Which biome is associated with a dense forest of conifers?

    1. Grassland
    2. Tundra
    3. Taiga
    4. Temperate deciduous forest

19. Which of the following correctly lists the phylogenic heirarchy?

    1. Kingdom, phylum, family, class, order, genus, species
    2. Phylum, family, order, class, kingdom, species, genus
    3. Kingdom, family, order, class, phylum, genus, species
    4. Kingdom, phylum, class, order, family, genus, species

20. The process in which a dipeptide is broken down into two amino acids is called

    1. hydrolysis
    2. dehydration synthesis
    3. peptide bonding
    4. hydrogen bonding

21. All of the following hormones are involved in the menstrual cycle EXCEPT

    1. progesterone
    2. estrogen
    3. testosterone
    4. follicle-stimulating hormone (FSH)

22. Which of the following graphs best describes the relationship between reaction rate as a function of the amount of substrate, if the amount of enzyme is limited?

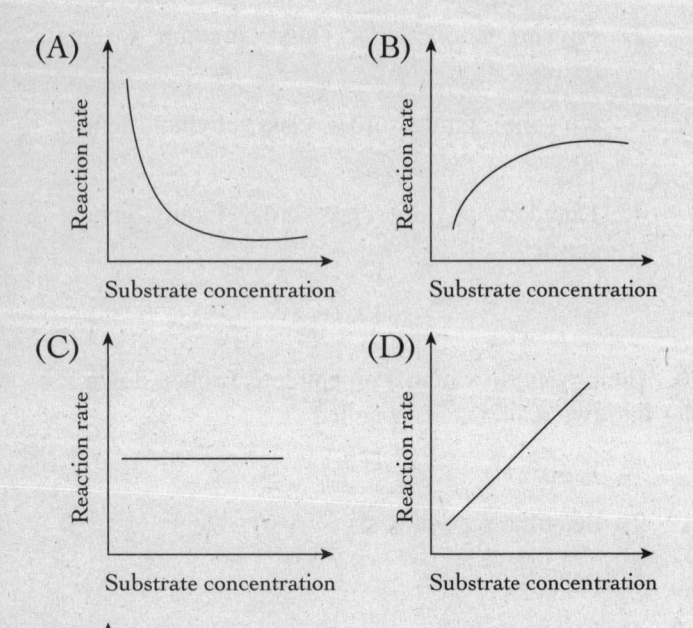

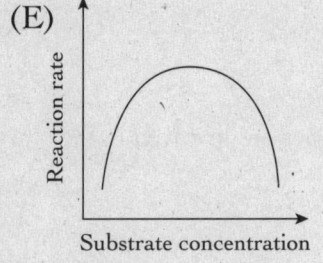

(A) [graph: reaction rate vs substrate concentration, decreasing curve]
(B) [graph: reaction rate vs substrate concentration, increasing curve leveling off]
(C) [graph: reaction rate vs substrate concentration, flat line]
(D) [graph: reaction rate vs substrate concentration, linear increasing]
(E) [graph: reaction rate vs substrate concentration, inverted U-shape]

23. Questions 23 and 24 refer to the data in the table below, resulting from an experiment concerning the rate of growth in a bacterial population over a 25-hour period.

Column I	Column II
Time (hrs.)	Number of bacteria
0	750
5	9,000
10	44,000
15	35,000
20	11,000
25	6,000

Which of the following graphs best represents the results set forth in the table above?

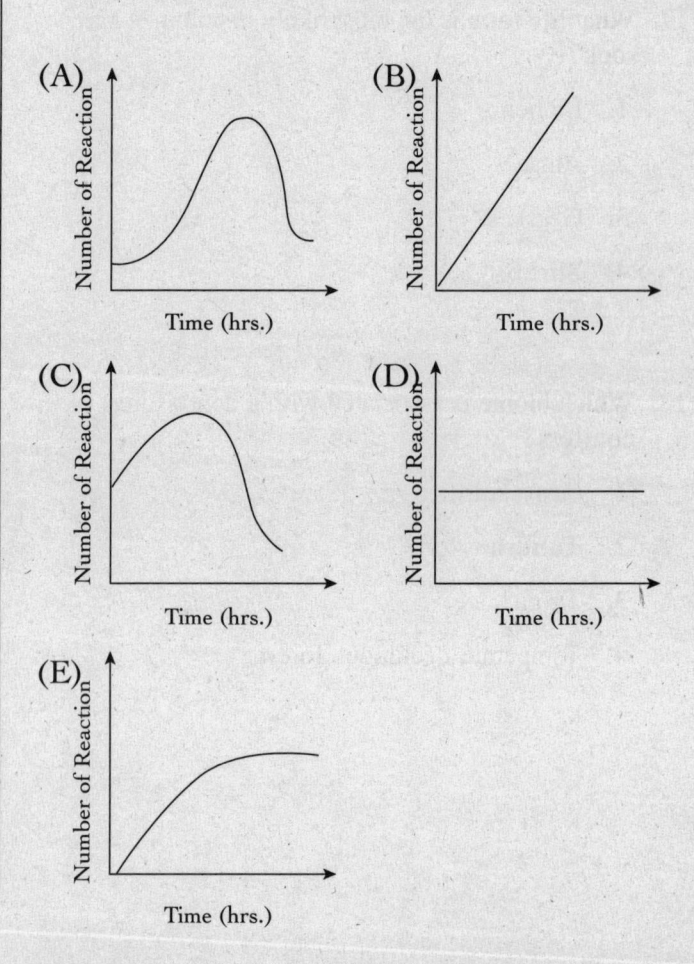

(A) [graph: Number of Reaction vs Time, bell-shaped curve rising then falling]
(B) [graph: Number of Reaction vs Time, linear increasing]
(C) [graph: Number of Reaction vs Time, rising peak then decreasing]
(D) [graph: Number of Reaction vs Time, flat line]
(E) [graph: Number of Reaction vs Time, increasing curve leveling off]

24. During which of the following time periods did the bacteria show the greatest percent increase in population?

    1. Between 0 and 5 hours
    2. Between 5 and 10 hours
    3. Between 10 and 15 hours
    4. Between 15 and 20 hours

25. The Krebs cycle in humans occurs in the

    1. cytoplasm
    2. mitochondrial matrix
    3. lysosome
    4. nucleus

26. During strenuous muscle exertion, an insufficient supply of oxygen will lead to a buildup of

    1. pyruvic acid
    2. glucose
    3. lactic acid
    4. ethanol

27. All of the following statements are correct regarding alleles EXCEPT

    1. alleles are alternate forms of the same gene
    2. a gene can have more than two alleles
    3. one allele can be dominant and the other can be recessive
    4. two identical alleles are said to be heterozygous with respect to that gene

28. Vitamins are essential to the human diet because they act as

    1. cofactors
    2. coenzymes
    3. enzymes
    4. hormones

29. DNA contains all of the following molecules EXCEPT

    1. adenine
    2. guanine
    3. deoxyribose
    4. uracil

30. All of the following are examples of chromosomal aberrations or mutations EXCEPT

    1. deletion
    2. sex linkage
    3. translocation
    4. inversion

WRITTEN-RESPONSE QUESTION

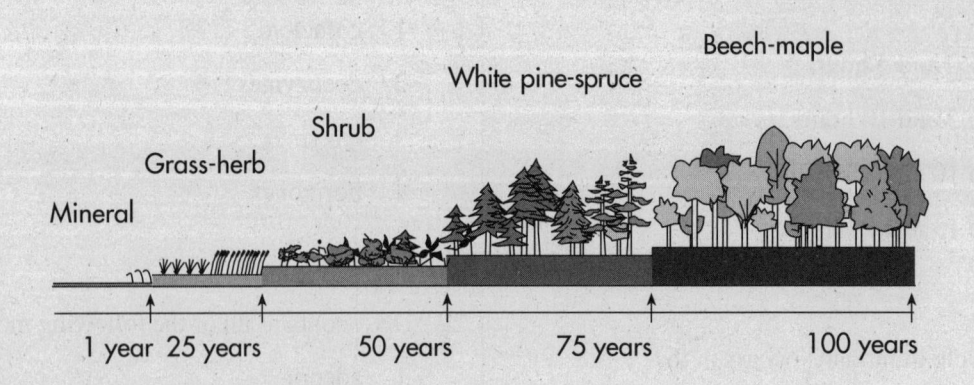

[Diagram showing ecological succession from Mineral (1 year) → Grass-herb (25 years) → Shrub (50 years) → White pine-spruce (75 years) → Beech-maple (100 years)]

A. Name and describe the process that's taking place in the drawing above. Use the following terms, but not exclusively: lichen, pioneers, climax community, invasion.

B. In the "grasses and shrubs" phases of the process above, you can see a rabbit feeding on the grass and a lion stalking the rabbit. Using the idea of the energy pyramid, describe the relationship between the grass, the rabbit, and the lion.

C. Describe these three types of symbiotic relationships: mutualism, commensalism, and parasitism.

ANSWERS AND EXPLANATIONS

1. Choice 4 is the correct answer. Prokaryotes are primitive cells that do not have a membrane-bound nucleus. Their DNA floats freely around the cytoplasm.
2. Choice 3 is the correct answer. When a plant is placed in a horizontal position, the cells will begin to grow toward the sky. This is a phenomenon known as geotropism, which refers to a plant's tendency to grow toward or away from the gravitational pull of the earth. This tropism is caused by the plant hormone auxin.
3. Choice 3 is the correct answer. To maintain a stable internal environment, animals must do several things: remove waste products, transport compounds throughout their bodies, and regulate bodily activities. Reproduction does not help maintain a stable internal environment.
4. Choice 1 is the correct answer. According to the heterotroph hypothesis, aerobes did not appear until oxygen was present in the atmosphere. Oxygen gas was produced by autotrophs as a byproduct of their metabolism.
5. Choice 4 is the correct answer. This statement best describes the concept of survival of the fittest. Organisms with favorable characteristics are able to successfully reproduce and pass on the favorable traits to their offspring.
6. Choice 4 is the correct answer. The theory of punctuated equilibrium says that evolution occurs due to stresses imposed by abrupt changes in the environment. These periods of relatively rapid change are followed by long periods of little or no evolutionary change.
7. Choice 1 is the correct answer. In aerobic respiration, organisms carry out fermentation, in which pyruvic acid is converted to either lactic acid or ethanol and carbon dioxide. Two ATP molecules are produced from each starting molecule of glucose in this process.
8. Choice 4 is the correct answer. The function of the guard cells, located on plants' leaves, is to regulate the opening and closing of the stomates, which in turn regulate gas exchange in the leaf.
9. Choice 3 is the correct answer. The plant in the diagram is exhibiting phototropism, which is caused by the plant hormone auxin. Phototropism is the tendency for a plant to grow toward the sun; here, growth appears as bending.
10. Choice 4 is the correct answer. Transfer RNA, or tRNA, picks up a free-floating amino acid in the cell's cytoplasm and shuttles it to the ribosome. Each tRNA is a personal messenger for one specific amino acid, and their specificity is defined by their anticodon.
11. Choice 2 is the correct answer. During metaphase of mitosis, sister chromatids begin to line up a the equator of the cell. Spindle fibers are responsible for this nice lining up of the chromosomes.
12. Choice 2 is the correct answer. Remember our chart from chapter 9? The skin, eyes, and nervous system all derive from the ectoderm; the digestive tract, respiratory tract,

pancreas, gall bladder, and liver derive from the endoderm; and the bones, muscles, gonads, excretory, circulatory, and reproductive systems derive from the mesoderm.

13. Choice 3 is the correct answer. Protein is broken down in the stomach by pepsin, which is an enzyme secreted by the lining of the stomach that breaks the peptide bonds between the amino acids that make up proteins.

14. Choice 2 is the correct answer. Hormones are chemical messengers secreted by the endocrine system in humans. Hormones act on target organs, signaling them to release or stop releasing certain substances; this helps regulate the internal environment.

15. Choice 4 is the correct answer. Symbiosis refers to a partnership between two organisms of different species. Parasitism occurs when one organism benefits from the association while the other is harmed; commensalism refers to when one organism benefits and the other is neither helped nor harmed; and mutualism refers to when both organisms benefit. As you can see, the common thread is that in symbiotic relationships, at least one of the organisms always benefits.

16. Choice 4 is correct. As we mentioned above, commensalism is a type of symbiosis in which one organism benefits while the other is neither helped nor harmed.

17. Choice 1 is the correct answer. Lichen are hardy organisms that can invade an area, even one containing only bare rocks, and erode rock surfaces, turning them into soil and rendering the site more susceptible to invading plants.

18. Choice 2 is the correct answer. The taiga is the biome that exhibits forests of conifers, stunted in growth. The taiga experiences very long, cold winters and its animals include caribou, wolves, moose, bear, rabbits, and lynx, all of which have a substantial fur coat.

19. Choice 4 is correct. Take a look at this: King Philip Came Over From German Shores—That's a handy mnemonic to help you remember the order of classification.

20. Choice 1 is correct. Proteins are formed of polypeptide chains, which are chains of amino acids. A dipeptide is two amino acids linked together by a peptide bond. Hydrolysis is a process whereby a peptide bond is broken and the amino acids are liberated. Water is released during this process.

21. Choice 3 is the correct answer. The menstrual process is a female phenomenon, and testosterone is a male hormone. It's easy to pick that choice out because it so clearly does not belong!

22. Choice 2 is correct. The enzyme is not saturated at first, so the addition of substrate will speed the reaction along. But once the experimenter has added sufficient substrate to make use of all of the enzyme, additional substrate won't affect the rate of reaction. This means you're looking for a graph that shows an initial increase in reaction rate, followed by a flat-line rate—choice 2 looks like this.

23. Choice A is correct. The table tells you that from 1 to 10 hours, the population increases. As time goes on, it decreases. So look for a graph that shows population first increasing significantly with time, and then decreasing significantly with time. Graph A is the only one that looks like that.

24. Choice 1 is correct. To increase from 750 to 9,000 is to increase by twelve times, which is equal to 1200%! Compared to the rest of the percent increases exhibited by the bacteria in the other time periods, this one stands out as being the highest. Don't forget that a percent increase would be different from a simple increase in number.
25. Choice 2 is the correct answer. The Krebs cycle occurs in the mitochondrial matrix. Don't forget to review the stie of each stage of aerobic respiration. Glycolysis occurs in the cytoplasm, the electron transport chain occurs in the inner mitochondrial membrane, and oxidative phosphorylation occurs from the intermembrane space to the mitochondrial matrix.
26. Choice 3 is the correct answer. During exercise, the muscles switch from areobic to anaerobic respiration, producing lactic acid.
27. Choice 4 is the correct answer. This statement is false because two identical alleles are said to be homozygous, not heterozygous, with respect to a gene.
28. Choice 2 is the correct answer. Vitamins function as coenzymes and assist enzymes in catalyzing reactions. Cofactors also assist enzymes, but they are inorganic molecules that usually include metals.
29. Choice 4 is the correct answer. DNA is made up of deoxyribose, a phosphate group, and four nitrogenous bases: adenine, cytosine, guanine, and thymine.
30. Choice 2 is the correct answer. Sex linkage refers to the inheritance of traits based on genes on the X or Y chromosome. All the other answer choices are examples of base mutations or chromosomal abnormalities.

WRITTEN-RESPONSE ANSWERS

a. The process taking place in the diagram is ecological succession. In ecological succession, there is a predictable procession of plant and animal communities that takes place over decades or centuries. Lichens are the hardy pioneer organisms—they invade and colonize a barren, rocky locale and render it habitable for other plant and animal life. Lichens are replaced by mosses and ferns, tough grasses, shrubs, deciduous trees, and evergreen trees. Evergreen trees represent the climax community—the final, stable community in the process of ecological succession.
b. In the diagram above, the grass is the autotroph—it is a producer. The rabbit feeds on the grass, and the rabbit is a primary consumer. The lion feeds on the rabbit, and is a secondary consumer. The grass possesses the most biomass (the total mass of all organisms in an area), the rabbit possesses the second highest biomass, and the lion has the least biomass.
c. Mututalism is a type of symbiosis in which both organisms benefit from the relationship. Commensalism is a type of symbiosis in which one organism benefits while the other is neither helped nor harmed, and parasitism is symbiosis in which one organism benefits while the other is harmed.

Chapter 19

THE PRINCETON REVIEW PRACTICE TEST II: SESSION II

PHOTOSYNTHESIS

On the table in front of you, you will find the following:

Elodea
Phenol red
25-mm test tubes
drinking straws
100-watt light source
hot plate
Lugol's solution
pipette
paper clips
filter paper

Read and follow the steps in the order given.

Record all observations, results, and answers to the questions as directed.

Immediately notify the proctor of spills or other problems.

Make your answers as complete as possible to demonstrate fully your knowledge of scientific principles and how to apply them.

1. In this section of the lab, you will study photosynthesis. Photosynthesis is the process by which green plants convert light energy into carbohydrates. Start by detecting the presence of carbon dioxide, CO_2, used by plants in the process of photosynthesis. Look at the following reaction, in which carbon dioxide dissolves in water to form carbonic acid:

$$CO_2 + H_2O \rightarrow H_2CO_3$$

Carbonic acid then dissociates in water:

$$H_2CO_3 \rightarrow H^+ + HCO_3^-$$

This dissociation of carbonic acid releases protons (H^+) into the water, lowering its pH. A plant undergoing photosynthesis in water will remove carbon dioxide from the water and prevent the formation of an acidic environment:

$$CO_2 + H_2O + light \rightarrow Sugar + O_2$$

Begin this experiment by filling two large test tubes with tap water. Use a straw to bubble water into the test tubes. Add phenol red to the water in each tube forcing bubbles into the water until it turns yellow.

Now place a section of Elodea, with the cut end facing upwards, into each test tube. Cork each tube, but leave space between the cork and the top of the water. Place one test tube near a 100-watt light source (but not too near), and place the other in a dark cabinet.

After half an hour, examine the color of the water and record the results below:

Test tube —Light   Color:

         —Dark   Color:

2. In this second section, we will study the relationship of chlorophyll to starch storage. Start by drawing the outline of the coleus leaf provided, in the space below:

Now place the leaf in a beaker and add about 2 cm of water; then boil this for about 1 minute. Use forceps to remove the leaf from the water, place it in another beaker, and add about 2 cm of alcohol. Boil this for about 5 minutes, and then use the forceps to place the leaf in a petri dish. Now apply Lugol's iodine to the leaf and examine it for the presence of starch.

In the space below, draw the outline of the blue-black area of your leaf. Starch should be pervasive, in the leaf.

3. In this section, we will study the pigments found in plants, including chlorophyll a (which is blue-green), chlorophyll b (yellow-green), carotene (orange), and xanthophyll (yellow).

First, use a pipette to apply spinach leaf extract to a spot about an inch from the bottom of a 7-inch long strip of filter paper. Keep pipetting drops in the same place to get a concentrated deposit of the extract. Attach the filter paper to a cork, with a paper clip, as is shown below. Now suspend the paper in a test tube that contains a little of the chromatographic solvent, making sure that only the bottom edge of the paper touches the solvent.

Let the tube stand for about 20 minutes, and remove the paper before the solvent reaches the top, then identify the pigments. They will have spread out, becoming separated according to their polarity and molecular weight.

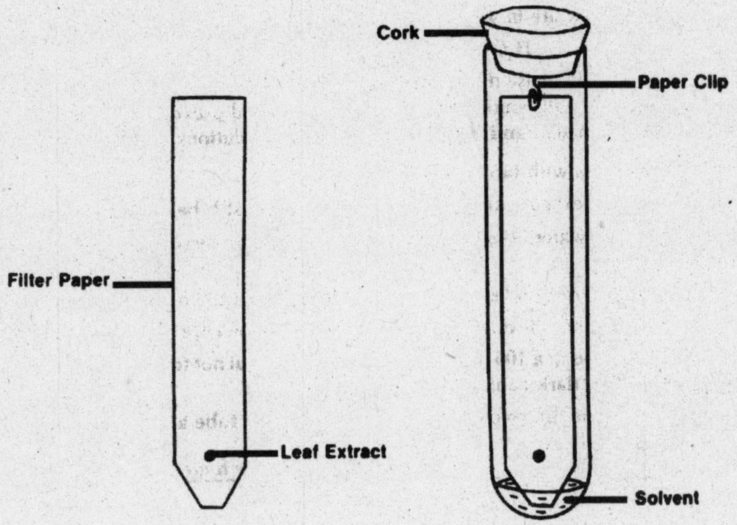
Filter Paper
Leaf Extract
Cork
Paper Clip
Solvent

Chapter 20

THE PRINCETON REVIEW PRACTICE TEST III: SESSION I

MULTIPLE-CHOICE QUESTIONS

Directions: The multiple-choice portion of the examination will give you an opportunity to demonstrate your knowledge of biology. You will answer 30 multiple-choice questions in 45 minutes. Allow yourself enough time to complete all 30 questions. Choose one of the four options for each answer.

1. Tendons are best described as
   1. tissue found between bones that protects them from damage
   2. cords that connect bone to bone and stretch at the point of attachment
   3. striated tissues that provide a wide range of motion
   4. fibrous cords that connect muscles to bones

2. In plants, glucose is converted to cellulose, and in human muscle cells, glucose is converted to glycogen. These processes are examples of which activity?
   1. Regulation
   2. Respiration
   3. Synthesis
   4. Excretion

3. Which process is correctly paired with its major waste product?
   1. Respiration – oxygen
   2. Protein synthesis – amino acids
   3. Dehydration synthesis – water
   4. Hydrolysis – carbon dioxide

4. Methyl cellulose is a chemical that slows the movement of *Paramecia* on a slide. This chemical most likely interferes with the movement of
   1. pseudopodia
   2. flagella
   3. setae
   4. cilia

5. Which adaptation found within the human respiratory system filters, warms, and moistens the air before it enters the lungs?
   1. Clusters of alveoli
   2. Rings of cartilage
   3. Involuntary smooth muscle
   4. Ciliated mucous membranes

6. Which part of the human central nervous system is correctly paired with its function?
   1. Spinal cord – coordinates learning activities
   2. Cerebellum – serves as the center of reflex
   3. Cerebrum – serves as the center of memory and reasoning
   4. Medulla – maintains muscular coordination

7. The production of a large number of eggs is necessary to ensure the survival of most
   1. mammals
   2. molds
   3. fish
   4. yeasts

8. In attempting to classify a newly discovered organism, the following characteristics were observed under a microscope: It is unicellular, heterotrophic, and contains a nucleus. Which kingdom is the organism most likely to be classified under?

   1. Protista
   2. Monera
   3. Plant
   4. Fungi

9. When viewed with a compound light microscope, which letter would best illustrate how the microscope inverts and reverses an image?

   1. A
   2. W
   3. F
   4. D

10. What process is taking place in the diagram below?

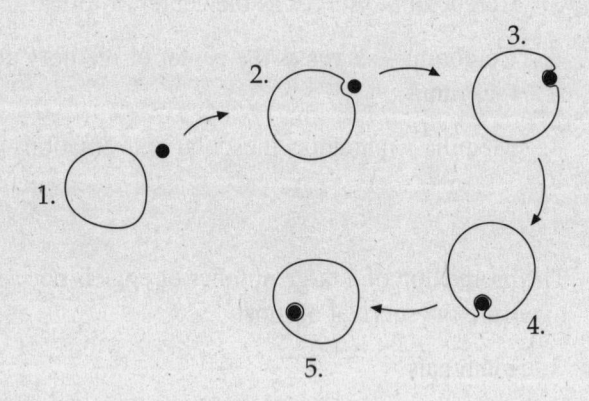

    1. Active transport
    2. Osmosis
    3. Facilitated diffusion
    4. Endocytosis

11. Which of the following is true of pyruvic acid?

    1. It contains little or no potential energy in its structure.
    2. It contains less energy than does glucose.
    3. It is created from acetyl CoA.
    4. It is formed in the mitochondria.

12. Located directly beneath the plant's cuticle are the

    1. upper epidermal cells
    2. lower epidermal cells
    3. palisade cells
    4. spongy cells

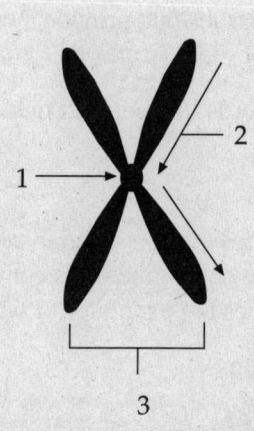

13. What can you say about the structure above with reasonable certainty?

    1. It is from a cell nucleus that has just completed mitosis and is ready to begin interphase.
    2. It is from a cell that has just completed replication and is ready to begin mitosis.
    3. It is a mutated form of sister chromatids.
    4. It is from a cell that has just completed interphase and is ready to begin replication.

14. All of the following take place during telophase of mitosis EXCEPT

    1. chromosomes decondense
    2. the nuclear membrane reforms
    3. the mitotic spindle disassembles
    4. sister chromatids move to opposite poles of the cell

15. All of the following are true about hemoglobin EXCEPT:

    1. it is a protein
    2. it is found in white blood cells
    3. it transports oxygen from the lungs to the rest of the body
    4. anemia results from its deficiency

16. Which of the following is (are) necessary in order for the thyroid gland to produce thyroxin?

    I. FSH
    II. TSH
    III. Iodine

    1. I only
    2. III only
    3. II and III only
    4. I, II, and III

17. The structure through which an ovum travels immediately following ovulation is the

    1. fallopian tube
    2. ovary
    3. uterus
    4. vagina

18. In chickens, the allele for long tail feathers (T) is dominant over the allele for short tail feathers (t). If a purebreeding long-tailed chicken (TT) mates with a purebreeding short-tailed chicken (tt), what percentage of their offspring (if mated with the correct genotype) could give rise to chickens with short tails?

    1. 25%
    2. 50%
    3. 75%
    4. 100%

19. The best definition of a species is

    1. a group of organisms that occupy the same niche
    2. a population that works together to defend itself from predators
    3. a group of organisms the can mate with each other
    4. a population that preys on other populations

20. The location on an enzyme where substrate binds is called the

    1. binding site
    2. reaction center
    3. allosteric site
    4. active site

Questions 21-22

A barren, rocky community near a lake has virtually no vegetation or animal life. After a period of approximately 75 years, the community boasts a wide variety of flora and fauna, including deciduous trees, deer, and raccoon.

21. The process that has taken place can best be described as
    1. progression
    2. succession
    3. evolution
    4. habitation

22. The stable community of deciduous trees and animals is known as the
    1. final community
    2. climax community
    3. apex community
    4. summit community

Questions 23-24

A population of birds (population A) on a remote, isolated island is studied to determine beak length. The resulting data is plotted in Figure 1.

Figure 1

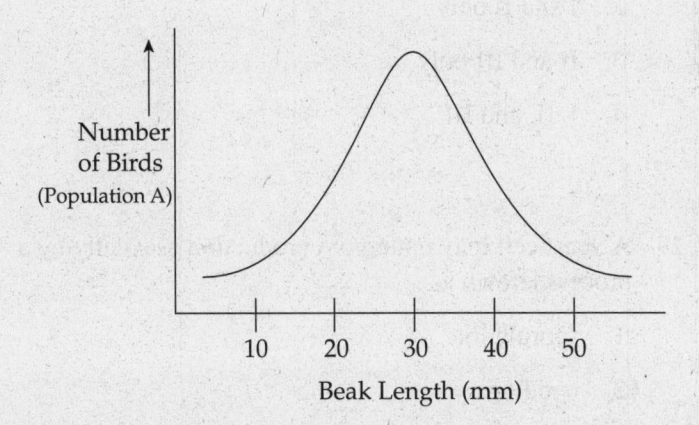

Suppose that 200 years later, the beaks of the birds on the island were again measured (population B). The data, when plotted, yielded a graph as in Figure 2.

Figure 2

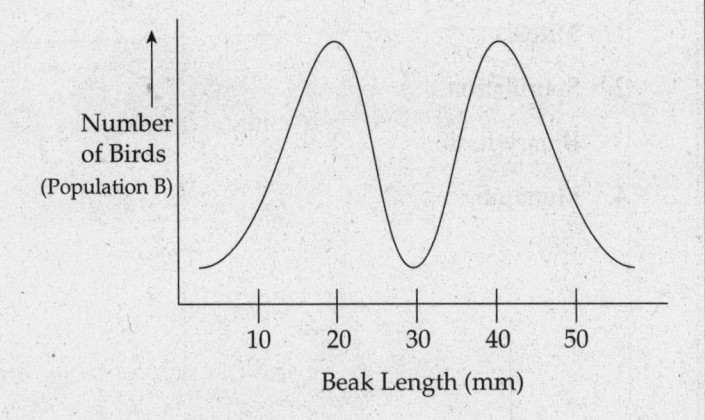

23. What is the average beak length (in centimeters) of the birds in Figure 1?
    1. 30 cm
    2. 15 cm
    3. 5 cm
    4. 3 cm

24. What is the most likely reason for the difference in distribution of beak lengths between the data plotted in Figure 1 and the data plotted in Figure 2?
    1. All birds with beaks of 30 mm flew to a new island over the 200-year time span.
    2. Birds with beaks of 3 mm were selected against.
    3. Predators consumed birds with beaks of 40 mm.
    4. Birds with beaks of 30 mm were selected for.

25. The following graphs show the growth of two closely related species of *Paramecia*, both when grown alone (Figure 1) and when grown together (Figure 2). Both species consume bacteria as their food source and reproduce by binary fission as often as several times a day.

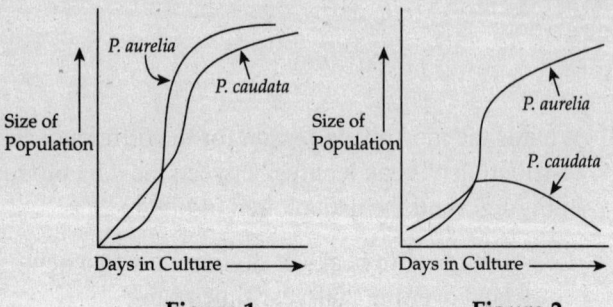

Figure 1

Figure 2

The data in Figure 2 indicates that

1. *P. aurelia* is preying on *P. caudata*
2. *P. aurelia* is a better competitor than *P. caudata*
3. *P. aurelia* and *P. caudata* are in a symbiotic relationship
4. *P. aurelia* is a parasite of *P. caudata*

26. All of the following are true about RNA EXCEPT:

1. it is single-stranded
2. its bases are adenine, thymine, guanine, and uracil
3. it has a sugar-phosphate backbone
4. its sugar is ribose

27. The nucleic acid that is translated to make a protein is

1. rRNA
2. mRNA
3. DNA
4. tRNA

28. Which of the following accurately states the principle(s) of cell theory?

   I. All organisms are composed of cells.
   II. All cells arise from pre-existing cells.
   III. Cells are the basic unit of biological function.

1. II only
2. I and II only
3. II and III only
4. I, II, and III

29. A yeast cell may undergo reproduction asexually by a process known as

1. sporulation
2. budding
3. vegetative propagation
4. binary fission

30. Which of the following contributes the MOST to genetic variability in a population?

1. Mitosis
2. Sporulation
3. Binary fission
4. Mutation

WRITTEN-RESPONSE QUESTION

Figure 1

Figure 2

a. Name the structure in Figure 1. In what stage of the cell cycle was this structure formed, and what will happen to this structure next if it goes through the process of mitosis?

b. What is happening in Figure 2? Name the overall process that is occurring, as well as the specific phase the cell is in. If this process is mitosis, will the resulting daughter cells be haploid or diploid?

c. Genetic variation is extremely important in the process of evolution. Define "crossing over" and state in which stage of mitosis it occurs. How does it contribute to genetic variation?

ANSWERS AND EXPLANATIONS

1. Choice 4 is the correct answer. Tendons are connective tissues that connect muscle to bone. Ligaments connect joints, which hold bones together.
2. Choice 3 is the correct answer. These processes are examples of synthesis, the making of complex compounds from simpler ones.
3. Choice 3 is the correct answer. The key phrase in this question is "waste product." During dehydration synthesis, water is a byproduct; it is given off.
4. Choice 4 is the correct answer. According to the question, methyl cellulose slows down the movement of *Paramecia*. This chemical must somehow have an effect on the cilia that *Paramecia* use for locomotion.
5. Choice 4 is the correct answer. As you already know, there are cilia in the respiratory tract that help keep foreign particles out of the body—they filter the air.
6. Choice 3 is the correct answer. The cerebrum, the largest part of the brain, controls memory and reasoning. This is a hard question, but you might just see something like this on the exam, so be sure to familiarize yourself with what the different parts of the nervous system do.
7. Choice 3 is the correct answer. Aquatic animals such as fish must produce large numbers of eggs in order to ensure that at least some of them are fertilized. This is because the eggs are fertilized externally, and many of them are lost because of harsh external conditions.
8. Choice 1 is the correct answer. The characteristics listed are found among organisms that belong to the kingdom Protista. Protists are one-celled organisms that are eukaryotic and heterotrophic.
9. Choice 3 is the correct answer. You need to pick a letter that shows a difference when inverted and reversed. *F* is the only letter here that appears different when it is inverted and reversed.
10. Choice 4 is the correct answer. Endocytosis refers to the process by which the cell takes in particles by forming a pocket from the cell membrane. The pocket pinches in and eventually forms either a vacuole or vesicle.
11. Choice 2 is the correct answer. Pyruvic acid contains less energy than glucose because it is the broken down form of glucose that is an end product of glycolysis. Keep in mind that two ATP are produced during glycolysis, which is the first step of cellular respiration.
12. Choice 1 is the correct answer. Take a look at the diagram in chapter 6 that shows a cross section of the leaf, and you'll see that the first layer of cells under the cuticle is the upper epidermal layer.
13. Choice 2 is the correct answer. This structure is a tetrad, a pair of sister chromatids. It is a chromosome that has just replicated prior to entering mitosis. The two sister chromatids will separate at the centromere, the dark circle that joins the two strands, and eventually migrate to two new cells.

14. Choice 4 is the correct answer. Sister chromatids move to opposite poles of the cell during anaphase. During telophase, a nuclear membrane begins to form around each set of chromosomes, and the cell membrane begins to pinch in and cleave in cytokinesis.
15. Choice 2 is correct. Hemoglobin is found in red blood cells, not white blood cells. The rest of the statements are true—hemoglobin is a protein complexed with iron, it transports oxygen throughout the body, and anemia is a result of its deficiency.
16. Choice 3 is correct. In order for the thyroid gland to produce thyroxin, the thyroid needs to be stimulated by TSH, which is secreted by the pituitary, but it also needs iodine. Iodine is necessary in the production of thyroxin, and goiters are a result of iodine deficiency in the diet.
17. Choice 1 is correct. The first stages of the menstrual cycle are as follows: the pituitary releases FSH and LH (causing the follicle to grow); the follicle releases estrogen; estrogen causes the pituitary to release more LH (resulting in a luteal surge); and the excess LH causes the follicle to burst, releasing the ovum during ovulation. At this point, the ovum travels through the fallopian tube. This marks the end of ovulation.
18. Choice 4 is correct. If a purebreeding long-tailed chicken (TT) mates with a purebreeding short-tailed chicken (tt), all of their offspring (the F1 generation) will have the genotype Tt (and have long tails). All of them, if mated with the correct genotype (Tt or tt), could produce offspring with short tails.
19. Choice 3 is correct. Two populations are considered separate species when they are so different from one another that they can no longer mate and produce viable offspring. Thus, organisms that can mate with each other must be of the same species.
20. Choice 4 is correct. The active site is the location on the enzyme where the substrate binds.
21. Choice 2 is correct. The development of a thriving ecosystem from a barren area is known as succession. Note that evolution has a much longer timeframe than does succession.
22. Choice 2 is correct. The climax community is the final, stable community in succession.
23. Choice 4 is correct. The question asks for the average beak length in centimeters, but the graph gives it in millimeters. Average beak length is 30 mm. 10 mm equals 1 cm. Therefore, 30 mm equals 3 cm.
24. Choice 2 is correct. Clearly, the birds with 30-mm beaks were not surviving too well. There is no reason to assume they flew to another island; remember, they are on an isolated island. There may not be another island near enough to fly to (so choice 1 is wrong). If predators consumed birds with 20-mm or 40-mm beaks, they would not be the prevalent populations in Figure 2 (so choices 2 and 4 are wrong).
25. Choice 2 is correct. Clearly *P. aurelia* can compete better and get more food than *P. caudata*, so it will grow while *P. caudata* is competed to extinction. Choice 1 is highly

unlikely, since the food source the *Paramecia* prefer is bacteria, not each other. This is not a symbiotic relationship, but a competitive one.

26. Choice 2 is correct. RNA bases do not include thymine; they are adenine, guanine, cytosine, and uracil. All of the other statements about RNA are correct.
27. Choice 2 is correct. rRNA helps form the ribosome, DNA is the genetic material of the cell, and tRNA transfers amino acids to ribosomes. mRNA is translated in the cytoplasm of the cell to make proteins.
28. Choice 4 is correct. The cell theory is the basis of modern biology, and the three statements are its principal components.
29. Choice 2 is correct. Yeasts belong to the kingdom Fungi. They reproduce asexually by budding: They shed a piece of themselves, and that piece becomes a new organism. Remember to associate "yeast" with "fungus" and keep in mind that yeasts, unlike most other fungi, reproduce by budding.
30. Choice 4 is correct. Mutations produce genetic variability. All of the other answer choices are forms of asexual reproduction.

WRITTEN-RESPONSE ANSWERS

a. The structure in Figure 1 is composed of two sister chromatids, joined at the centromere; also called a double stranded chromosome. This structure came about when the strand of DNA that made up one of the chromatids replicated, in the S phase of the cell cycle. This structure will now take place in the process of mitosis, in which the two sister chromatids will be separated at the centromere and migrate to the opposite poles of the cell. Eventually the cell will split in two, creating daughter cells with the same genetic material as the parent.

b. The cell in Figure 2 is undergoing cytokinesis to produce two identical daughter cells, either in mitosis or in the second round of meiosis (meiosis II). Cytokinesis occurs at the end of telophase. If this process is mitosis, the resulting cells will be diploid, but if it were meiosis, the daughter cells would be haploid zygotes.

c. Crossing over is the process that occurs during meiosis. It is the reciprocal exchange of genetic material between non-sister chromatids of a tetrad, during synapsis of meiosis I. Crossing over contributes to genetic variability because new genetic combinations are created.

Chapter 21

THE PRINCETON REVIEW PRACTICE TEST III: SESSION II

GRAPHING AND DATA MANIPULATION

In this lab, you will practice graphing and manipulating data.

A student performed a laboratory investigation to determine the effect of temperature on the heart rate of *Daphnia* (water flea). The following temperatures and heart rates were recorded:

20 °C—270 beats/min
10 °C—150 beats/min
15 °C—180 beats/min
25 °C—300 beats/min
5 °C—108 beats/min

Organize the data by filling in the data table below. Complete both columns so that temperature either increases or decreases from the top to the bottom of the table.

Data Table

Temperature (°C)	Heart Rate (beats/min)

Now, using the data you've organized, construct a line graph on the grid below.

Heart Rate (beats/min)

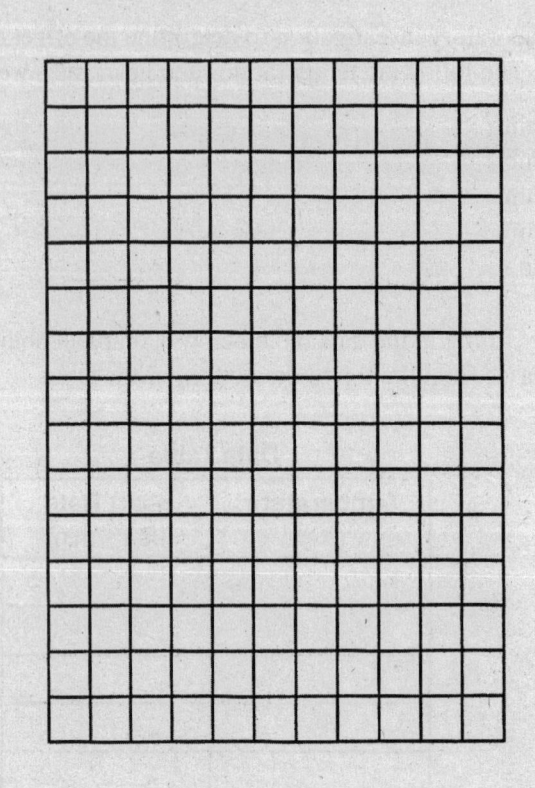

Temperature (°C)

During which temperature interval did the greatest change in heart rate occur? According to the graph, it looks like it occurred between 15 °C and 20 °C.

Data Table	
Temperature (° C)	Heart Rate (beats/min)
5	108
10	150
15	180
20	270
25	300

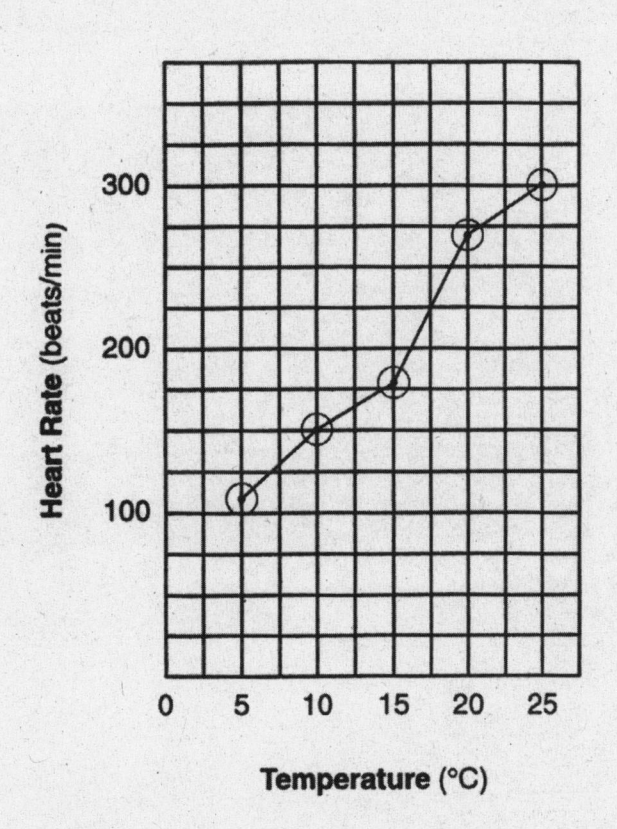

Chapter 22

THE PRINCETON REVIEW PRACTICE TEST IV: SESSION I

MULTIPLE-CHOICE QUESTIONS

Directions: The multiple-choice portion of the examination will give you an opportunity to demonstrate your knowledge of biology. You will answer 30 multiple-choice questions in 45 minutes. Allow yourself enough time to complete all 30 questions. Choose one of the four options for each answer.

1. Which statement is true regarding plants produced by vegetative propagation?

    1. They normally exhibit only dominant characteristics.
    2. They normally have the monoploid number of chromosomes.
    3. They normally obtain most of their nourishment from the seed.
    4. They are normally genetically identical to the parent.

2. In a rabbit, the embryo normally develops within the
    1. placenta
    2. uterus
    3. yolk sac
    4. umbilical cord

3. The correct sequence between genes and their expression is
    1. RNA → DNA → protein → trait
    2. DNA → RNA → protein → trait
    3. trait → DNA → protein → RNA
    4. protein → trait → protein → DNA

4. The diagram below represents a sample of crushed ion cells that was centrifuged. Cell and cell components were dispersed in layers as illustrated:

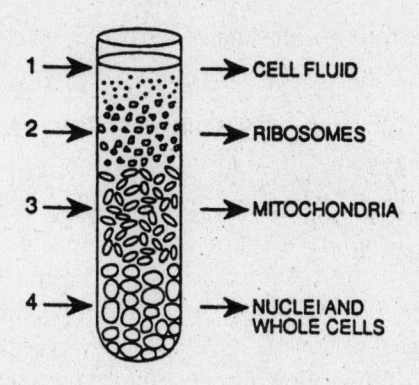

    1 → CELL FLUID
    2 → RIBOSOMES
    3 → MITOCHONDRIA
    4 → NUCLEI AND WHOLE CELLS

    The organelles that act as the sites of protein synthesis are found in the greatest concentration within layer

    (1) 1
    (2) 2
    (3) 3
    (4) 4

5. Which technique enabled scientists in the 1800s to identify cell organelles?
    1. Electron microscopy
    2. Ultracentrifugation
    3. Staining
    4. Dissection

6. Which of the following correctly orders the early stages of embryonic development?

   1. Zygote → fertilization → cleavage → gastrula → blastula
   2. Gastrula → blastula → cleavage → fertilization → zygote
   3. Fertilization → blastula → gastrula → cleavage → zygote
   4. Fertilization → zygote → cleavage → blastula → gastrula

7. Which of the following sets of hormones act antagonistically (oppositely) to one another?

   1. Epinephrine and norepinephrine
   2. Glucagon and insulin
   3. Adrenaline and epinephrine
   4. TSH and thyroxine

8. The lining of the uterus is shed during which of the following events?

   1. Maturation
   2. Ovulation
   3. Fertilization
   4. Menstruation

Questions 9-10 refer to the following energy diagram:

Marine algae → minnow → mackerel → seal → killer whale

9. The primary consumer above is

   1. marine algae
   2. minnow
   3. mackerel
   4. seal

10. Which of the following is true concerning the flow of energy in this food chain?

    1. The minnow has access to more energy than does the mackerel.
    2. The mackerel has access to more energy than does the minnow.
    3. The seal has access to more energy than does the mackerel.
    4. The killer whale has access to the most energy.

11. The final outcome in the ecological succession of a pond is a

    1. grassland
    2. bare rock
    3. forest
    4. lake

12. Which of the following RNA sequences would be transcribed from the DNA sequence ATGCCTAGGAC?

    1. TACGGATCCTG
    2. UAGCGAUCCUG
    3. AUGCCUAGGAC
    4. UACGGAUCCUG
    5. GCAUUCGAAGU

13. Two organisms live in close association with one another. One organism is helped by the association, while the other is neither helped nor harmed. Which of the following best describes this relationship?

    1. Mutualism
    2. Commensalism
    3. Symbiosis
    4. Parasitism

14. Immediately after fertilization, the zygote begins to undergo rapid cell division. This process is known as

    1. blastulation
    2. gastrulation
    3. cleavage
    4. implantation

15. The function of the Golgi apparatus is to

    1. package and store proteins for secretion
    2. synthesize proteins
    3. function in cellular respiration
    4. help the cell expel waste

16. The plasma membrane is a semipermeable organelle composed chiefly of

    1. lipids and sugars
    2. sugars and proteins
    3. proteins and lipids
    4. lipids and carbohydrates

17. According to the heterotroph hypothesis, the atmosphere of the earth before the beginning of life contained all of the following gases EXCEPT

    1. hydrogen
    2. water
    3. oxygen
    4. methane

18. The basic principles of genetics were established in the nineteenth century by

    1. Jean Lamarck
    2. Louis Pasteur
    3. Charles Darwin
    4. Gregor Mendel

19. A yeast cell may undergo reproduction asexually by a process known as

    1. sporulation
    2. budding
    3. vegetative propagation
    4. binary fission

20. A principal difference between mitosis and meiosis is that

    1. mitosis involves physical division and meiosis does not
    2. mitosis involves replication of chromosomes and meiosis does not
    3. mitosis occurs only in sex cells and meiosis occurs only in somatic cells
    4. mitosis gives rise to diploid daughter cells and meiosis gives rise to haploid daughter cells

21. The organ that secretes the main digestive juices for complete digestion is known as the

    1. mouth
    2. esophagus
    3. pancreas
    4. small intestine

22. In a marathon runner, painful muscle fatigue may be caused by the products of

    1. carbon fixation
    2. aerobic respiration
    3. anaerobic respiration
    4. lipolysis

23. For a guinea pig, black coat (B) is dominant over white coat (b). If two guinea pigs mate and produce 75% offspring with black coats and 25% offspring with white coats, then the genotypes of the parent organisms are most likely

    1. BB x BB
    2. Bb x BB
    3. BB x bb
    4. Bb x Bb

24. Which of the following biomes has fauna that includes moose and black bear?

    1. Tundra
    2. Tropical forest
    3. Desert
    4. Taiga

25. Which of the following contains the enzymes of the Krebs cycle?

    1. Ribosomes
    2. Mitochondria
    3. Lysosomes
    4. Cell membrane

26. Which of the following is the site of DNA transcription?

    1. Ribosomes
    2. Mitochondria
    3. Nucleus
    4. Lysosomes

Question 27 refers to the following diagram of a flowering plant:

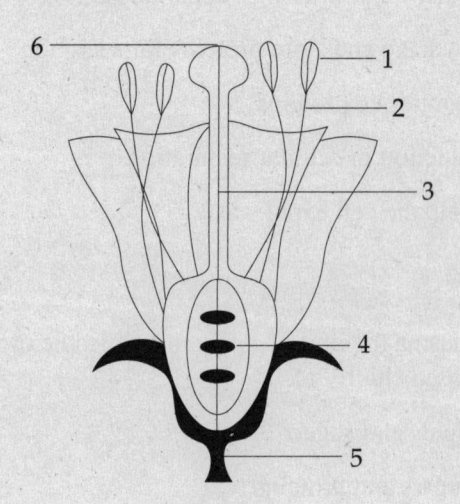

27. Pollen grains are produced by

    1. structure 1
    2. structure 3
    3. structure 4
    4. structure 6

28. Which of the following is a characteristic of arteries?
    1. They are thin-walled blood vessels.
    2. They contain valves that prevent the backflow of blood.
    3. They always contain oxygenated blood.
    4. They carry blood away from the heart.

29. Movement of materials against a concentration gradient is accomplished by
    1. diffusion
    2. active transport
    3. osmosis
    4. facilitated transport

30. In general, animal cells differ from plant cells in that animal cells
    1. have membrane-bound organelles
    2. have a cell wall
    3. have vacuoles
    4. have centrioles

WRITTEN-RESPONSE QUESTION

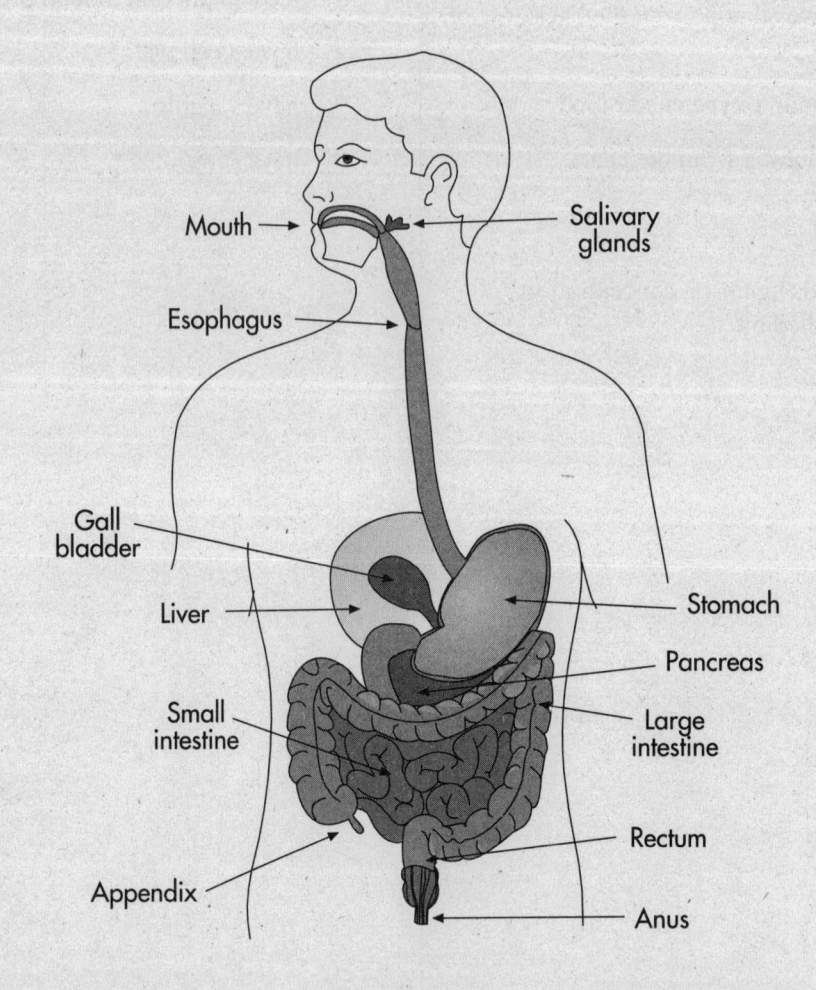

a. Say the person in the above drawing has just consumed a hamburger. Describe how the starch, protein, and fat of the hamburger will be digested as the hamburger passes through the digestive tract. You should state the sites of each of the substances' digestion, as well as any mechanical or chemical processes that occur.

b. Explain the causes of symptoms of constipation and diarrhea.

c. State the location of most of the absorption of nutrients in the digestive tract, and explain how nutrients are absorbed. Make sure to clearly name the structures involved.

ANSWERS AND EXPLANATIONS

1. Choice 4 is correct. Vegetative propagation is a method used by some plants to reproduce asexually. The offspring are therefore identical to the parent.
2. Choice 2 is correct. The rabbit embryo develops in the uterus of the mother. The rabbit is a placental mammal.
3. Choice 2 is the correct answer. The sequence always begins with DNA and ends with the expression of the trait. The only answer choice that begins with DNA is choice 2.
4. Choice 2 is the correct answer. The diagram shows a sample of crushed onion cells that was centrifuged (i.e., spun so that the cell components separated according to density). This question tests your ability to recognize that protein synthesis occurs in the ribosomes. Ribosomes are found in level 2.
5. Choice 3 is correct. Staining enables scientists to identify organelles by providing a contrast between the cell and its structures.
6. Choice 4 is correct. The correct order of events is fertilization: formation of the zygote; cleavage (cell division); formation of the blastula; formation of the gastrula; and finally, formation of the neurula. These are the very early stages of embryonic development.
7. Choice 2 is correct. Glucagon increases the amount of glucose in the bloodstream; it tells the liver to break down some of the glycogen it's storing. Insulin, on the other hand, signals the cells to take up glucose from the bloodstream. These two hormones act antagonistically to each other.
8. Choice 4 is correct. Menstruation refers to the time in the menstrual cycle during which the built-up tissue in the uterus sloughs off and exits via the vagina. Menstruation lasts anywhere from 2 to 7 days.
9. Choice 2 is correct. The primary consumer feeds on the producers in a food chain. The producer here is the marine algae. The secondary consumer (the mackeral) feeds on the primary consumer (the minnow), and the tertiary consumer (the seal) feeds on the secondary consumer.
10. Choice 3 is correct. The final outcome in the ecological succession of a pond is a forest. The stages of succession would be as follows: bare rock or field, to grassland, to shrubs, to evergreens, to deciduous trees.
11. Choice 4 is correct. In RNA, the base thymine (T) is replaced with uracil (U), so choice 1 can be eliminated. Further, adenine (A) will always pair with U, and guanine (G) will always pair with cytosine (C). The only choice that has the bases paired correctly is choice 4.
12. Choice 3 is correct. When the concentration of substrate far exceeds the concentration of enzyme, all the enzyme active sites are saturated with substrate, and the product is being formed at maximum rate. The only way to increase product

formation at this point is to increase the concentration of the enzyme. Note that enzymes should not be used up in the course of the reaction (choice 1 is wrong). Furthermore, product formation is still occurring, only at a stable rate (so choices 2 and 4 are wrong).

13. Choice 2 is correct. This symbiotic relationship describes commensalism. In mutualism, both partners benefit; in parasitism, one partner benefits while the other is harmed; and symbiosis is a general term used to describe two species in a close arrangement.

14. Choice 3 is correct. Rapid cell division after fertilization is known as cleavage. Blastulation is the formation of a hollow ball of cells; gastrulation is formation of the three primary germ layers; and implantation is when the morula (the solid ball of cells) burrows into the uterine lining.

15. Choice 1 is correct. Ribosomes synthesize proteins; mitochondria function in respiration; and vacuoles help the cell expel waste. The Golgi apparatus is the packaging and secretion center of the cell.

16. Choice 3 is correct. The plasma membrane, also called the cell membrane, is made of something called a lipid-protein bilayer. This means that it's made of lipids and proteins. Whenever you see the phrase "lipid bilayer," think "plasma membrane."

17. Choice 3 is correct. According to the heterotroph hypothesis, life began when the earth's atmosphere contained little or no oxygen, but instead contained a great deal of hydrogen, water, ammonia, and methane.

18. Choice 4 is correct. You should probably be familiar with some of the names associated with key discoveries for the GSE Biology. When you think of genetics, think of Mendel and his garden peas.

19. Choice 4 is correct. The most crucial difference between meiosis and mitosis is that meiosis produces haploid cells and mitosis produces diploid cells. The haploid cells then go on to join other haploid cells in fertilization to form diploid cells. The meiotic process occurs in both sexes. Human spermatozoa and ova, for example, result from meiosis—they're haploid. When they join, they form a diploid zygote.

20. Choice 3 is correct. Most of the enzymes that are produced for digestion are made in the pancreas, including pancreatic lipase and pancreatic amylase. These enzymes are released into the small intestine.

21. Choice 3 is correct. If one exerts muscles to the point that circulation cannot deliver enough oxygen to maintain aerobic respiration, the muscles begin to perform anaerobic respiration. The muscle fatigue and pain that results is caused by a buildup of lactic acid, the byproduct of anaerobic respiration.

22. Choice 4 is correct. This is a Mendelian cross. In order for any of the offspring to show the recessive trait, they'd have to be homozygous for it. This means that both

parents would have to be carrying the recessive gene. The only choice that shows parents who both possess the recessive gene is choice 4.

23. Choice 2 is correct. The carbohydrate glucose does not decompose into lactic acid. (Anaerobic respiration of glucose may produce lactic acid as a byproduct, but glucose isn't composed of lactic acid, so it can't decompose to produce it.) All of the other paired substances represent organic compounds and the smaller entities from which they are synthesized.

24. Choice 4 is correct. The taiga is a class of biome located in North America, Europe, and Asia. It has short summers and extremely long, cold winters. Flora consists of conifers or evergreens, and animal life consists of moose, bears, and caribou, among others.

25. Choice 2 is correct. The mitochondria are the sites of aerobic cellular respiration; they are the cell's "powerhouse." It's in the mitochondria that the cell performs the aerobic phases of respiration—the Krebs cycle, oxidative phosphorylation, and the electron transport chain—all in order to produce ATP. When you see "mitochondria," think "cellular respiration."

26. Choice 3 is correct. The cell's genetic information is contained in the nucleus, specifically within the chromosomes. Transcription refers to when DNA is used as a template to create mRNA. mRNA travels out of the nucleus, and into the cytoplasm, where it is used to create protein in a process known as translation.

27. Choice 1 is correct. Pollen is produced and stored in the anther (structure 1). Pollen grains are haploid and is the male part of the plant; it fertilizes the ovules located in the ovary.

28. Choice 4 is correct. Arteries are thick-walled vessels that carry blood away from the heart.

29. Choice 2 is correct. Active transport occurs against a concentration gradient and requires ATP. All of the other examples represent movement along a concentration gradient.

30. Choice 4 is correct. Unlike plant cells, animal cells have centrioles. Both plant and animal cells have membrane-bound organelles and vacuoles. Plant cells have plastids and cell walls, which animal cells do not possess.

WRITTEN-RESPONSE ANSWERS

A. The digestion of starch begins in the mouth, where salivary amylase (an enzyme secreted in saliva) breaks starches into maltose. This is where the bun of the hamburger will begin its breakdown. In the stomach, protein begins to be broken down by the enzyme pepsin. Pepsin breaks the peptide bonds between amino acids and is activated by the acidic environment of the stomach. In the small intestine, starch, protein, and fats are all broken down. Many digestive enzymes are secreted by the pancreas into the small intestine: protease digests proteins into amino acids, lipase breaks down lipids, and amylase breaks down starch.

B. Constipation is a disorder in which peristalsis moves the feces through the colon, or large intestine, too slowly. An excess of water is reabsorbed by the colon, and the feces becomes compacted. In diarrhea, the lining of the colon is irritated, possibly by a viral or bacterial infection, and less water than usual is reabsorbed by the colon, resulting in watery stool.

C. Most of nutrient breakdown and absorption occurs in the small intestine, where tiny, finger-like projections from the wall of the small intestine increase the surface area significantly. Within each villus is a capillary, across the wall of which nutrients are absorbed to enter the bloodstream.

Chapter 23

THE PRINCETON REVIEW PRACTICE TEST IV: SESSION II

DATA MANIPULATION AND GRAPHING

In this lab, you will practice creating data tables and graphs, and interpreting graphs.

A group of biology students extracted the photosynthetic pigments from spinach leaves using the solvent acteone. A spectrophotometer was used to measure the percent absorption of six different wavelenths of light by the extracted pigments. The wavelengths of light were measured in units known as nanometers (nm). One nanometer is equal to one billionth of a meter. The following data were collected:

>Yellow light (585 nm)—25.8% absorption
>Blue light (457 nm)—49.8% absorption
>Orange light (616 nm)—32.1% absorption
>Violet light (412 nm) 48.9% absorption
>Red light (674 nm)—41.0% absorption
>Green light (533 nm)—17.8% absorption

Complete all three columns in the data table on the following page so that the wavelength of light either decreases or increases, from top to bottom of the data table.

Color of Light	Wavelength of Light (nm)	Percent Absorption by Spinach Extract

Now, using the information in the data table, construct a line graph on the grid provided.

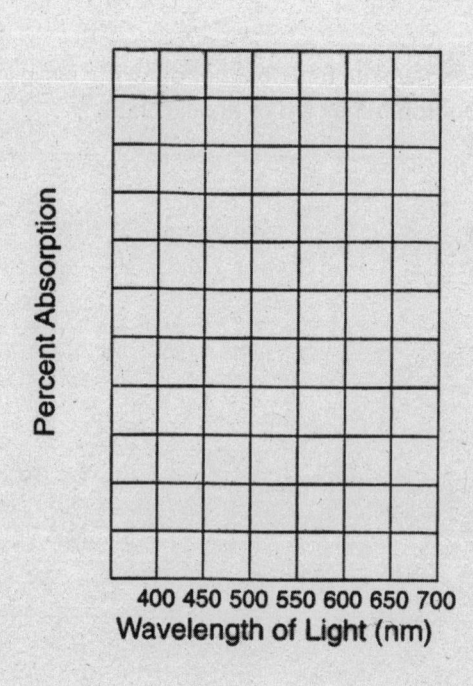

What could you conclude from the data obtained in this investigation? For one, you could conclude that photosynthetic pigments in spinach plants absorb blue and violet light more efficiently than red light. In this lab, we put the graphs on the other side of this page so that you have a chance to test your skills out.

THE PRINCETON REVIEW

YOUR NAME: _____
(Print)   Last   First   M.I.

SIGNATURE: _____ **DATE:** ___/___/___

HOME ADDRESS: _____
(Print)   Number and Street

_____
City   State   Zip Code

PHONE NO.: _____
(Print)

Completely darken bubbles with a No. 2 pencil. If you make a mistake, be sure to erase mark completely. Erase all stray marks.

Practice Test I

1. Ⓐ Ⓑ Ⓒ Ⓓ
2. Ⓐ Ⓑ Ⓒ Ⓓ
3. Ⓐ Ⓑ Ⓒ Ⓓ
4. Ⓐ Ⓑ Ⓒ Ⓓ
5. Ⓐ Ⓑ Ⓒ Ⓓ
6. Ⓐ Ⓑ Ⓒ Ⓓ
7. Ⓐ Ⓑ Ⓒ Ⓓ
8. Ⓐ Ⓑ Ⓒ Ⓓ
9. Ⓐ Ⓑ Ⓒ Ⓓ
10. Ⓐ Ⓑ Ⓒ Ⓓ

11. Ⓐ Ⓑ Ⓒ Ⓓ
12. Ⓐ Ⓑ Ⓒ Ⓓ
13. Ⓐ Ⓑ Ⓒ Ⓓ
14. Ⓐ Ⓑ Ⓒ Ⓓ
15. Ⓐ Ⓑ Ⓒ Ⓓ
16. Ⓐ Ⓑ Ⓒ Ⓓ
17. Ⓐ Ⓑ Ⓒ Ⓓ
18. Ⓐ Ⓑ Ⓒ Ⓓ
19. Ⓐ Ⓑ Ⓒ Ⓓ
20. Ⓐ Ⓑ Ⓒ Ⓓ

21. Ⓐ Ⓑ Ⓒ Ⓓ
22. Ⓐ Ⓑ Ⓒ Ⓓ
23. Ⓐ Ⓑ Ⓒ Ⓓ
24. Ⓐ Ⓑ Ⓒ Ⓓ
25. Ⓐ Ⓑ Ⓒ Ⓓ
26. Ⓐ Ⓑ Ⓒ Ⓓ
27. Ⓐ Ⓑ Ⓒ Ⓓ
28. Ⓐ Ⓑ Ⓒ Ⓓ
29. Ⓐ Ⓑ Ⓒ Ⓓ
30. Ⓐ Ⓑ Ⓒ Ⓓ

The Princeton Review

YOUR NAME: _____
(Print)   Last   First   M.I.

SIGNATURE: _____ DATE: __/__/__

HOME ADDRESS: _____
(Print)   Number and Street

_____
City   State   Zip Code

PHONE NO.: _____
(Print)

Completely darken bubbles with a No. 2 pencil. If you make a mistake, be sure to erase mark completely. Erase all stray marks.

Practice Test II

1. Ⓐ Ⓑ Ⓒ Ⓓ
2. Ⓐ Ⓑ Ⓒ Ⓓ
3. Ⓐ Ⓑ Ⓒ Ⓓ
4. Ⓐ Ⓑ Ⓒ Ⓓ
5. Ⓐ Ⓑ Ⓒ Ⓓ
6. Ⓐ Ⓑ Ⓒ Ⓓ
7. Ⓐ Ⓑ Ⓒ Ⓓ
8. Ⓐ Ⓑ Ⓒ Ⓓ
9. Ⓐ Ⓑ Ⓒ Ⓓ
10. Ⓐ Ⓑ Ⓒ Ⓓ

11. Ⓐ Ⓑ Ⓒ Ⓓ
12. Ⓐ Ⓑ Ⓒ Ⓓ
13. Ⓐ Ⓑ Ⓒ Ⓓ
14. Ⓐ Ⓑ Ⓒ Ⓓ
15. Ⓐ Ⓑ Ⓒ Ⓓ
16. Ⓐ Ⓑ Ⓒ Ⓓ
17. Ⓐ Ⓑ Ⓒ Ⓓ
18. Ⓐ Ⓑ Ⓒ Ⓓ
19. Ⓐ Ⓑ Ⓒ Ⓓ
20. Ⓐ Ⓑ Ⓒ Ⓓ

21. Ⓐ Ⓑ Ⓒ Ⓓ
22. Ⓐ Ⓑ Ⓒ Ⓓ
23. Ⓐ Ⓑ Ⓒ Ⓓ
24. Ⓐ Ⓑ Ⓒ Ⓓ
25. Ⓐ Ⓑ Ⓒ Ⓓ
26. Ⓐ Ⓑ Ⓒ Ⓓ
27. Ⓐ Ⓑ Ⓒ Ⓓ
28. Ⓐ Ⓑ Ⓒ Ⓓ
29. Ⓐ Ⓑ Ⓒ Ⓓ
30. Ⓐ Ⓑ Ⓒ Ⓓ

The Princeton Review

The Princeton Review

YOUR NAME: _____
(Print)   Last   First   M.I.

SIGNATURE: _____ DATE: ___/___/___

HOME ADDRESS: _____
(Print)   Number and Street

_____
City   State   Zip Code

PHONE NO.: _____
(Print)

Completely darken bubbles with a No. 2 pencil. If you make a mistake, be sure to erase mark completely. Erase all stray marks.

Practice Test III

1. Ⓐ Ⓑ Ⓒ Ⓓ
2. Ⓐ Ⓑ Ⓒ Ⓓ
3. Ⓐ Ⓑ Ⓒ Ⓓ
4. Ⓐ Ⓑ Ⓒ Ⓓ
5. Ⓐ Ⓑ Ⓒ Ⓓ
6. Ⓐ Ⓑ Ⓒ Ⓓ
7. Ⓐ Ⓑ Ⓒ Ⓓ
8. Ⓐ Ⓑ Ⓒ Ⓓ
9. Ⓐ Ⓑ Ⓒ Ⓓ
10. Ⓐ Ⓑ Ⓒ Ⓓ

11. Ⓐ Ⓑ Ⓒ Ⓓ
12. Ⓐ Ⓑ Ⓒ Ⓓ
13. Ⓐ Ⓑ Ⓒ Ⓓ
14. Ⓐ Ⓑ Ⓒ Ⓓ
15. Ⓐ Ⓑ Ⓒ Ⓓ
16. Ⓐ Ⓑ Ⓒ Ⓓ
17. Ⓐ Ⓑ Ⓒ Ⓓ
18. Ⓐ Ⓑ Ⓒ Ⓓ
19. Ⓐ Ⓑ Ⓒ Ⓓ
20. Ⓐ Ⓑ Ⓒ Ⓓ

21. Ⓐ Ⓑ Ⓒ Ⓓ
22. Ⓐ Ⓑ Ⓒ Ⓓ
23. Ⓐ Ⓑ Ⓒ Ⓓ
24. Ⓐ Ⓑ Ⓒ Ⓓ
25. Ⓐ Ⓑ Ⓒ Ⓓ
26. Ⓐ Ⓑ Ⓒ Ⓓ
27. Ⓐ Ⓑ Ⓒ Ⓓ
28. Ⓐ Ⓑ Ⓒ Ⓓ
29. Ⓐ Ⓑ Ⓒ Ⓓ
30. Ⓐ Ⓑ Ⓒ Ⓓ

THE PRINCETON REVIEW

YOUR NAME: _____
(Print)   Last   First   M.I.
SIGNATURE: _____ DATE: ___/___/___

HOME ADDRESS: _____
(Print)   Number and Street
_____
City   State   Zip Code

PHONE NO.: _____
(Print)

Completely darken bubbles with a No. 2 pencil. If you make a mistake, be sure to erase mark completely. Erase all stray marks.

Practice Test IV

1. Ⓐ Ⓑ Ⓒ Ⓓ   11. Ⓐ Ⓑ Ⓒ Ⓓ   21. Ⓐ Ⓑ Ⓒ Ⓓ
2. Ⓐ Ⓑ Ⓒ Ⓓ   12. Ⓐ Ⓑ Ⓒ Ⓓ   22. Ⓐ Ⓑ Ⓒ Ⓓ
3. Ⓐ Ⓑ Ⓒ Ⓓ   13. Ⓐ Ⓑ Ⓒ Ⓓ   23. Ⓐ Ⓑ Ⓒ Ⓓ
4. Ⓐ Ⓑ Ⓒ Ⓓ   14. Ⓐ Ⓑ Ⓒ Ⓓ   24. Ⓐ Ⓑ Ⓒ Ⓓ
5. Ⓐ Ⓑ Ⓒ Ⓓ   15. Ⓐ Ⓑ Ⓒ Ⓓ   25. Ⓐ Ⓑ Ⓒ Ⓓ
6. Ⓐ Ⓑ Ⓒ Ⓓ   16. Ⓐ Ⓑ Ⓒ Ⓓ   26. Ⓐ Ⓑ Ⓒ Ⓓ
7. Ⓐ Ⓑ Ⓒ Ⓓ   17. Ⓐ Ⓑ Ⓒ Ⓓ   27. Ⓐ Ⓑ Ⓒ Ⓓ
8. Ⓐ Ⓑ Ⓒ Ⓓ   18. Ⓐ Ⓑ Ⓒ Ⓓ   28. Ⓐ Ⓑ Ⓒ Ⓓ
9. Ⓐ Ⓑ Ⓒ Ⓓ   19. Ⓐ Ⓑ Ⓒ Ⓓ   29. Ⓐ Ⓑ Ⓒ Ⓓ
10. Ⓐ Ⓑ Ⓒ Ⓓ   20. Ⓐ Ⓑ Ⓒ Ⓓ   30. Ⓐ Ⓑ Ⓒ Ⓓ

NOTES

NOTES

NOTES

NOTES

NOTES

# NOTES

NOTES

NOTES

We have a smarter way to get better grades in school.

Find a tutor in 3 easy steps:

Find.
Log onto our website: **www.tutor.com**

Connect.
Sign up to find a tutor who fits all your needs

Learn.
Get **tutored** in any subject or skill

Visit www.tutor.com

www.review.com

Expert Advice

Talk About It

Pop Surveys

Paying for it

www.review.com

www.review.com

THE PRINCETON REVIEW

Getting in

Word du Jour

www.review.com

Find-O-Rama School & Career Search

www.review.com

Finding it

Best Schools

www.review.com

More Expert Advice
on all your important exams

THE PRINCETON REVIEW

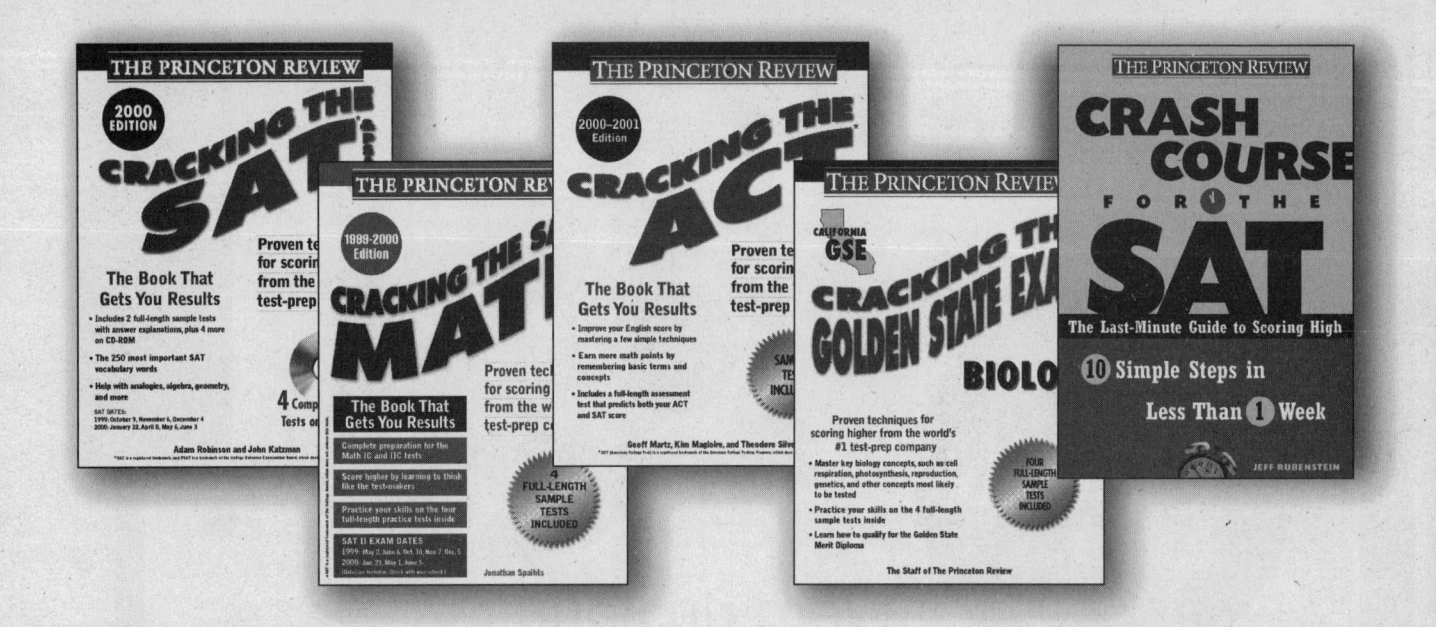

**CRACKING THE SAT & PSAT
2000 EDITION**
0-375-75403-2 • $18.00

**CRACKING THE SAT & PSAT WITH
SAMPLE TESTS ON CD-ROM
2000 EDITION**
0-375-75404-0 • $29.95

SAT MATH WORKOUT
0-679-75363-X • $15.00

SAT VERBAL WORKOUT
0-679-75362-1 • $16.00

**CRACKING THE ACT
2000-2001 EDITION**
0-375-75500-4 • $18.00

**CRACKING THE ACT WITH
SAMPLE TESTS ON CD-ROM
2000-2001 EDITION**
0-375-75501-2 • $29.95

CRASH COURSE FOR THE ACT
10 Easy Steps to Higher Score
0-375-75326-5 • $9.95

CRASH COURSE FOR THE SAT
10 Easy Steps to Higher Score
0-375-75324-9 • $9.95

CRACKING THE CLEP 4TH EDITION
0-375-76151-9 • $20.00

**CRACKING THE GOLDEN STATE EXAMS:
1ST YEAR ALGEBRA**
0-375-75352-4 • $16.00

**CRACKING THE GOLDEN STATE EXAMS:
BIOLOGY**
0-375-75356-7 • $16.00

**CRACKING THE GOLDEN STATE EXAMS:
CHEMISTRY**
0-375-75357-5 • $16.00

**CRACKING THE GOLDEN STATE EXAMS:
ECONOMICS**
0-375-75355-9 • $16.00

**CRACKING THE GOLDEN STATE EXAMS:
GEOMETRY**
0-375-75353-2 • $16.00

**CRACKING THE GOLDEN STATE EXAMS:
U.S. HISTORY**
0-375-75354-0 • $16.00